Finding the *Wild* Inside

Exploring Our Inner Landscape
Through the Arts, Dreams, and Intuition

MARILYN KAY HAGAR

SHE WRITES PRESS

Published 2019
Printed in Canada
ISBN: 978-1-63152-608-4
ISBN: 978-1-63152-609-1
Library of Congress Control Number: 2019906664

Interior design by Tabitha Lahr

For information, address:
She Writes Press
1569 Solano Ave #546
Berkeley, CA 94707

She Writes Press is a division of SparkPoint Studio, LLC.

To my sons, Erik, Gabriel, and Eli
And to my four precious grandsons, Andrew, Alex, Chase, and Cole
Into their hands, I entrust our future.

Contents

PART III: ELDERHOOD

Part I

The First Half of Life

*Nature, psyche, and life appear to me like
divinity unfolded—what more could I ask for?*
—Carl Jung

Introduction:

Our Wild Home

Our lives move at a dizzying pace. We rush through our days, exhausting ourselves in our mad scrambling. We fall into bed each night for a few precious hours of sleep and then get up the next morning and do it all over again. But as we scurry, filling our calendars and making our lists, another life is living itself inside each one of us. That life is invisible and moves at a different pace. It runs through us like a deep underground river, its source the crystal-clear waters at the center of our being. It lives inside us from the day we are born until the day we die and is the source of our deepest knowing. I call that river and the inner landscape it traverses our wild home.

Most of us are not taught to navigate this terrain, nor do we know how to understand the language it speaks as it tries to guide us toward fulfillment. Instead, we stumble into adulthood, trying to build our lives by following the familiar structures we see around us. Ideally, we succeed in creating a satisfying and meaningful existence. But in a culture that hawks the material plane as the only route to finding joy and fulfillment, we are doomed to struggle, and many of us end up in a crisis of meaning.

This book chronicles my own struggle over seven decades to find meaning and purpose in a world that begged me to look outward, rather than inward. In my midthirties, when my beloved grandmother died, I began to wonder if there was more to life than met my eye. In grieving her passage, I turned my gaze inward to see what I might find. While I wasn't aware of it at the time, that was a completely rebellious act—one that transported me into a wild, unknown world where I had to find new eyes and new ears and learn a completely different way of being present in my life in order to make sense of it. A language beneath my words began to reveal itself. It came to me through my music, my dreams, my art, my imagination, and the uncanny synchronicities that I began to recognize as they rained down around me. This new form of communication was rich in feeling, tone, image, and metaphor and was communicated more often through my body than through my mind.

It took many years to make sense of my childhood intuition about my wild home. I was just living my life. I grew up, got married, became a mother, and found my path as an expressive arts therapist. This book chronicles the deeper story that was being told. Because I was not guided by the institutions that most often shepherd us, I traveled through uncharted waters and wandered in a wilderness without trails. There, I learned to follow the ever-unfolding mystery of my wild soul as it guided me through life's great adventure.

My story unfolds as a series of reflections on my inner life, from the time I was a tiny child until this book's publication. Exploring my inner landscape opened me to the gift of creative imagination, a gift available to each one of us. My wild inside took me cascading down rushing rivers, through dark green valleys, and high up onto mountaintops. I communed with the fish and learned from the bears. I came to see that I am a child of Nature, made of the earth, a small speck of the Great Mother herself. I gave birth to my children, and I witnessed my aging parents as they stepped close to death's door. Standing in the circle of life, I learned that accepting life's endings is as important as welcoming its beginnings.

The giant redwood trees that surround me in my forest home in Northern California have taught me that if my roots are not firmly planted in the soil of Mother Earth, I cannot reach for the sky. As I learned to traverse this wild land inside me, the boundary between my inner world and my outer world began to dissolve, expanding my notion of my place in the universe and challenging me to reconsider what it means to be human.

I've sprinkled my dreams and my art amid the stories told here because they are all of one piece inside me now. The stories cannot be told without them. The images that arise from our unconscious minds are gifts from our wild self. If we pay attention, they remain alive inside us and continue to provide insight and meaning throughout our entire lives. I hope that including this part of my journey will inspire you to look anew at what dreams and the arts have to offer. Perhaps you have already opened to these ways of exploring; if not, just know that they await you with wonderful blessings and ask only that you turn in their direction.

I believe with everything in me that looking inward is never an end in itself. I'm deeply committed to using what I find inside as a guide and trust that when I am in communion with my wild home, I will find right action in my world. I want to live with that kind of authenticity. We are each on our own journey in this life. My story will not be yours, and your story is for you to explore. I hope, though, that reading about my dogged attempt to live as my truest self, struggling first to recognize and then to accept all the ways in which the larger energies around me support me, will assist you in doing the same. Our beautiful world deserves our own deepest expression of who we were meant to be.

❦ *Reflection*

At the end of each chapter, I'll offer ideas for reflecting on your own story. Have ready an unlined journal, some larger art paper, colored construction paper, markers, oil pastels, chalk pastels, colored pencils, or paints. If you are thinking, *I don't do art!* give it a try. Open to the first page of your journal and scribble all over it. You're off to a great start. Don't worry about whether what you create here is perfect or beautiful—what's important is what your art says, not what it looks like.

Chapter 1:

In the Beginning

Our birth is but a sleep and a forgetting . . .
—WILLIAM WORDSWORTH

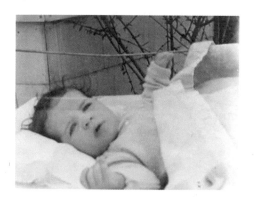

Memories are spun from the threads of our experience and woven into the fabric of our lives through the stories we tell. What makes certain experiences remain with us and others fade into oblivion remains a mystery, but I am convinced that the stories we carry are jewels in the treasure box of our inner lives and are important clues about what gives us meaning.

In my life, one of those jewels is my earliest memory. In it, I am tiny. I am outside, watching the leaves on the trees above cast dancing shadows over me as they flutter in the breeze. I am immersed in the experience, lost in the sounds, and mesmerized by the shadows.

Most would say that remembering something from infancy is impossible, but clearly those shadowy leaves fluttering overhead made a deep impression on me. It was as if their movement and my physical response were somehow in sync. Then and now, the recollection fills me with deep peace.

As I grew, there were other times when I seemed, out of nowhere, to melt into my experience, as I did that day with the shadows. It felt like falling down a rabbit hole into another world. All my senses were amplified, and that filled my body with pleasure. I was witness to the experience but still somehow very much a part of it. I couldn't make it happen, but I would have loved to.

From an early age, I learned that I could surrender to this bliss. Surrendering prolonged the feelings once they started. I couldn't move, speak, or interact, or the spell would be broken. Nothing special in my external reality triggered these moments; they often occurred as I observed someone doing something ordinary. For instance, I have a clear memory of watching the parent of a friend change a lightbulb in the room where I was playing. Every sound, every movement—all the visuals—sent me into this blissful state. These moments lasted for just a few minutes, which seemed not long enough to me. I was always saddened when the experience began to fade.

I have come to believe that my experience with the shadowy leaves was an early moment of this expanded awareness. Some months after my own birth, I found myself simply there, under a tree, awake, in a moment of solitude, deeply experiencing the breeze, those leaves, those shadows, and me, alone there, in that quiet moment, at the very beginning of my life, communing with Mother Nature. It may have been one of my earliest encounters with the natural world. It stands out like a beacon pointing to a time when, having had my world turned inside out, which is what birth does, I began my long journey of trying to reorient myself.

The questions "Who am I, where did I come from, and why am I here?" have been my companions, and I have asked and answered them again and again over my lifetime. My spiritual quest led me far away from my source in Mother Nature before leading me toward home again.

In our patriarchal culture, we have a troubled connection with Mother Earth. It is no wonder that I had trouble finding my way, as the feminine principle is ignored and even denigrated at all levels of our society. We take our lives for granted, forgetting that Mother Nature's great blessings support us in every way. We even feel free to exploit her gifts without thought for the future. We would rather not look at the fact that we are all subject to her indiscriminate power to determine whether we live or die. Wanting to find some control over our fragile situation, we spend far more time imagining ourselves as separate from her realm than acknowledging our belonging within her sphere.

But, contrary to what we might like to believe, we do not arrive on Earth descending from the sky world. Rather, we emerge from the cave of our mother's womb. We are literally made of the earth, embedded in the earth, and born out of the earth. As we emerge from the womb and our umbilical cord is severed, we exist on our own, accepting our more removed belonging to the world around us. Though we are made of the earth, we are now our own unique being, no longer attached to our personal mother, who was our external root in the larger story of human existence. When we separate from our mother, we separate from much more—so many umbilical cords severed in the long chain that connects us to the first humans and then goes further back, to the life force as it expressed itself before humans even existed. We spend little time honoring the immensity of this larger separation. But I wonder if we have some inkling, some kind of distant awareness, that we are also separating from that long chain of being that created us. Is it possible that this separation marks the beginning of our spiritual quest, our yearning to know something of the source from which we came?

As a young girl in a culture cut off from its roots in Mother Nature, I received confusing messages about the value of growing up female. There were overt indications that my father's life had more value than my mother's. But in my daily experience, my mother's life was far more important to my well-being than my father's life was. Yet her role was taken for granted. In that way, she was like the ground we walk on. Rather than being lauded in any way, mothers are just assumed to be—like the Earth itself.

Of course, it wasn't only in my family that I found women cast in a supportive role, instead of as the star of the show. It was simply the milieu I was raised in during the 1950s in the American culture at large. This situation was mirrored in my church, where Christianity, one of the guiding mythologies of American society, was all about God and Jesus, while the feminine characters more often seemed like servants of powerful men. With the exception of Mary giving birth to Baby Jesus, the image of the sacred feminine lived in the shadows. And

Mary was completely desexualized, a virgin who had somehow magically had a baby. This lack of a full-bodied, divine feminine presence left me without a compass with which to direct my spiritual wanderings.

When I think now about who I was as a young girl, it is as if I were trying to plant myself in some kind of artificial turf, instead of the rich, loamy soil that is my birthright. My essential being embodies the deep feminine energy of Mother Earth, but nothing about my life encouraged me to look in her direction. In fact, society taught me to be embarrassed and ashamed of that part of myself, to find her inferior and maybe even dangerous. That led to copious amounts of mistrust in an essential part of my own being.

Not seeing as sacred the essential nature of my womanhood and the creative essence I shared with the world, I looked skyward for my spiritual guidance. But, in spite of myself, as my life lived itself forward, I found myself stumbling toward the realization that I needed to plant my feet firmly on the ground, look down rather than up, and sink more deeply into life, instead of trying to rise above it.

What I couldn't see and didn't yet fully understand is that life on this Earth, in and of itself, is sacred. The experience of being in a woman's body, being pregnant, giving birth, and becoming a mother carried me forward. Thankfully, as I matured, I learned to sink beneath the chatter of my mind and listen to a voice that originated deeper in my body. That deeper voice whispered to me the teachings of wild Nature and reminded me again and again that my larger Mother and I had some long-lost, important, but unremembered relationship with each other. My task was to rediscover that connection.

I've learned to treasure that deep voice inside me. It is the voice of my own wild self. She is untamed and speaks in a variety of ways, but she always speaks freely. She exists outside the patriarchal influences of my culture and works to tame my inner patriarch, who seeks to silence me. Owning my wild self has been my life challenge. It takes courage to surrender to her ways, but the great reward is being able to live life more authentically and with greater trust in the love that rests in the core of my being. I believe if there is hope for our planet, it will come because we allow our deep feminine energy to arise and find balance with the masculine energy that has been running amok. If we can do that, I know we can create a better world.

In finding my wild home, what I know now to be true about my relationship with divine energy lives inside me as embodied experience. All of my inner explorations have made visible for me what was once invisible. One day, on a morning beach walk, I watched as a flock of shorebirds up ahead appeared and disappeared before my very eyes. When they flew in one direction, their feathers caught the light and they appeared out of nowhere, bright white against the deep blue water. When they reversed direction, they were completely camouflaged once again, disappearing in the dark blue background. Though I tried hard to catch even the slightest hint of their movements, I couldn't see them at all. I watched in awe, enjoying this natural magic show, as they swirled around and around, catching the light and then disappearing over and over again. Finally committed to a direction, they disappeared down the beach and I didn't see them again.

As I walked on, I thought how much my experience with those birds mirrors the moments when flashes of insight from my wild self suddenly appear as if out of nowhere. When it happens, I always feel as if magic is afoot. Over the years, these moments have added up. They have become something of substance and have challenged me to find my sense of belonging in a world that is much more expansive than I ever imagined.

We all have a wild self at the core of our being, just waiting there for us to come near. When we open to that part of ourselves, we begin to discover the uniqueness that we are, and that is the first step toward finding our own authentic contribution to our world.

I have always loved this quote from Martha Graham, urging us toward our own deepest expression of who we are: "There is a vitality, a life force, an energy, a quickening that is translated through you into action, and because there is only one of you in all of time, this expression is unique. And if you block it, it will never exist through any other medium and it will be lost. The world will not have it. It is not your business to determine how good it is nor how valuable nor how it compares with other expressions. It is your business to keep it yours clearly and directly, to keep the channel open."

❦ *Reflection*

Reflect on an early memory of being in nature. On a walk or hike, collect sticks, leaves, rocks, seeds, moss—whatever calls to you. With thread, string, tape, glue, etc., fashion a representation of yourself as a doll or in a natural collage. In your journal, begin a conversation with this earthy part of yourself.

Chapter 2:

The Bear Is Coming. He's Coming for Me!

I've dreamt in my life dreams that have stayed with me ever after,
and changed my ideas; they've gone through and through me,
like wine through water, and altered the color of my mind.
—EMILY BRONTË

One night at bedtime, my mother walked by my room and saw me kneeling beside my bed, my little hands clasped in front of me, saying my evening prayers. Then she heard me say, "Dear Jesus, please help me to be a better girl and help my mama be a better mama." I was three years old.

When I was that age, my mother was the source of my religious instruction. We hadn't started going to church yet, but there were strong messages in my family about being bad and being good. Regrettably, those messages were backed with spankings, sometimes with a board, which left me trying hard to be very, very good. Not only was I supposed to be good, I had concluded that we were all supposed to try to be our very best selves. Thinking back to my little-girl prayer, I must have been aware that the harsh discipline in my family was a violation. It seems that from the time I was a tiny child, I thought about very big things. I see all the signs that I was a seeker right from the start.

Around the same time my mother heard my childhood prayer, I had a dream that remains

My Childhood Dream, 1948

one of the strongest memories of my early childhood. It was so completely real to me that I was incensed when those around me dismissed it as a fantasy. I have since come to see it as a big, life dream, one that remains relevant to me even now. *My Childhood Dream,* 1948 depicts my dream.

In my dream, I was sitting in the window seat of my Sparks, Nevada, home, looking out a large bay window at my front yard and my neighborhood beyond. A bear dressed in striped blue denim overalls came riding down the street on a shiny red motor scooter. He stopped right in front of my house, got off his scooter, and walked through my gate, heading straight for my front door. Terrified, I ran to the closet in the entryway. The smell of green bananas wafted over me as I opened the closet door. My father had brought them home from the rail yard and hung them there to ripen. I scurried under the bananas and folded myself into a tiny ball in the back corner of the closet. Shaking and trying my best not to cry, I heard the front door creak as it opened. The bear was coming. He was coming for me!

I woke up crying. My mother came rushing into my room and tried to comfort me. I was not easily comforted. In fact, I was beyond comfort once I realized that she didn't believe that what had happened was real. Through my sobbing, she must have heard the words "bear" and "closet." "There isn't a bear in the closet, Kay. Look," she told me, as she opened the closet door in my bedroom. "No bear." Now I was crying inconsolably. There was no hope here. She was not going to listen to me.

Because I insisted that my dream bear was real, it became a topic of conversation in the family for days afterward.

"Look, Kay," my mother said. "That was just a dream. Dreams seem real, but they aren't. That was not a real bear! It was just in your imagination."

I adored my grandparents, who lived nearby. When they came to visit, I climbed up into my grandmother's lap, seeking comfort. Certainly, she would believe me, I thought, but that was not to be. "It was just a dream," she told me. "Just a dream," she repeated, as she ran her fingers through my long, curly hair, trying to comfort me. The veil between this world and my dream world was very thin, if not nonexistent, at that early age. Amazingly, the fact that no one believed me didn't make me question what I had seen. I knew what was real for me, and no one was going to persuade me otherwise.

I eventually learned to separate my dream reality from waking life. It was vital that I learn to distinguish between the two, but it would have been lovely if, in that process, the truth of both worlds could have been validated.

Perhaps I could have been told that I had a day world and a night world and that both were very real. My night world could have been explained as the home of my dreams, visions, and intuition. I could have been told that they were as important as, but different from, my waking life experiences and that I could learn from each one. But for a child growing up in small-town America in the 1950s, that wasn't the way things were. So, instead of learning to honor this less rational part of myself, I absorbed the message of the culture around me: There is only one reality that matters, and that is our very rational waking reality. It wasn't until much later that I began to have experiences that made me wonder just how separate those parts of me really were. Only then did I begin to consider that maybe that three-year-old girl knew something that those of us much older have forgotten.

On a personal level, I know now that my dream may have been addressing my family situation and my budding independence. But every dream speaks to multiple layers of meaning. I believe this big, life dream spoke to more than the little girl I was at the time. There was no way to have known it then, but, almost seventy years later, as I write this book, I now see my dream as a blueprint for what was to become my spiritual quest.

When I look at it from that perspective, I see that this dream held important clues about my spiritual predicament at the time. It spoke to the juxtaposition between the vulnerable little girl I was and the wildness of the natural world from whence I came. At three, I was learning to split off from my instinctual, animal nature. In fact, I was being actively taught to make that split, and necessarily so. But that doesn't happen without consequence. As we leave our roots in Mother Nature, we leave much behind.

In his essay "Marginalia on Contemporary Events," Carl Jung acknowledged that the development of our conscious minds necessitates splitting with the instinctual connection we have with the natural world around us. But he cautioned that in modern society, that split has gone too far, that we are out of balance with natural forces. Because energy doesn't disappear and what we leave behind doesn't just go away, those elements simply retreat into our unconscious minds. Our blindness to the fact that those energies still affect us puts us in jeopardy, as those repressed instincts can burst out in destructive ways. Though Jung spoke of this concept in 1945 after the rise of the Nazis, his comments are relevant for us today. There is much to say about the broader aspects of the repression of our instinctual selves and the implications that has for our society, but for now I want to focus on the consequences I have discerned for myself as I tried to negotiate that separation in my own little life. My dream speaks directly to that struggle.

In my dream, I looked out the window at the civilized, domesticated world I called home. A wild creature arrived, with the trappings of town life—his overalls and his red motor scooter—but I wasn't fooled. I saw his wild and uncontrolled essence, something I was in the process of disowning. My dream bear was a perfect representation of who I was at the time, a wild little instinctive creature with just a few trappings of civilization plastered over my essence. In my struggle to give up my wild roots, I gave the bear all my instinctual power, all my ferocity, and all other connections to the wildness that I was. Yikes—what a terrifying creature he had become with all my gifts! As I faced the bear, my instinct in the dream was to hide, and I did. I didn't want this wild creature to find me. My fear was over the top. And so I fell into my life as a human being here on Earth. I knew what was being asked of me, and I made myself into the tiniest manifestation of who I really was. The symbolism is not unlike that of the creation story, the fall of Adam and Eve and their expulsion from the garden. The fact that I could make up my own version of that story at age three attests to the power of our dreams to access the gifts of the collective unconscious at any age.

My dream ended smack dab in the middle of all my fear. Having given away my home in the arms of the Great Mother, I was undone, and no wonder. Is it possible that something buried deep inside me knew the bargain I had struck? I tried to communicate to my mother with the only words I had: the language of the dream, the bear, the closet, my fear, my sobbing.

Jeremy Taylor, a mentor of mine who dedicated his life to working with dreams, held that nightmares don't come to torture us or leave us in the miserable situation in which we find ourselves, but rather to shock us awake because some situation in our psyche has become urgent. When the dream awakens us with all its terrifying vitality, we remember it. A dream remembered offers the possibility of bringing our conscious minds to the conflict we are experiencing.

My dream left me curled in a tiny ball in the closet, but I was not left without hope; I was surrounded by the ripening bananas. The darkness of the closet was not unlike the darkness of the womb. I was like a seed planted there. It was indeed time to develop my rational side at age three, but my dream offered the promise that as I grew in that way, a piece of me was still planted there in darkness. That promise still hangs over me, with all its sweet wonder. I can even smell it. Perhaps it was that scent that carried me forward as I struggled to live into the task this early experience set for my lifetime.

It would be many years before I would discover the wisdom of my night world. Everything in my culture told me nothing of value existed there. In fact, it would try to convince me that there was nothing there at all. Like a salmon, I would need to swim against the current to find my way home again. When I began to honor my night world, it was like learning to see in the dark.

The power of the less rational part of us goes unrecognized in our culture. In our never-ending fascination with the light of the mind, anything we can't see or can't understand is threatening. We have even come to associate darkness with evil, rather than the unknown, a great mystery. Anne Baring, in *The Dream of the Cosmos*, suggests that when we humans moved from a consciousness in which "the Great Mother *was* heaven and earth" to a consciousness where a transcendent "God became the *maker* of heaven and earth," spirit and nature were torn asunder. Spirit and the rational became ascendant over darkness, and the body. Western civilization was built on this split. Our rational minds have brought and continue to bring us many wonders, but I want to encourage us to look at what we have forgotten.

As a tiny child, I fell in love with the night sky. One night in rural Nevada, I lay in the back of a pickup truck as we drove back to my aunt and uncle's ranch after visiting with relatives nearby. The valley had not yet been electrified, and the absence of city lights for miles and miles made the stars brilliant, the Milky Way easily visible. As we drove on that warm summer evening, my cousins and I giggled and made wishes, watching one falling star after another streak across the sky. We were laughing and singing:

Twinkle, twinkle, little star,
How I wonder what you are!
Up above the world so high,
Like a diamond in the sky.

When the blazing sun is gone,
When he nothing shines upon,
Then you show your little light,
Twinkle, twinkle, all the night.

When I listen more deeply now, I realize that this song teaches us about finding our way in the darkness when the brilliant light of consciousness has moved below our horizon—when we have exhausted the bright light of the mind and can no longer use its strategic powers to find our way. Then we are called to look with different eyes.

When, as an adult, I became curious about my night world, many questions arose. *What have we left behind?* I wondered. *What about our dreams and the messages they bring from our unconscious minds? What about intuition and the wisdom in our bodies? What about our instincts and the emotions born of them?* I wanted to know more.

When I began to open myself to the mysteries of my night world, my connection to my wild home revealed itself to me. In my art, my dreams, and all the other ways I learned to access the less rational parts of myself, images of the night, of animals, and of nature poured forth. My art began to be pictured under the night sky, complete with stars, the full moon, and often the aurora borealis. I didn't make that happen; it was simply the natural unfolding of my inner imagery as it emerged from my unconscious mind. My pastel drawing *Receiving the Blessing of the Night* shows me trusting into that landscape, opening to the gifts offered there.

When I was first learning about guided imagery and music, a process of listening to specially selected classical music and letting images appear in my mind, I was listening to the adagio of Beethoven's Piano Concerto No. 5 in E-flat Major. As the orchestra began its prelude, I found myself gazing into the inky darkness of a night sky studded with stars. When the first notes of the piano entered, the stars began to melt. I saw pure white drops of liquid starlight falling from the heavens like rain. As I reached out, they landed in my outstretched

Receiving the Blessing of the Night

hands. Quite literally, I felt like I was receiving the blessing of the night. This moment was a clear marker of when I began in earnest to trust in a whole new part of myself.

I see now that I was allowing the divine feminine to awaken in me. My life became a practice in letting both my day world and my night world speak. The arts, once I found them again, served as a bridge between what was inside and what was outside, bringing the darkness within into shape and form in the light of day, my unconscious self and my conscious self finding communion at long last.

But in a culture that represses the feminine aspect, it takes courage to look into the darkness to see what we might find there. History has taught us to turn away. Though it is now a distant memory, we know that our sisters just a few centuries ago were killed for their knowledge and abilities in these deeply feminine ways of knowing. Little is taught about that dark spot in our history, but as I have grown older, I have become convinced that the slaughter of those "witches" taught us not to trust into this deeper part of ourselves.

As I opened to my own feminine wisdom, I was surprised to find the mark those terrible times left buried inside my own body. Images of being hanged or burned at the stake first emerged in my consciousness during freeform body movement sessions. For eight years when I was in my fifties, I belonged to a circle of women who practiced Authentic Movement. This process originated in the 1950s, when Mary Starks Whitehouse, a dancer and psychotherapist, began asking her clients to listen inside and let their bodies move with their own inner urges. Authentic Movement is a deeply intimate experience between the one moving and another, the witness, who holds a safe space for the mover and witnesses her movement from a place of complete nonjudgment. For me, Authentic Movement sessions often felt like waking dreams, as they asked my conscious mind to step back and allow my unconscious body to speak.

It was in one such session that an image of myself being hanged as a witch arose from my unconscious mind. An entry from my journal describes the story that unfolded. It is possible that my participation in a circle like ours is what triggered the image. Had we been meeting at the time of the witch hunts, all of us might have been tried as witches, as our sessions resembled experiences that women were killed for in that dark time in our history.

In this session, I found myself immobilized, my hands bound behind my back, a noose around my neck, my feet dangling just off the ground. The sounds in the room were strangely removed from me, as if I were there and not there, in limbo between this world and another. Inside me, I knew that I was dead, that I had been hanged, but I felt no angst about my situation. I was waiting. I felt fire all around me. The sounds in the room came closer. Another mover was making an unearthly sound that I imagined to be that of a wounded animal. The creature was crying out to the wild emptiness, telling its tragic tale of neglect, abandonment, and betrayal. In a moment of deep compassion, a sob passed through my body. Afterward, I began to shake, starting at my feet. As I surrendered to the sensation, it moved upward, its intensity increasing until my whole body was shaking with such force that my hands fell free. Now the shaking was so intense that it began to move my feet. I moved about the floor, my feet pounding. It was not a movement that I was making consciously. I couldn't have done such a thing if I had tried. It was too erratic and too quick for my conscious mind to direct. I was conscious only of not trying to stop it. I moved for quite some time, before I stopped from sheer exhaustion. I wanted to fall to the ground and rest, but a voice inside forbade me: *Stay on your feet!* I obeyed and caught my breath. *Walk in the world with that energy. Give it to others!*

Experiences like this one convinced me that, just as our bodies carry the knowledge of our evolutionary past, our psyches can carry knowledge of events outside the era in which we live. From ancient times to modern day, shamans and mystics have transcended our normal human experience of time and space in this way. I believe this experience in Authentic Movement touched on that kind of awareness. The physical energy I released in the experience could well have been my body letting go of past trauma recorded in my cellular memory, freeing the energy for myself and for others.

As I worked to heal the wounding I carried inside from the brutality of those long-ago times, many paintings about the witch hunts emerged onto paper.

In *Remembering*, I paint a new dawn. Pictured oddly like the crucifixion, the three crosses are now gallows where the witches hang. The priest stands below and behind me with his noose ready for the next persecution and hanging. In the center, I stand with legs now grown long enough to touch the earth. Nature fills the background as my bound feet touch the grass. The image unfolded in that order, with the figures painted first, the natural world surprising me when it spilled out into the stark white space behind. The Great Mother Bear, long-legged like I am, stands beside me, embracing me, holding the world in her heart. Though I am still bound

Remembering

and the noose remains around my neck, I am finding my way back to my home on Mother Earth and emerging into a new day. Experiencing this new day and freeing the energy trapped in these old wounds leaves me ready to trust more deeply into the energies of the night world inside me.

My father used to tell a dramatic story of a night he spent camping with a friend in the wilderness of the Ruby Mountains in northeastern Nevada. After fishing from dawn to dusk, they built a campfire, cooked dinner, and settled in for the night. The fire brought warmth and a ring of light in the darkness. As they sat around their campfire, talking about their adventures that day, my father suddenly saw the eyes of a wild creature emerge from the darkness just outside the ring of light created by their little fire. Those eyes moved around the circle, now here, now there, now in front of them, now behind them, never stepping farther into the light but never disappearing into the darkness for long. They sat spellbound throughout the night, unable to sleep, looking into the darkness, and desperately stoking their fire to keep the animal at bay. Finally, as night passed and the sky began to lighten, they went to explore and learned that it was a mountain lion that had been circling their camp.

My father's story recalls the poem "You Darkness" by Rainer Maria Rilke. It is one I have memorized. It speaks to the great power of darkness to hold everything as one before we shine a light on this aspect or on that one. It has guided me as I have come into better relationship with the power of the night inside me, with all that cannot yet be seen and with all that has yet to take form.

You Darkness
Rainer Maria Rilke

You darkness from which I come,
I love you more than all the fires
that fence out the world,
for the fire makes a circle
for everyone
so that no one sees you anymore.

But darkness holds it all:
the shape and the flame,
the animal and myself,
how it holds them,
all powers, all sight—

and it is possible: its great strength
is breaking into my body.

I have faith in the night.

(Translation by David Whyte from *River Flow: New and Selected Poems*)

I have lived my adult life trying to find my way to the grounded truth of that last line. The poem shatters years of prohibitions against trusting our dreams and visions, our intuition, our imaginations, and our unconscious minds. That little girl who awakened convinced that the bear in her dream was real had a certain kind of faith in her night, though it terrified her. She didn't yet know what to do with the reality she was grasping.

What we have left in the darkness is a vital part of who we are. Once we open that door to our wild home, the enchantment we find there awakens us and revitalizes our lives. Life becomes faded without it. Through honoring the power of our intuition and our sacred imagination, we invite color and vibrancy to return to our waking lives. Our creative inheritance just waits inside for us to recognize that it is there. In embracing divine feminine energy, we join the circle of life. Our lives aren't one or the other, day or night, light or darkness, sun or moon, masculine or feminine, but rather are about healing all of those splits inside us and making our world whole.

❦ *Reflection*

Record your nightly dreams in your journal. Write in the present tense. Start a dream group with friends. Respond to each dream you hear as your own. That way, what you say will be about you. The dreamer can take what fits. Two helpful books: *The Wisdom of Your Dreams*, by Jeremy Taylor, and *The Art of Dreaming: Tools for Creative Dream Work*, by Jill Mellick.

Chapter 3:

Loving, Losing, Reclaiming the Arts

All the arts we practice are apprenticeship.
The big art is our life.
—M. C. RICHARDS

As a tiny child, I lay in the grass under the maple tree in our big backyard. My older brother had my parents' old hand-crank RCA Victrola phonograph outside. He placed the needle on the record and turned the handle, and "Cruising Down the River" floated out into the warm summer afternoon. Hearing that particular song can still take me back to that afternoon in an instant. The scratchy sound of the old record player, the breeze rustling in the trees, and the smell of a warm Nevada afternoon all come alive in me as one piece, somehow carried in those vibrations. Later, I had my own little red record player and would play my Golden Records, singing along for hours on end. I was drawn to music from my earliest beginnings and keenly remember the joy it brought me.

When, just a few years later, I was enrolled in dancing lessons, I loved everything about them. Moving my body to music was right up my alley. I especially enjoyed all the trappings that went along with my lessons: my sweet little yellow tutu and soft ballet slippers, my shiny black patent-leather tap shoes, and the sparkly sequins on my blue taffeta recital costume. I can see the vibrant colors, feel the slippery-soft textures of the fabrics, and remember the leathery smell of the shoes. I remember the shy but sensual and joyous little girl I was, wearing those fancy costumes and performing in dance recitals with confidence, completely at ease doing those things I had taught my body to do.

These precious memories are of a time before the arts in me became domesticated. My delight sprang from the simple pleasure of expressing myself in the moment. It was a time before my culture had laid its heavy hand on me, sorting my friends and me into boxes—some of us declared to have talent, others shamed into not participating. In those times, expressing myself through singing, dancing, and making art was the most natural thing in the world for me to do. I did it simply because I was human.

While my parents were not involved in music, they marveled that their children had an interest. They tried to support that in their own way, even if just with their amazement. "I don't know how we ended up with children who can carry a tune," my mother would say. "My first grade teacher told me just to move my lips!"

I learned many years later that my father had actually played the saxophone as a young man, but by the time I knew him, all he would say about his own creativity was, "I don't have a creative bone in my body." They observed our interest in music as if studying aliens from another planet. Feeling as if they didn't know what to do with us in this regard, they turned us over to the experts.

By third grade, I was taking piano lessons with Mrs. Padgett, a dear woman who was kind, gentle, and encouraging. At first, I was thrilled. My little red piano book made me feel grown-up. The fairy songs in the beginning books captured my imagination, but the recitals were deadly for me and I hated when my parents asked me to play for others. A year or so into my piano lessons, the curtain was beginning to close on the innocence of my early artistic expression. Sadly, I mark this time as the end of my feeling entirely free to express myself through the arts.

With the classes came expectations of accomplishment and requirements of practice. I began looking outside myself, measuring and being measured against the achievements of others. These comparisons took the place of experiencing, and I lost that sense of joyful participation in the present moment that I had had when I was younger.

By the time I was twelve, my artistic life had grown far more complicated. Critical now of my own artistic abilities, I wanted out. I quit all my lessons and turned my exuberant physical energy toward sports, playing basketball, volleyball, and baseball. I was happy to leave my participation in the arts behind—at least, I thought so at the time. I see now that while I left disillusioned, my original love of the arts hadn't disappeared; I had just buried it in a safe place deep inside me.

After such a fiery rebellion, I surprised myself when on occasion I felt moved to play the piano. When I was in high school, I taught myself to play the songs I loved from *West Side Story*, *South Pacific*, and *Doctor Zhivago*. In college, I found a few pieces that I wanted to play, even though they were way above my ability level. In times when I was emotionally stirred, I'd find an empty practice room in the music building on campus and play Chopin's Marche Funèbre from his Sonata No. 2 in B-flat Minor, sometimes for hours on end.

It is clear to me now that stomping away from my lessons was a declaration of independence. Being responsible to others had tainted my connection to my own musical desires. I wanted to be the one who decided when I would play, what I would play, and how I would play it. I like to think that my insistence was a little spark from my wild child, leaping forth to protect something very precious. That place inside that music touched so deeply was a sacred space. I didn't want others colonizing it, even if they had my best interests at heart.

My older brother introduced our family to classical music. The depth of emotion expressed in that music drew me in and reconnected me with my urge to dance. As a teenager, when no one was home, I would put Tchaikovsky's *Romeo and Juliet* Fantasy-Overture on our hi-fi and dance wildly around the room, expressing with my body the emotional energy I heard in the sound. This became my secret and spontaneous pleasure well into adulthood.

My mother and my aunt were excellent artists. When they made art, it seemed like magic to me. While I loved my crayons, I soon realized that I couldn't draw realistically. When I was in fifth grade, I tried to enter a drawing contest I found in a magazine. I did my very best replication of the person the publication wanted me to draw and showed it proudly to my mother. She had lots of suggestions for how I could make it better. In the end, I erased so much that I made a hole in the paper. I ripped my drawing to shreds and tossed it in the trash. That experience ended my thinking that maybe I could be an artist, too. But, remarkably, the urge to draw didn't leave me. I kept my eye out for something that might be easier to render. Driving through the Mojave Desert to visit my grandparents in Reno, I spent hours studying the power lines as they stretched across the desert landscape on the eastern side of the Sierras. I was inspired to try to draw the towers where many lines came together. Pumps for oil wells attracted my attention as well. I guess I thought maybe straight lines and angles were more controllable.

We had art classes in school in which we were instructed to realistically portray a bowl of fruit or a bouquet of flowers, but I never really learned to draw. It wasn't until I took art appreciation classes in college that I was encouraged to discover that art didn't always have to be realistic. One summer, while home from college, I felt an urge to paint in the same expressive way in which I was dancing to classical music. I went to the art store, bought oil paint, brushes, and some canvases, went home, and started painting. It felt like a rebellious act to paint without any skill or talent, without knowing what I was doing.

My paintings were dark. I remember one in which a woman's face, barely visible in the shadows, peeked out from behind a dark green curtain. At the time, I was very shy. It was hard for me to make myself visible. I was undaunted when, looking at my artwork, my mother's friend told my mother that she thought I might be depressed. My paintings spoke to me. I found them comforting. That was all that mattered.

On my very own, I had discovered that the arts were a place where I could express something about what was happening inside me, and I came to know the pleasure in doing that. I had never heard of art therapy, dance therapy, or music therapy, and expressive arts therapy hadn't even been born yet. I stumbled into what lies at the heart of each one of these therapies all on my own.

I don't think I am alone in the wounding I received in the arts arena as a child. In a culture that teaches the arts as achievement, rather than as expression, only a gifted few survive the curriculum, and, amid all the competition, many of those fall by the wayside. The creative child inside each one of us is discouraged when our enthusiastic creative expression isn't met with openness and support, and when criticized we can easily feel shame about our creative exuberance. That shame can last a lifetime. When we quickly become convinced that being creative belongs to others, we are separated from a vital part of ourselves.

All of my early explorations and the wounding I received in the arts planted the seeds that would one day grow into my life's work as an expressive arts therapist. My tangled relationship with the arts as a young one eventually led me to ask an important question: Who would we be if we allowed ourselves to accept that the gift of being creative comes with being human? Each one of us receives this gift. None of us is excluded. I eventually discovered that my life calling was to spread that good news. I wanted to do that in a way that would keep the wild child inside us alive and growing through childhood and beyond.

❦ *Reflection*

Keep a photo of your very young self somewhere you can see it often. With your nondominant hand, make a drawing of that naturally creative little one inside you. Make a pledge to that child that you will never again tell yourself that you are not creative. Write the pledge somewhere on your drawing. Date it and sign it, then tape it to the back of your photo.

Chapter 4:

Jesus Loves Me

If the Buddha . . . had been asked whether he believed in God,
he would probably have winced slightly and explained—with great courtesy—
that this was not an appropriate question.
—Karen Armstrong

I was born to a family that had little understanding of the complexity of my inner world. My mother was a very practical person. It wasn't easy to talk with her about my deep thoughts and feelings. If I was sad or upset, she urged me to overlook my feelings. "Buck up," she would say. "You have so many things to be grateful for. Other kids have it much worse than you do." That was just how she dealt with life, but the message that came through to me was that I shouldn't be having any feelings at all.

My feelings were a problem for my father as well. He traveled frequently for work, and I was very upset about his being gone so much of the time. Taking him to the airport was such a routine part of our life that even as a very young child, I knew how to get there by heart. As we turned off the freeway to navigate the city streets that would take us to LAX, a bottomless pit would open in my stomach and my tears would begin to flow. As we pulled up to the curb to drop him off, my parents would look in the backseat and find me in a heap. "Oh, she's crying again," my father would say to my mother with consternation. Although this scene repeated itself again and again, I don't remember ever having been comforted.

But the truth is, even when my father was home, he wasn't very available to me. That didn't keep me from feeling an innate connection with him. Whether he believed that I belonged to him, I knew that he belonged to me. I sensed that we had a great deal in common. My mother and my older brother were very much alike and were close. Coupled with my father's aloofness and his physical absence, their connection left me the odd one out. I know I felt very alone, misunderstood, judged, and unprotected in my family.

The milieu of our family life affects us deeply in positive and not-so-positive ways. Fortunately, as we grow, we begin to step outside that tight little circle of family and a larger community opens to us. Relatives, friends and neighbors, schoolmates and teachers, and community groups can all play a part in shaping who we become. If we are fortunate, we find encouragement in our expanding world for parts of us that are neither recognized nor supported at home. When my family moved to Southern California in 1952, my church became one of those places for me.

In the newly created suburb of West Covina, we found ourselves in a close-knit neighborhood that felt like an extended family network. Among the families there were three girls my age and three just a year older. Our parents were all good friends, and the children were all close. Soon after we settled into our tract house, we discovered the First Baptist Church. I don't remember the adults attending services, but on Sunday mornings they sorted us kids into our various denominations and sent us off.

In services and at Sunday school, I learned all the important Bible stories, reflected on the moral teachings, and participated in all the activities. My church was not of the fire-and-brimstone variety; it emphasized right thought and right action. I loved that we had serious conversations about how we should treat one another and how we might struggle to find right action in that regard. I felt challenged to come to terms with a deeper knowledge of who I was on the inside. Of course, as a child I had little life experience on which to reflect, whereas in hindsight I question some of the dilemmas we contemplated.

For instance, one morning we were discussing the story of Daniel in the lion's den. After he read it to us, our teacher asked, "If the communists take over our country today, knowing you would be persecuted for your beliefs, would you have the moral courage to admit that you are a Christian?"

A lively discussion ensued. Some wise guys responded quickly with, "Are you kidding me? Heck no!" As an innocent, idealistic young girl, I genuinely tried to consider whether I could do that or not. *What if that confession meant my death?* I wondered. I concluded that I could and would claim Christianity in that scenario, but I also certainly hoped it would never come to that. While I question the topic, that day has stayed with me. I can't help but think that being encouraged to grapple with finding my bottom line and contemplating my ability to stand for what I believed in planted a seed for my much later activism in the 1960s.

I took all this in, and, over time, this church began to feel like a place where I belonged. While so many are disenchanted with or even traumatized by their childhood church experience, I found a genuinely supportive environment for my budding spiritual life from third grade through high school. I feel blessed that, instead of hypocrisy, rigidity, and piousness, I found a home for my inner life.

You could not become a member of the church and be baptized until you reached an age when you could make that decision for yourself. When I turned twelve, in my own, very serious childlike way, I decided I was ready to make that commitment. It was a rite of passage for me and a blessing that I found this way to honor my growing maturity, my big thoughts, and my complex emotional makeup in my church experience.

In our church, at the end of every service, John Gunn, our minister, made an altar call, asking the congregation if anyone wanted to "come forward" and dedicate their life to Christ. This meant that you were ready to accept Jesus Christ as your personal savior, be baptized, and join the church. Accompanied by our organist, the congregation sang as we waited for those who might feel ready to respond. As I write, all these years later, I can hear the hymn "Have Thine Own Way, Lord" and feel the expectant energy of the congregation all around me.

Through the innocent eyes of childhood, I watched people walk down the aisle, responding to the call. I imagined that, like I had, they had been particularly inspired by the music and the sermon that morning. When they reached the front of the church, Reverend Gunn greeted them warmly. He exuded kindness. Standing in his flowing black robe, arms outstretched, he welcomed them lovingly into the fold.

Now, as an adult, I realize the innocence of my childhood perceptions. I'm sure there were, among those "going forward," lives that had gone seriously astray. It wasn't so much the music or the sermon that was pulling them down the aisle as it was hitting rock bottom in their lives and hoping for some redemption.

I remember clearly the Sunday morning when I decided that I would "go forward." Sunlight filtered through the long windows along one side of the sanctuary. I remember the music, the openhearted feel of the congregation, and the terrible butterflies in my stomach. I was shy and didn't much like making myself the center of attention, but my decision had been building inside me for weeks. I wanted to be baptized. Teetering on the edge of what I thought was possible for me, I was jittery with excitement.

Without thought, my body chose the right moment and I found myself stepping out of the pew and walking toward the front of the congregation. I was aware that I was stepping toward belonging to something much larger than I was. In a certain way, "going forward" was like going home after being away for a long time—people had been waiting to welcome me.

Soon after that, John Gunn invited me to a series of evening meetings for those of us who had come forward. This was a step up for me and proof that I was mature enough to have made this decision. Until then, Reverend Gunn had seemed far away, definitely part of the adult world at the church. My connection with adults in the church had been with my Sunday school teachers, who met us at our level. Reverend Gunn was much more dignified, clearly the leader of the group. His thick, black-framed glasses gave him a professorial air. He was always neatly groomed and very well dressed. Whether donning his silky black robe for services or wearing a dark suit and tie, he moved among his flock like one in charge. He was tall and handsome and seemed rock solid. Though I didn't really know him at all, it was very easy for me, a young girl with a missing father, to unconsciously project the image of a father onto this man who seemed so passionate about teaching us about our Father in Heaven.

When the evening of the first meeting arrived, Reverend Gunn's small, dark office glowed with warm golden light as my friend and I entered. We were the first to arrive. The walls were covered with books. There was nothing childlike about this room. While we waited for the others, I wondered what was in store for me. I felt like I was diving off a cliff into very deep water. Would I be able to meet all the challenges I might encounter?

Though there was just a handful of us present, both children and adults, the office was crowded. Reverend Gunn congratulated us on taking this big step and told us he was there to let us know about the important tenets of the church and the rules and expectations of church membership. He never spoke down to the young ones; he made me feel absolutely equal to the adults sitting around me. That was new and made me feel very powerful. I see now that I was being handed a precious gift, the knowledge that my inner life was something real and special. It belonged to me and only to me. I was now old enough to hold it for myself. In this part of my life, I was in charge.

This was the first of many gifts that I received from John Gunn, and only the beginning of a relationship with a man whom I have held in my heart over many years now. So many people pass through our lives, and, while we learn something from every one of them, only a few become our mentors. John Gunn was to become one of mine. As a child, I was grateful for his presence in my life but also unconscious of the true meaning of what I was receiving. Not until much later, when I grasped the depth of his symbolic presence as a loving father, did I realize the full impact he had on my life.

Our meetings progressed and affirmed the choice I had made. I wanted to commit my life to Jesus, which for me meant being conscious of my actions and trying to live my life on the side of good, rather than evil. It also meant that all my sins were to be washed away. What sins I thought I had at twelve years of age is beyond me, as I was already trying to be a very good girl, but I know this possibility of purification was my central focus.

The Baptist church believes in total immersion for baptism to be accomplished. I had watched our baptismal ceremonies many times. In our classes, we had rehearsed the practical aspects of how to negotiate immersion itself, as, even in water, the human body is heavy and we had to be able to right ourselves. We learned that baptism meant dying with Christ, dying to what separates us from God, and then being resurrected into the newness of life with Christ.

The ceremony happened on a Sunday evening. The church was candlelit. Organ music assured the solemnity of the event. The baptismal pool was behind the altar at the front of the church and had a curtain that would be opened and closed throughout the ceremony to allow for the transition from one person to the next. I changed into my white baptismal gown in the women's dressing room at one side of the church. Steps from that room went down into the baptismal pool. The ceremony began with a short teaching about the baptism of Jesus, and then, soon, it was my turn.

The water rippled as I stepped down into the pool, my gown billowing around me. Reverend Gunn, in white as well, was waiting there for me. The curtain opened, and the ceremony began. Reverend Gunn announced to the congregation my wish to be baptized and then, turning to me, asked, "Are you ready to accept Jesus Christ as your personal savior?" I looked up at him and replied in the affirmative. He responded, "I now baptize you, in the name of the Father, the Son, and the Holy Spirit."

I held on to Reverend Gunn's wrist as he gently placed a handkerchief over my nose and mouth with one hand and put his other hand behind me. I bent my knees, as I had been instructed to do, and down I went. I reemerged and found my footing, and, as water poured off me, the curtain closed. I slowly made my way out of the pool and back to the dressing area. I am certain I was crying.

I was a very impressionable young girl, and at age twelve my body was coming alive in a whole new way. The sensual nature of being completely immersed in a body of water during this ritual was not lost on me. Whatever I had thought about it beforehand, this was not an experience of the mind; it was an experience in my body, my whole body, from head to toe, inside and outside. The trust and surrender embodied in these precious moments was probably the closest I have come to experiencing what the ancients experienced in participating in ritual. Something very real happened that night. Perhaps symbolically, I did enter the tomb with Jesus. Like the initiates in shamanic cultures I later studied, I had to die to the world of my ordinary reality and be reborn into the life of the sacred.

The ritual of my baptism served as a bridge between my ego consciousness and something much larger, a great mystery, beyond my understanding. The way I see it now, as I sank beneath the surface of the water that night, the ordinary child in me stepped aside, and, when I emerged, I was wedded to that great mystery. At that time, the Christian path was the only path to the divine I knew anything about. That night, I believed I had a direct line to God through Jesus. It was a magical moment in the most profound sense of the word. I remember walking home under the canopy of a night sky filled with stars, in awe of the great blessing I had received.

I went home wearing the cloak of that magic. I'll never know what dreams visited me during the night, but when I awoke the next morning I was catapulted back to Earth from the moment I opened my eyes. It was a crash landing. My experience of the night before had evidently overwhelmed me. Clearly focused on the fact that I had been cleansed of all my sins, I became obsessed with the problem of how I was going to keep it that way. My runaway perfectionism had me in its grasp. Near tears, I managed to get up and get dressed. All I could think was that if I allowed myself to step back into my reality as an early-adolescent girl, I would certainly do or say something that would spoil my newfound purity.

I was unable to speak of my concerns. They built over the morning while I got ready for school, haunted by the possibility of sin waiting for me at every turn. I managed to choke down some breakfast but knew I couldn't go any further. I went into the living room and huddled behind the big occasional chair that sat in the corner of the room. My tears came as I heard my friend arrive to walk to school with me, as we did every morning. I heard my mother call my name: "Marilyn, Judy is here. Time to go." I was silent. She called again, this time more loudly: "Marilyn?"

Now, puzzled by my lack of response, she began to search the house for me. I heard her footsteps go down the hallway to my bedroom. "Marilyn?" she called again. Eventually she made her way into the living room and found me hiding behind the chair. I began sobbing.

"Marilyn, what's wrong?" she asked.

When I caught my breath, I blurted out, "I can't go to school, because I'll mess everything up. I know I'll make a big mistake."

I cried and cried as my mom tried to decide what to do next. She sent my friend on to school without me, and I began to relax. When she returned to the living room, I had specific questions.

"I've been forgiven for all my sins. What happens now if I do the wrong thing?"

Her wrinkled brow let me know that she had been genuinely trying to figure out the issue, and once she determined that it was religious, the tension in her face dissolved. She had the answer. "Don't take things so seriously," she told me. "If you do something wrong, you just ask Jesus to forgive you. It is no big thing. Come out from behind the chair. You'll be late for school."

Reflecting now on that chaotic morning, I realize that my violent crash back to Earth after my profound spiritual experience was natural and completely normal. It only validated the profundity of what had happened the night before. As an adult, I have had many experiences that I hold as sacred and that have overwhelmed my perceptions of normal reality, but negotiating my return to normal life is something I had to learn to do. It's much easier now.

That morning after I was baptized, I fell back into the life of my ego after being awed, but I didn't know then that my new, larger reality didn't cancel out the smaller me. Both worlds need to be lived at the same time. I wish I could travel back to that long-ago morning and hold that young Marilyn in my arms. Maybe this writing is a love letter sent back through time, letting her know that she is perfectly fine just the way she is and that if she continues to listen deeply inside herself, she will never lose the golden threads she found the night of her baptism. They will only multiply.

As I entered the world of adolescence, my emotional world became increasingly unstable. My cousin, who had been left as a baby in the care of my grandmother, came to live with us for three years. She was a year older than I was. My mother was close to her family and wanted to help, but she took on my cousin as a project that needed fixing, and that guaranteed her failure. My mom did not have the skills she needed to cope with a young girl whose foundations were shaky and who was acting out in various ways. The tension in our family increased tenfold at that time.

Though I was excited when I learned that my cousin would become my new sister, in the fallout of the situation, I was pushed further into the shadows of my family's life. I became ever more the good girl who didn't cause trouble, except for one thing: I couldn't stop crying. I cried over big things—disappointments, mistakes, a cross word from someone—and I cried over small things—a slight, a frown, a joke. It became a problem at school. A B grade instead of an A on a test, the slightest suggestion from a teacher that I wasn't performing as I should, missing the mark athletically, trouble with my friends—to all of this, crying seemed to be my only emotional response. No one inquired about the underlying cause of all those tears. Rather, I received lectures at home and at school about how I needed to learn to have "emotional control." There were no suggestions about how to get that. I was just given the message that mine was sorely lacking, and thus I concluded that I had a major personality flaw.

My parents' struggle to cope with our new family situation was reflected in their marriage as well. They often fought. I came to expect that when my father sat down at the dining room table, pushed back the lace tablecloth, and began balancing the checkbook and paying the bills. "Where's your checkbook, Rosy?" he'd ask my mom. She would search through her various purses while my father began to fume. Finally handing it over, she would go about her work in the kitchen while my father shouted questions about the incomplete information he was finding on her check stubs. "Who was this check for ten dollars to?" Becoming increasingly frustrated with her errors of omission, he would soon be shouting. "You haven't written anything on this one! Who did you write it to? How much was it for?" Soon my father would utter a string of profanities, throw down his pen, and scatter the papers on the table, in complete disgust at my mom's inability to pay attention to these details.

Eventually, all would be quiet and he would fall into a silent rage that his every pore exuded. These tension-filled intervals lasted for hours and sometimes even days. They weighed on me, compressing my chest so tightly, I could hardly breathe. I tried to stay out of the way by going to my room and listening to music. If I could, I would leave the house to visit friends, hoping that when I returned, the atmosphere would have cleared.

Scenes like this repeated themselves again and again. And God forbid that my father tried to repair something in our house. In those situations, curse words would fly, as well as the tools he was using. "Goddamn son of a bitch!" he would shout.

My mother would scurry around, trying to stop his rages. "Tom, you're losing your temper!" she would shout. "Control yourself!"

My stomach would twist into knots, and my heart would ache. *Oh no—here we go again.*

When my family dynamic grew oppressive, my church was a safe haven where I had access to adults, other than my parents, who cared about my well-being. Some of those people became my treasured advisors. For several summers, I worked at the church nursery school and later was offered a job helping the church secretary in the main office. It was then that I began to witness what went on behind the scenes at our church. As I did my clerical tasks, adults I recognized from services filed past me on their way to their appointments with the minister. I registered the emotional states of those folks, the tension between the couples, the feeling of isolation and despair in others. Once they were inside John Gunn's office, I would sometimes hear crying or raised voices. But I also noted a distinct lightening of the atmosphere around them when they emerged an hour later. Sometimes they were even laughing. I came to feel as if, even if I didn't know or understand the details, something important was happening in that office.

At times, I found myself unable to hold the intensity of what I witnessed. I was ill prepared for the emotional toll that being so close to true tragedy took on me. One day, there was a funeral for a young woman who had died. As the time for the service neared, her family, dressed all in black and overcome with grief, walked by me on their way down the hallway to see the minister. Sorrow weighed down everyone I saw that day—the teachers, the secretary, even John Gunn himself.

When I went home later that afternoon, I was emotionally exhausted. I ate some lunch and then went into our living room, which we didn't use all that often. I lay down on the turquoise couch and let my mind wander. I was trying to gather some peace, when my mother called from the kitchen, "Marilyn, your room is a mess. You promised you would have it cleaned over the weekend, and you didn't do it. Time to get it done."

Lost in the emotional trauma of the day, I ignored her nagging.

"You didn't keep your promise, and that's not fair. I'm tired of waiting. It's such a mess," I heard from afar.

She was determined that I was going to clean my room, and I could tell she wasn't going to let up. I felt a fiery rage move through my body, and then I burst into tears. Leaping up from the couch, I ran for the front door. As I slammed it behind me, I yelled back over my shoulder, "Don't you know that a woman died today?!" Such drama—but I didn't know any other way to express all that I had absorbed.

In all these ways, I came to see that my minister could be called upon to help people when life became overwhelming; so, feeling pretty overwhelmed in my family life, I reached out to him for help. His kind, accepting presence calmed the worried voices inside me. Focusing on me as if I mattered, he listened to me in a deep and loving way. He let me know that what I was feeling inside and my conclusions about those feelings were definitely worthy of exploration. I felt validated, supported, and held emotionally, perhaps for the first time in my life. I know I was receiving parenting that I sorely needed, parenting that my own parents, while good people, didn't seem equipped to provide. My time with Reverend Gunn attests to the healing power of being fully present with another person and witnessing their life stories in a nonjudgmental way. That quality of presence outweighs the importance of any words spoken. I developed a deep trust in John Gunn and, more important, a deeper trust in myself. He was a big part of whatever emotional stability I had in my high school years.

When I graduated from high school and went off to college, we corresponded. It was the mid-'60s, and while things hadn't broken loose, as they did a bit later, the culture around me was rumbling. John F. Kennedy was assassinated in the fall of my freshman year. I remember writing letters to my minister as I struggled to manage my transition to college life and process the chaos in the world around me. Replies arrived, words of calmness and reassurance handwritten on yellow lined paper. I read them again and again whenever my anxiety arose.

I was home on summer vacation the day in 1965 when the Watts riots broke out in Los Angeles. I was watching the news on television with my family, and my father burst out, "They oughta just go in there with machine guns and mow them all down." His violent reaction sent me running down the street to John Gunn's house and asking for help. Now I cringe to think of the invasion of his privacy, but he welcomed me with loving care. Having access to him at that time in my life meant having a little island of sanity where I could touch base with all that was right in the world.

At the University of California, Santa Barbara, when I was nineteen, I took one class called, "The Sociology of Religion," and another called, "The Bible as Literature," the latter of which was taught by an avowed atheist. UCSB was not a religious college, but these two classes were in high demand. By the end of that semester, after looking at the Bible as rich in symbolism and metaphor and studying the world's religions and their influence on our societies, I noticed that the spiritual beliefs I grew up with began to dissolve. I read Camus and Jean-Paul Sartre in a class segment on existentialism, and that exploded my old beliefs into a million tiny pieces. As much as I wanted to believe what I had been taught as a child, I simply couldn't. My world had expanded, and there was no going back.

I could no longer believe that there was an old man in the sky watching over me. I couldn't believe in the virgin birth or that Jesus had risen from the dead. I equated those notions with believing in Santa Claus. I was convinced that religion was the opiate of the people. As a species, we couldn't face the fact that we are born and then we die and that is all there is, so we made up the idea of eternal life. I had come to believe that life required me to struggle with my existential angst, rather than try to escape it.

I wanted to be brave enough to look into the bleakness of my own existential aloneness and not flinch, but in the face of the dissolution of my beliefs, I felt as if the ground had fallen out from under me. I so wanted to retreat to the feathery nest of my old belief system, but my rigorous mind would not allow it. I was convinced that I needed to be brutally honest with myself and toughen up to my new reality. There was a war going on between my heart and my newly powerful mind. I desperately wanted to reconcile the differences between the two.

The next time I was home, I made an appointment with John Gunn, which I awaited with great anticipation. Stomach fluttering, I entered his office and was immediately enveloped by the feeling of safety that that place had come to represent for me. As I sank down into the familiar, big, green, leathery chair, I knew I was not the young girl who had sat there before, so certain of my belonging in this church community. In my mind, I was an outsider now, maybe even a traitor. I looked across the desk at this man I had so come to trust and began to cry. "I no longer believe in God," I confessed. "I just can't believe any of it anymore. I don't believe that Mary gave birth as a virgin or that Jesus died and came alive again. It's all just a bunch of hocus-pocus."

I peered across at him, fully expecting that if anyone could, John would be the one to help me recapture my faith, stitch it all back together, and make it whole again. When I finished my tearful story, he was silent at first. Then he looked at me and said simply, "Congratulations! Now you can set out in your own life and decide what it is that you truly believe. You are free. Now the real story begins."

We may have talked longer, but I don't think I was there for a full hour. The work was finished. He wished me well, and I walked out the door. I left holding my spiritual life in my own hands. *What I believe is mine to discover?* That was a whole new way of seeing things. As confused as I was at the time, I recognized a kernel of truth in what he was saying, and off I went. I had found a certain peace, not in the way I had hoped, but in a grounded optimism that I would figure things out. Of course, the rest of my life has told the story.

I have carried that encounter with me all these years, as one of my most important moments, and have recounted to many the events of that meeting. Each time I come to my minister's response, even the most jaded are moved, and I relive again the blessed freedom my minister gave me as a young girl to find myself in a most essential way. Now, some fifty years later, this writing, which traces the golden threads of the sacred as it has woven itself through my life, was inspired by the freedom and the challenge John Gunn gave me that day.

With that meeting, I left my Heavenly Father and my beloved Jesus behind. I made no more attempts to retrieve my beliefs, but life did go on. I was convinced that in leaving my church, I had severed all ties to religion. Like so much else that we cast aside as we mature into adulthood, my religion was simply another piece of my childhood that I had left behind.

❦ Reflection

How have your early religious experiences affected your life? If you didn't go to church, what did you consider sacred? Make two collages, one about your childhood spirituality and the other about your relationship with the sacred today. Try this even if you are now agnostic or an atheist.

Chapter 5:

Finding My Knight in Shining Armor

Our marriage license turned out to be a learner's permit.
—JOAN RIVERS

I understood from a very young age that I was destined to grow up and get married. In the 1950s, that message was part of the air that little girls breathed. "One day you'll fall in love, you'll see. It will happen. It happens to everyone," my mother promised. My grandmother assured me, starting when I was very small, that when I married, her china and her silver would be mine. In my mind, that was my future, unless I was undesirable and ended up being an old maid.

In those days, getting married was the first step toward manifesting my real purpose as a woman, and that was to become a mother. My family valued education, so I had gone to college and received my bachelor's degree. But the emphasis was on getting the degree and not on how I would use my education to support myself in the world. When I was a child, I didn't have one friend whose mother worked to support herself. All were stay-at-home moms with a husband to support them. I had only to look around to understand that motherhood was the real purpose of my existence.

Getting married required making myself attractive to men so this prophecy could be fulfilled. It was devastatingly clear to me throughout my adolescence that I was failing miserably in this area of my life, as boys did not seem to be attracted to me. I suffered through junior high school dances without being asked to dance and went all the way through high school without being asked out on a single date. The shame I felt permeated my being and devoured my self-esteem. I squirmed when my grandmother, tilting her head and raising her eyebrows, asked, "Do you have a boyfriend yet?"

"No, no boyfriend," I responded, looking away, knowing that my life was not proceeding as was expected. But, try as I might, I couldn't make it happen as it should.

I know it didn't help that I was five feet, eight inches tall by sixth grade and six feet by high school. In addition, I was still exceedingly shy. Besides that, I had a mother who discouraged makeup and laid down the law about what kind I was allowed to use.

"You can wear Tangee lipstick, but that's it. And wipe most of it off," she told me. Tangee was more like lip balm than lipstick.

"But, Mom, everyone is wearing real lipstick and using mascara. I want to, too," I begged.

"You have such long, beautiful eyelashes, you don't need any eye makeup. I don't care what everyone else is doing. You're not one of those girls. I don't want you to be a hussy."

By controlling my access to money, my mother also exercised considerable control over my wardrobe, which did not help me wear clothes that were considered stylish at the time. Growing up in Southern California, where image was everything, I did not fit the mold that was all that mattered at the time. My struggles seemed destined to repeat themselves in college, as I lived through my first year with the same curse I'd had in high school.

When I was a child, nineteen was my favorite number. It felt magical to me. Naturally, I couldn't wait to be nineteen years old. Sure enough, during my sophomore year of college, when I reached that magical age, my relationship fortune shifted for the better. In the fall of that year, not one but two guys suddenly wanted my attention. Of the two, I chose John in a spontaneous moment, standing up the other guy, Wally. Wally was as shy as I was. I selfishly left him in the dust on the occasion of our first date in an almost animalistic fashion, deciding my fortunes were better served by casting my lot with John. With that choice, I did indeed set my future, though I didn't know that at the time. What I did know was that, at long last, my life seemed to be righting itself.

John lived in the dorm where my brother was a resident assistant, and my brother introduced us sometime before Christmas. The night we got together, there was a door-decorating contest in the dorm, and the halls were filled with students checking out all the doors and voting for their favorites. I had arranged to walk around with Wally, who was by now a little late. I waited patiently in my room, listening for a knock on my door. My excitement built as I heard the students flooding down the hallway, laughing and having a good time. When the knock finally came, it was John, not Wally, who stood there waiting.

"Well, hello," I stammered.

"Hi," he replied, a bit stiffly, looking like maybe he didn't know what to say next. Time stopped for a moment as we each waited for the other to speak.

"You want to walk around with me?" he managed to ask.

"Sure," I replied, without a moment's hesitation. I had waited years for this, and no part of me wanted to let it slip away. I was only vaguely aware that I was deserting Wally as I stepped out the door, so flattered was I by what was unfolding in the moment. Lost in the sheer joy of being seen and desired by someone, I was finally off on my first date. *Will he become my boyfriend?* I wondered, as he took my hand and we walked down the hallway.

That is what happened, and in the following months, many of my long-held desires were fulfilled. Being home in high school when I knew others were out and about together, especially at dances that required dates, had been excruciating for me. Staying home alone in deep mourning, I had imagined what it might have been like to be there, to be invited and accepted. Now, I had a date for all the important events. I felt like Cinderella, finally recognized for my royal roots, finally loved, cherished, and desired, finally participating in a world I had only watched from afar.

Memories of my early times with John live in me as snapshots of events and feelings, without any sense of order or continuity. Soon after that magical first evening, I was walking across campus with a girlfriend. Hearing a scuffle in some bushes nearby, we turned to see what was causing the ruckus and found John scrambling out from the undergrowth. He claimed to be checking on some quail nests he was monitoring for one of his science classes, which no doubt was true, but my friend and I found it hilarious and amazing and responded to that meeting as a meaningful coincidence, long before I had the word "synchronicity" to describe such an event.

John and I began seeing a lot of each other. We took long walks around the lagoon and watched sunsets from the headlands across from our dorms. There were dances and parties, including a beach party where a whole pig was roasted right there on the sand. One night we went into the Santa Barbara hills, where part of the old UCSB campus had been repurposed as a movie theater, and saw the incredibly romantic French film *The Umbrellas of Cherbourg*. I fell in love with the movie and the music, just as I was falling in love with John.

Afterward, we found an overlook where the twinkling lights of Santa Barbara proper stretched out below us, all the way out to the sea. We made out in the steamy car, kissing and beginning to open our bodies to each other. Allowing his hands to fumble with my bra and offering my breast for his exploration, I felt a rush of warmth sweep through me and instantly understood that I was playing with fire. This much passion was wild and exciting, but I knew it was something I would have to learn to control.

It all seems so innocent now, but in those days, that exploration took place under a great shadow, with severely threatening consequences. The pill was not yet easily available, so everyone was afraid of getting pregnant, but the shame I would surely endure if I became pregnant gave me much greater motivation to control my desires than any thoughts about having a child and becoming a mother at my young age. That was unthinkable, and abortion came with a possible death sentence. The times weren't yet pressuring us in the direction of a more open sexuality, but, just few years later, it would be an entirely different story.

I didn't have a car, but John had an old Peugeot, which gave us lots of freedom. We took day trips into the mountains, enjoying nature together. I liked to go with him on his biology field-study excursions into the Santa Ynez Mountains just outside Santa Barbara. One unforgettable night, we were wading up a creek bed in the dark, trying to catch frogs with a butterfly net, when we heard a scream so close and so wild, it sent us scrambling back to the car. Hearts pounding, we slammed the doors shut, stared at each other wide-eyed, and burst into hysterical laughter. We didn't ever learn what made that feral sound, but I imagine it was a mountain lion. Looking back, I see that evening as a perfect mirror for the adventure we were involved in—our passionate sexual connection and our frantic attempts to slam the door shut in order to deal with all that wildness inside our own bodies.

Making out in the back seat of John's old Peugeot was next to impossible for our tall bodies, but down back roads and in the vastness of the great outdoors, we could lay a blanket on the forest floor and spend hours exploring each other in greater comfort. In those days, making love was tantalizing and very, very slow. Neither John nor I was into risking our future by getting me pregnant, so we were both extremely careful and considerate as we built mutual trust. Kissing and his fondling my breasts were only the beginning. Soon I was unzipping his Levi's and reaching into his Jockey underwear to free his penis. Having never explored a penis before, I was curious about how it went from soft and floppy to long and hard. I felt like I had magic in my hands. It was a miracle to me that I could bring his penis alive and offer so much pleasure with my touch, as evidenced by his sighs. Watching it grow to full size was a bit frightening at first, as it was so substantial that I had trouble imagining how it would one day enter my body. I didn't let that stop me, though; I came to trust that it would all work out as it should.

All of this sent my body into rapture. Before long, he was reaching under my dress and into my panties, stroking my clitoris and exploring my depths with his long fingers. After some time, we were undressing each other, fondling each other everywhere, using our hands and mouths to bring each other to climax.

Often, we would stop in the midst of these encounters, take some deep breaths, and calm ourselves, wanting so to control our desire to consummate our lovemaking by having intercourse. In retrospect, I don't know how we were able to stop it, but it's easy to forget now how enormous our fear was back then.

As we fell in love, I wanted nothing more in the world than to spend time with John. I wanted to know everything about him—what he was interested in, who he had been, and what his plans for the future were. I was excited to learn that he was very smart and had graduated at the top of his class in high school. The fact that math and science were his focus seemed admirable and very manly, and I translated his interest in biology into a fascination with nature. I also learned that he went to church every Sunday and considered himself a Christian. The fact that he still went to church was bothersome, and his plan to become a dentist and work for his father's dental practice in Fresno after graduation was downright repulsive to me. I hated dentists!

I met his father, Sherman, early in our time together. I learned that he was a man with strange boundaries. As we stood on the headlands, looking out over the ocean, he told me he once knew a woman with hair on her breasts. That day, Sherman also gave me a warning: "You know, I don't want you to disturb John's studies. He's a serious boy, dedicated to his religious beliefs and on a challenging career path. I don't want that messed with because he's falling in love with you."

Sherman's assumption that he was running John's life felt overbearing and uncalled for. It made John seem like a boy, not a man. Yet I didn't challenge his father. "Yes, all those things are important," I assured him. I did want the best for John, but I didn't see how our relationship would get in the way of his accomplishments or mine. I valued independence, and my own parents certainly weren't watching over me in that way.

Despite Sherman's lecture, soon after our meeting, I suggested a different career path for John. "Have you ever thought of becoming a doctor, instead of a dentist?" I asked one afternoon as we walked out of the dorm on our way to the dining hall. "I mean, you're a really great student—you could easily do it. Do you really want to be a dentist in Fresno with your dad?"

"That's just always been my father's dream," he told me. "He's been talking about that since I was a little boy."

"Yeah, but do you really want to be a dentist?" I repeated.

"You know, I think I'd probably like it OK, and he has everything all set up. I guess I've never really thought about it much, but no, I'm not really thrilled about moving back to Fresno."

At the time, I probably thought I was helping John find his independence. I don't know why I thought that was my job, but I took it on quite naturally. Perhaps back then I didn't think I had the power to manifest my own dreams, so I thought I'd help him with his. I did know that I was trying to direct his future in a way that was more pleasing to me. Aside from the fact that I hated dentists, I had already lived in Fresno as a young girl. I had no desire to return.

The 1960s hadn't come into full bloom yet. Neither of us knew how our world would soon explode, how so much of the innocence of the generation before would soon be tossed away. It's amazing to me now that, so early in our relationship, I saw marriage as a possibility and was aiming my actions in that direction. I was struggling for my own maturity and independence, and I wanted a partner who was yearning for those things as well. Along with his unquestioning surrender to his father's plans for his future, I saw John's unexamined religious beliefs as a mark of his immaturity, another way in which his father was overbearing and not allowing John to chart his own path.

"So, do you really believe there's a God up there in the sky?" I asked one day as we sat overlooking the ocean.

"Well, I haven't thought about it much. I've just always gone to church and been part of all that."

"I'm just wondering how, since you're into science and all, you come to terms with things like the creation story in Genesis, and what you do with the idea of Jesus rising from the dead," I said. "I just don't buy all that anymore."

"I guess I just don't take it all that seriously. My dad always took us to church. It's just what we did. I don't much like all the rules," he said. "In the church I went to at home, we weren't allowed to dance, and anything having to do with sex was evil. That was hard on my social life. I guess that's where I've had the most trouble with the church, all the rules. And now, here, I don't really fit in with the campus Christians. It's really not that big a thing for me. Besides, I'm busy, so it's hard to make time for church."

Aha! I thought. He *was* stepping away, albeit a little more slowly than I had, but I could see he was headed in that direction.

Little did I know that this world in which all seemed right wasn't actually reality; rather, I had merely entered the world of romantic love. My culture had been selling me this worldview since I was a tiny child. In this realm, I was told, a knight in shining armor on a snow-white horse would one day swoop down, pick me up, and save me from all worry and concern, my protector forever. When I met him, we would marry, have children, and, like the kings and queens of old, live happily ever after. John was my knight in shining armor. He rescued me from a world where I felt like a misfit, where I was unseen and unloved. His presence in my life catapulted me into my future. I immediately saw him as the fulfiller of all my dreams.

This was a problem, however, when he didn't actually fit the image of the man of my dreams. For instance, on the night of our first formal dance, he presented me with a corsage, as was expected. He had made reservations at a restaurant in the harbor in downtown Santa Barbara. I imagined our dinner out as a romantic interlude by the water. When we arrived at the restaurant, however, I saw that it was on the other side of the busy beachfront highway. Once inside, in my formal dress and wrist corsage, I was mortified to discover that it was a cafeteria and that John was pleased to have a coupon for our dinner. I can laugh now at my predicament, but it was no laughing matter at the time to be with a man who thought this was "a great place, a special bargain" on this important night. Clearly, I was in someone else's dream, not my own.

During our courtship, I periodically broke up with John when he didn't meet my expectations, but we were never apart for long. After a bit, we would end up back together again. My heart and my body kept me returning.

Near the end of college, we felt our lives transforming as we prepared for our next steps. I was accepted to serve in the Peace Corps in Micronesia, and John was accepted at the University of California, San Francisco, for medical school. As it all became more real, I must have realized that going to Micronesia would be a reach for me. My heart rebelled against the plan, and I started to realize that what I really wanted was to get married.

We lived in our own apartments in our last year at UCSB. John had only one roommate, so we spent plenty of time at his place. After our last breakup, we had become quite serious. Life was moving forward quickly, and we had talked about a possible future together, but it was all very vague. That winter, the Peugeot conked out and would have required extensive repair to get it back on the road again. I saw my chance. "John, don't spend your money on that old car. Save it and buy me an engagement ring instead. Let's get married. I'm ready for that," I announced.

"You mean you would give up going into the Peace Corps and come to San Francisco with me?" he asked excitedly.

"Yes," I said. "I can get a job and support us while you're in school. Let's do it."

John took me up on the idea without hesitation, and soon we were picking out rings together and planning a simple wedding after our graduation.

We were enough on the early edge of the sexual revolution of the '60s that we never considered living together, instead of marrying. We also still hadn't consummated our relationship by having intercourse. In the late spring, once I had legally obtained birth control pills from my doctor because I was about to be married, we decided we couldn't wait any longer. We made a reservation at a hotel in downtown Santa Barbara, and there, at long last, his penis entered my vagina and we both experienced the real thing. As the world had changed around us, I think we felt left behind in our cautiousness. That night gave us some credentials in the new age, but my simultaneous realization that there was an art to having intercourse made the encounter a bit of a letdown for me.

June 24, 1967

One week after we graduated, John and I walked down the aisle in the new sanctuary at the West Covina Baptist Church and said our vows. John Gunn presided over our union. We borrowed my parents' extra car, and off we went to Carmel for a weeklong honeymoon. Upon returning, we settled in San Francisco. It was 1967, the Summer of Love. Though we dressed and looked like hippies, we weren't dropping out. John was just beginning medical school, and I found a job working for the telephone company and became our sole financial supporter.

We were both only twenty-one years old. Emotionally, we were but children setting out into our adult lives, as if we were stepping into a fairy tale. Neither one of us had witnessed good examples of coupling in our own families. John's parents were divorced, mine living in a long-term marriage without much apparent emotional connection.

Memories are elusive, and what we hold as the truth about our past is often inaccurate. While I was writing this book, I wanted to look more deeply at who I was when I entered my marriage, so I dug out my wedding photographs and reread all the entries in my wedding memory book. I found myself there, a young woman full of innocence and trust, letting my life move on to its next expected phase. I seemed to be much more concerned with external things—the wedding, the shower, the gifts—than with what was happening to me internally. Still, I do recall sometimes wondering if I should go through with it all. It was evidently all right for me to question that inside myself, but when my college roommate asked me what I was doing, I was furious. I was headed down the road of marriage and family, and no one was going to talk me out of it. I didn't have the slightest clue that the reality I was entering was a fairy tale.

My grandmother had sewn all my clothes for me when I was a little girl. When the time came to select my wedding dress, I begged her to sew it for me. After her initial resistance, she agreed. The pictures from my wedding show me in the gown that she made—a regal dress, complete with a crown and an extralong train. The night of our wedding, I knew I was a queen, marrying my king. I slipped easily into the fairy-tale life that I had been promised and was fully expecting to live happily ever after.

Of course, there is much more to the story. Not until I stumbled upon the writings of Carl Jung did I understand that my "knight in shining armor" stood out to me because he embodied many aspects of me that I didn't recognize as my own—namely, my own male energies. The story didn't mention that, looking into John's eyes, I would see my own masculine side and fall in love with him. Likewise, in me, he would see his own feminine side and fall in love with her. Jung identified the masculine side of a woman as her animus and the feminine side of a man as his anima. They exist in the psyche as powerful archetypes and take on godlike proportions. When we project them onto mere mortals, we set the stage for great disillusionment.

I think it is accurate to assume that this was the state of my psyche when I married John. He would have to tell the story of what he saw in me that would complete the picture of what we projected onto each other, but I'm certain the projections were there for both of us, as we were not unique in this process. I believe it is how we all come to relationship in a culture that believes in and fosters romantic love.

By the time we married, I had thrown out all belief in a divine energy that presented itself as God. I had moved through my agnostic phase and identified myself quite certainly as an atheist. I never once thought that in falling in love with John, I was falling in love with another god, though my enchantment with the situation might have been a hint about the mythic nature of what was happening. As Jung would say, my animus projections blinded me to the real human being. Having given up on a God in Heaven, I created a god here on Earth, within my own mind, a god constructed of my own unlived life energy, and then I named him John and we began relating to each other. In this way, my relationship with John and my marriage became my unrecognized spiritual path.

Of course, life is not a fairy tale and human beings are not gods. Reality has a way of challenging us to come down from the sky world and plant our feet on Mother Earth. John was not placed here to play the role in which I cast him, nor was I to do that for him. He was not here to make my life easy or to protect me from the suffering that is inevitably part of living. He was here to pursue his own interests, desires, and goals, to live his own life. And so was I!

Every couple enters a process of needing to pull back these projections and enter more deeply into their own lives. It is at that point that our fairy-tale lives come to an end and we begin seeing the actual person we have chosen to live with. The real work of relationship starts then, when the give-and-take of working out a life together commences. There can be a deepening of love and commitment as we learn to hold ourselves and that real person we have chosen to marry. That is what we hope for most, but disillusionment and disintegration can also ensue if we can't find our way to that new reality. As our life together unfolded and our fairy-tale courtship began to dissolve, John and I began our struggle to meet that challenge.

Some years into my marriage, I had an important dream. In my dream, I was standing alone in a wide-open landscape. Off in the distance, I saw a rider galloping toward me on a white horse. I could hear the hoofbeats coming closer and closer. I saw dust clouds gathering around the rider. I was relieved, thinking that he was coming for me and would take me home. Imagine my surprise when he galloped on by, headed for some distant destination.

I've never forgotten that dream. It marks the time when, having already given up on an old man in the sky watching over me, I was perhaps also ready to give up on a knight in shining armor as well. It was the beginning of my understanding that it was my own wholeness I was seeking. It would be many years before I would begin to integrate the fact that I didn't need to look outside myself for that fairy-tale magic. I had both a king and a queen, as well as gods and goddesses, residing right inside me. If I was going to find my own genuine relationship with the divine, I needed to look within.

June 24, 1967

❧ *Reflection*

We fall in love again and again, with people, work, pets, activities, places, things. Make a long, thin piece of paper. Create a timeline that traces the periods when that kind of magical experience visited your life. Use photos, collage, paint, glitter, whatever you like to express the exuberance of those openings. In your journal, write what you learned about yourself and how each of those experiences changed you.

Chapter 6:

Revelations from the Fertile Darkness

What is this talked-of mystery of birth
But being mounted bareback on the earth?
—ROBERT FROST

Two years after John and I were married, I felt an irresistible force pulling me toward motherhood. All my thoughts and fantasies expressed my deep longing to become pregnant, have a baby, and start our family.

When I held a friend's newborn in my arms, it was as if I had fallen under a spell. I was in the clutches of a biological imperative so powerful, it was impossible to ignore. I see now that being pregnant and giving birth began many years of apprenticeship to the Mother God, Mother Earth, the Goddess, She of Many Names, but I didn't think of it that way at the time.

Only in looking back do I see the thread of the sacred woven solidly into this time of my life. All my earlier spiritual seeking had me looking skyward, not down toward the earth; it had been all about ascending, not descending. In fact, I was taught subtly, if not blatantly, that living the life of the body, especially a woman's body, was not to be trusted. It risked descent into hell.

Creation

I certainly received those messages about my sexuality. Having sex outside marriage was a mortal sin. While my church didn't emphasize that, the message had been absorbed into the culture. Whether we would actually go to hell in a biblical sense, my friends and I understood that we would be living in hell on Earth if we became pregnant before we were married.

When my grandmother learned that I finally had a boyfriend, she warned me, with a wink and a nod, "Be good and be careful." She said it in a kindly fashion, but there was a deadly seriousness behind her words that took me by surprise. However, Grandma had reason to warn me. I learned when I was much older that my father was born seven months after my grandparents were married. She must have borne terrible shame for her transgression.

In so many ways, I learned that living in a woman's body required much carefulness. Everything had to occur in just the right order. I had managed to be careful and pretty much do things in that expected order. Finally, all the lights were green and, now married, I could safely proceed down the road of motherhood.

Rationally, I knew it would have made much more sense to hold off on starting our family until John had finished his training, but that would have been years. We lived in married-student housing at the university. Others there were having babies and making it work. *They're doing it; I'm sure we can, too*, I thought. I came up with a plan and presented my idea to John. "If I get pregnant now, I can work until the end of my pregnancy. We would just need a loan for your last year. It will be tight financially, but I know we can make it work." I was thrilled that John didn't resist.

Once our decision was made, the few months it took to become pregnant seemed like an eternity. My excitement when it finally happened was over the top. I loved being pregnant! Even morning sickness, while pretty miserable to deal with in the moment, seemed like part of the magic. I experienced my body taking charge in a dramatic way, transforming before my very eyes.

My physical reality came to dominate my life, and I was fine with letting that be. There was pleasure in having my biological destiny fulfill itself, though the feminist in me is a bit embarrassed to admit that. It was a relief, a kind of coming home to an essence of who my body meant me to be. While I was not thinking of it as a spiritual experience, I did realize that being pregnant catapulted me into a new sense of belonging in the world. I felt as if I was stepping into a circle of women that had been forming since the time of my earliest ancestors.

I felt aligned in a new way with all creation. In being pregnant, I was living with one foot in this world and one foot in another, much more expansive reality. My body was the bridge between the two. Having three sons, I experienced this precious state three times in my life. I knew it was miraculous, but I don't think I ever put the word "sacred" on it or saw it in any way as connected to the religion I had disavowed.

I know the exact moment when I no longer considered myself an atheist. It was at 12:46 in the afternoon on September 28, 1970. I was at the University of California Medical Center in San Francisco, having just given birth to my first son, Erik. My water had broken early that morning. It was a big surprise, as it was a full month before my due date.

Labor started immediately after my water broke, but early that afternoon, an intern examined me and told John that if the process didn't pick up after lunch, they would have to induce me. The door to my labor room had barely closed when my next contraction began to tighten my belly. As it reached its peak, I felt a distinct urge to push. I told John, who was my labor coach. We were confused, after having just heard the intern's report, and we both decided that it couldn't be so. But as I struggled to manage the next contraction, the need to push returned strongly. I announced again, more urgently this time, that I wanted to push. I had no doubt about what I had just experienced, but John remained unconvinced. Very soon, the next contraction was upon me, and this time the need to push was so strong and my announcement so undeniably certain that John fled the room to seek help.

I had never had a clearer message from my body about anything. I knew my baby's birth was imminent. I knew it with everything in me. The doctor rushed in to examine me, and in no time, he and his staff were in position at the bottom of the delivery table. That was fortunate, because once I had permission to push, my son slithered out of me and into the world after only a few more contractions.

I got my first look at Erik when they laid him on my belly while they dealt with the umbilical cord and the afterbirth. Reaching down to touch my slippery, tiny little baby and hearing him cry, I wondered, *How it could be that this perfectly formed little person grew inside me?* It wasn't that I didn't know or had forgotten the scientific explanation of what had just occurred; it was that everything related to the mind seemed so small in comparison with what I had just learned in my body. *Wow*, I thought, *if this is possible, there is way more to this life than I ever imagined. I don't know what it is, but whatever it is, I know now that it exists and that I'm part of it!*

I didn't call it God—I had no name for it—but I knew for certain, as certain as I had been about that need to push, that there was some larger power, some larger energy, some force of nature that might as well be called God if it had a name at all. It was massive and unfathomable, like trying to hold eternity in my mind. It wasn't something out there that I had to believe in. There was nothing to look for, or hope for. I didn't have to conjure up images of or a relationship with an old man in the sky, nor did I have to try to make myself believe all those religious stories I had been told. It was made not of air or sky or the Holy Spirit, but rather of something from the earth itself. It was inside me, inside everyone, and inside everything. We were all deeply entwined with it and created by it.

The births of each of my children remain the high points of my life. While Gabriel's and Eli's births were not followed by such a deep spiritual transformation, they were equally powerful. Each left me with enormous confidence and a deeper belief in my own power as a woman. The memories of those times are not sugarcoated. It was hard work, probably the hardest work I have ever done in my entire life, but it was manageable. In fact, it became increasingly clear that my body, which I judged harshly in so many ways, was perfectly designed for this experience. For me, giving birth was a deep meditation on the force of nature at the core of my existence and a matter of learning to surrender to it. In each of my births, once I could push and meet that force with my own energy, I felt sheer ecstasy. My large frame was built for this part to be easy. At no other time in my life have I experienced such pure joy as I did when I heard their first little gurgles and then their hearty cries. As my little ones took their first breaths, I was returning to this world, as if coming back from a wilder place where flesh and blood were all that mattered. My animal body reigned there, and my time in that wild world left me vibrantly alive, shaking, laughing, and crying from the beauty of it all, while it also left my mind feeling very small.

Giving birth brought me maturity, a taste of the biological power of my womanhood, and a glimpse into our deep, dark past, when, rather than being taken for granted, this power we women hold was celebrated. I had a new understanding of how others' fear of this awesome power contributed to the subjugation of women, how the ancient cultures that celebrated those powers needed to be vanquished in order for the patriarchy's reign to take hold.

The weeks following the births of my sons were challenging for me. I was thrilled with my new little ones and awed each time by the experience of giving birth, so I was confused by the sadness inside me in those early days. I didn't understand it, but I did accept it, because it was undeniable. I knew I was in a time of major transition, that my pregnancy was over and life was moving on, and that my hormones were taking me for a wild ride, but my sadness seemed self-centered and unreasonable. I puzzled over these disparate feelings and felt a good deal of shame about it all.

Only in hindsight did I come to understand those feelings as genuine mourning. After all, the baby in the womb is lost to the mother. Though my arms were now full, my uterus was not. Naturally, I felt the emptiness. While pregnant, I was a part of something much larger than I was. My body was the conduit and container for the creation of life. I had embodied the Great Mother's energy; I was as close as I would ever come to connecting with the source of all creation. Then, suddenly, upon the completion of my pregnancy, I was not. I was falling back into my ordinary reality. As with the sadness I felt as a child when my moments of expanded awareness ended, as with my rude awakening from the magic of the night of my baptism, the ordinary Marilyn reappeared and was the one who needed to meet the daunting demands of her little ones.

Touching the wellspring of creation through my own body was a gift beyond all measure, but it has taken a lifetime to extract the full meaning of the experience. On one level, it was all so ordinary, and on another, completely extraordinary. I had received a scientific description of what to expect from pregnancy and childbirth, but nothing in my life had prepared me to think of anything connected to my feminine body as sacred until I grew a baby inside my own womb. It left me with an embodied understanding that the process of creation is ongoing, ever present, and always revealing itself. It taught me that we are all one with the creative energies of the universe.

Indeed, living life is itself a creative process. We humans are creating our own lives from moment to moment, whether we perceive it that way or not. Our genetic makeup and our life experiences sculpt us, but we are not the rigid structures we sometimes perceive ourselves to be. We live inside a universe that is alive and always changing, powered by an energetic flow that presents us with the opportunity for new life at every turn. This promise of regeneration and renewal rests at the core of our very existence.

When we speak of "visions," we are most often talking about brilliant illuminations of the mind. The Bible is full of stories about old men having these kinds of revelations. The revelation I received in being pregnant and giving birth didn't present like a fiery bolt of lightning from the sky but rather grew over months of time, in the darkness of my womb. In its time, and with great force, it broke into my consciousness when I gave birth. The energy behind that revelation took place in the darkness, not in the light. It clearly came from below and not from above, from inside me and not outside me. But, like the visionaries of old, I was literally left shaking, my world redefined.

❦ *Reflection*

When have you felt closest to the creative power of the Great Mother's energy? Make a collage, drawing, or sculpture titled, "I Am a Child of Nature." In your journal, let that child speak to you about the creative process of which we are a part.

Chapter 7:

What Are Little Boys Made Of?

*Sometimes when you pick up your child you can feel the map of your own bones
beneath your hands, or smell the scent of your skin in the nape of his neck.
This is the most extraordinary thing about motherhood—finding a piece of
yourself separate and apart that all the same you could not live without.*
—Jodi Picoult, *Perfect Match*

Even though my pregnancies and my births carried their own light, that light didn't scare away the dark patterns that were emerging in my marriage. I had imagined that starting our family would bring John and me closer together; instead, it did the opposite. When Erik was born, I became acutely aware that while John and I had conceived him together, we were not both in charge of his care. Our lives were diverging. My life was becoming centered at home, John's immersed in the outer world. Compared with the transformation that motherhood inspired in me, John's life seemed to go on almost without missing a beat. As a result, I felt very alone with all my new responsibilities.

I was a nursing mother, so feeding the baby was mine to manage, but it seemed everything else was, too. When I was pregnant, I had expected that I would nurse Erik in the night, but when he was born a month early, I didn't realize how often he would need to eat. As that reality unfolded, I lost confidence. *Wait a minute*, I thought. *I expected to feed him at 2:00 a.m. and 6:00 a.m. But midnight and 4:00 a.m. as well? How can that be?* I remember standing in the doorway of our apartment, saying goodbye to friends who had stopped by to see our new baby. It was my second day home from the hospital. I was trying to describe my surprise at just how impossible this all seemed, but words could not contain how incredulous I was. I felt as if I were stepping outside the realm of human possibility. Those first few days with Erik gave me a crash course in the level of self-sacrifice mothering would ask of me. I wasn't at all sure I was up to the task.

When John's fall term began, he continued to add to his already demanding schedule. "They're offering a Spanish class now with a medical emphasis. It's voluntary but very important. I'd like to be able to communicate directly with Spanish-speaking patients, so I'm going to enroll."

"OK," I said. But inside, I felt abandoned. The class met in the evening, which was our only time together. I didn't challenge him, as I still believed that his needs were more important than mine. Though I had read Betty Friedan's *The Feminine Mystique* near the end of college and had removed the word "obey" from our wedding vows, clearly, I had not yet integrated the feminist message. *Besides*, I thought, *I signed up to support John through medical school, and I was the one who suggested we have a baby in the midst of it all.* The Spanish class seemed like just one more sacrifice I needed to make for John's training.

When Erik was only ten days old, he was readmitted to the hospital because he was jaundiced. When the doctors broke this news to me, John was in his Spanish class, somewhere in the UC medical center's multistory building. While the doctors were readying Erik for admission, I left the emergency room and wandered from floor to floor, looking for John so I could alert him to this turn of events. Trying not to cry and becoming increasingly frantic, I peeked in every classroom where I saw a light and asked everyone I saw if they knew where the Spanish class was being held. I was unsuccessful in my search. Returning to the emergency room, I was directed to the nursery, where I found Erik in an incubator in a room with other sick babies. John did not learn about what had happened until later that night.

Erik remained in the hospital for ten days, being tested for all sorts of scary conditions, none of which seemed to be the cause of the problem, which eventually righted itself. While he was there, I nursed him when I could and expressed milk so he could continue to have breast milk when I was not there. I sat by his incubator for as many hours as I could possibly manage, holding him when I was allowed to and going home only to sleep. John came and went as he could. Mostly, I sat alone.

These iconic moments remain present for me because they tell the story of our divergent paths as I entered motherhood. The image of me wandering in the halls of academia, looking for my husband and my children's father, perfectly describes the next several years of our lives together. John was the missing piece in the puzzle that I was trying to put together, and I just couldn't find him.

He was absorbed in his life as a student. There was no end to the possible studying that he could do. That left him not very present to what was happening at home, even when he was there. Because doctors in training spend days and nights away from home, I often believed his allegiance was elsewhere. His physical and emotional absence was difficult for me to manage. I wasn't so aware of it at first, but I eventually came to realize that I had managed to duplicate the family pattern I had grown up with: first the absent father, now the absent husband.

I begged for more time and attention to come our way. "John could you just take a break?" became my mantra. I had no end of ideas about what we could be doing that would be much more fun. Our apartment in married-student housing was tiny. We made a nursery out of the bedroom and put our king-size bed in the living room. That left barely enough room for John's desk, a small couch, and a collapsible table that we set up only for our meals. The kitchen had room for one person to cook. It was easy to get cabin fever, and on sunny weekend days, I just wanted to get outside.

"Let's go take a walk in Golden Gate Park. It's a beautiful day," I'd suggest.

There would be a pause while John, sitting at his desk with his nose in a book, would finish what he was reading. Looking up as if I had dragged him away from another land, he would respond, "I can't. I've got a big exam coming up on Monday, and I've hardly paid attention to one of the main topics. I need to stay focused here today."

My heart would sink. I'd pack up what I needed and get the baby ready, and off we would go, on our own. I could tolerate being put off for a while, but when it happened time after time, I felt abandoned. I see now that in my desperation for John to be a part of our family, I sometimes found it hard to have compassion for his predicament. Likewise, he didn't have compassion for mine, but the difference was that our society supported his lack thereof. We women were expected to do whatever was necessary to support our men. Men were to provide support by working, but not so much in other ways.

After all of Erik's early problems, imagine my despair when I took Gabriel for his first checkup and learned that, although I thought nursing was going well, he had not gained enough weight. He was diagnosed as a "failure to thrive." Because of my experience with Erik's prematurity and his hospitalization, I was counseling other breastfeeding women through a local nursing-mothers organization. I was supposed to be the expert. I knew the size of my own nipples was a problem for my newborns, but I thought I was dealing well with that problem. After that doctor's visit, all the confidence I had flew out the window. I was clearly the cause of this problem; there was no other way to look at it. I had failed at my number-one job. I immediately began expressing milk after I nursed and feeding it to Gabriel with a bottle. Eventually he got a little bigger, and the problem resolved itself.

Because we were moving every couple of years for John's training—first medical school, then his internship, and then his pediatric residency—my social support system was small and made up of new friends, mostly other doctors' wives with struggles similar to my own. Once we moved to Mendocino and settled in our community, that began to change. In addition, as the years passed, I became dedicated to the feminist cause. I joined a conscious-ness-raising group when I was pregnant with Gabriel and later began organizing such groups for the National Organization for Women. I had become an ardent feminist, though I often laugh when I remember that while I was working with NOW, I was still ironing John's clothes. Clearly, it takes a while for consciousness to actually change—in truth, perhaps a whole lifetime.

With my newfound awareness, when Eli was born, I began asking, or perhaps I should say insisting, that John participate more in our family life. Once his training was completed and he had started his own practice, I demanded that he make more time for family, that he take an extralong lunch hour (since we lived close by), and that he work only four and a half days per week. Between that and his call schedule, he was still often left with a more than forty-hour workweek. I wanted time for John and me to nurture our relationship, which was in trouble from sheer neglect, but, perhaps more urgently, I wanted my boys to have a father who was present in their lives.

The Joy of Parenting X 3

Whatever struggles I was having in my marriage, and whatever difficulties John and I had parenting together, I loved being a mother. There was no part of me that wasn't absorbed in it. For me, it was biological. Yet when I held my babies in my arms, I couldn't help feeling like Mary holding the baby Jesus. *Ridiculous*, I told myself, but that didn't stop the thoughts from coming, especially in quiet moments with my little ones, as I admired every inch of their perfect little bodies. And even though I no longer believed all those Bible stories, when their first Christmases rolled around, visions of the true meaning of the season flooded me.

I excused my thoughts and feelings as inescapable mental images of the culture in which I was raised and assured myself that they were meaningless. But it is telling that I recall them so clearly these fifty years later. If I had known then to pay attention to my inner imagery the way I do now, I might have realized that a voice from deep in my body was trying to let me know that in becoming a mother, I was standing on sacred ground.

When my babies were tiny, I was completely immersed in the physical realm. My body had just gone through an incredible transformation, birth had taken me more deeply into my physical reality than I had ever imagined possible, and now my breasts were pouring forth milk, that life-giving, perfectly formulated food for my babies. Except for those haunting images of Mother Mary, there was no part of me that saw what I was experiencing as sacred. Rather, I simply felt like I was living my biological destiny. The responsibility of being in a woman's body was now fully mine. It was a massive responsibility.

I know now that I wasn't ready to be a mother, though I would have argued with anyone who tried to tell me that at the time. Now, I would argue that no one is ever ready. I don't think it is possible. Rather, motherhood is something we dive into, like jumping off of a cliff, surrendering to the mystery, and somehow finding trust midfall that it will all come out all right in the end. I don't think it matters how much we have thought about it or planned for it—even if we yearned for it with all our heart, we cannot be prepared. While all those things may help, the fact is, we have no idea what will really be asked of us. We just have to jump in and give it a try. And so I did. A great deal of faith was called for, not in something external, but in my own ability to hold a precious new life in my hands and guide it toward maturity.

Of course, our hormones set us up with the best possible conditions for motherhood to flourish. That is in our DNA. But our psychological preparation depends on so many things. I wanted to do it perfectly, like I wanted to do everything else in my life at that time. I even believed maybe I could. But we are not perfect beings, and we will not raise perfect children. It sounds ludicrous to me now even to write those words, but I know that the innocent young woman I was back then hoped that might be possible. It didn't take long to put me in my place. It was a laughable goal.

When I first brought Erik home from the hospital, I wondered if the "powers that be" really knew what they were doing entrusting this life to me. I felt like an impostor, making it up as I went along. It was a giant experiment with really high stakes. As it turned out, the rocky beginnings for Erik and Gabriel proved just how high they were. I'll never forget the day when Eli was sitting peacefully in his infant seat in the backyard when a soccer ball, which had been kicked from some distance away, landed right on top of him. He was not injured, but I felt lacking in not having seen what was coming so I could have protected him. All of that had only to do with their *physical* survival—I was also in charge of shepherding these three lives on mental, emotional, and spiritual levels.

That's the problem with motherhood: Our culture pays lip service to the fact that motherhood is special and puts us on a pedestal, but that recognition backfires on us. We are held to standards so high that meeting them is impossible, and when we can't, we take the blame. Most of us internalize this dynamic and hold ourselves responsible.

Humility is perhaps the biggest lesson I learned in becoming a mother. We strive for our highest self to meet each challenge, but, more often than not, the ordinary human being that we are shows up. To make matters worse, it is guaranteed that occasionally even the worst of us will appear. When that happens, there is hell to pay internally. In the end, everything I ever thought about myself was challenged at one point or another over the time of my active mothering. I don't think there's any way around it. Being a parent is truly humanizing. If it isn't, I think we're in trouble and our children will be, too.

I tried with all my heart to be the very best mother I knew how to be. I'm sure at times I got close and my children thrived, but I also know that in other moments I was the worst possible mother and my children suffered. The good mother and the bad mother, the stuff of fairy tales, is right there playing itself out as we live our ordinary lives. In the end, it's all about balancing and hoping that the scales tip in the direction of the "good enough mother," a term coined by Donald Winnicott, a famed British pediatrician and psychoanalyst. If we strike that balance, our children learn to deal with our darkness yet remain open to all the good things life has to offer.

Now that I am in my seventies, active mothering is a long time in my past. I was twenty-four when Erik was born, and I was forty-nine when Eli graduated from high school. That means that active mothering spanned twenty-five years of my lifetime, almost one-third of my life as of the publication of this book. I know it's easier to make a list of the things I did wrong than it is to recount the things I did right and that making either of those lists is useless at this point in time. I know I loved my children. I respected them as unique individuals and learned over the years to trust their way of seeing the world and their place in it. My sons are grown and have their own, very independent lives. They also have light and dark sides of their own, just like everyone else. When I stand back and look at these young men, all seems to have turned out well in the end.

As the years rolled by, it was a challenge to recognize what I now see as the innate differences between my sons. What was appropriate parenting for one was not appropriate parenting for another. It was a constant challenge to keep up with their growing maturity. What was right at one time was completely wrong sometime later. That kept me dancing lightly on my feet, trying to be flexible, spontaneous, creative, and present.

Discovering that that creative approach was my own parenting style was an important piece of my mothering, but, even as it was emerging, I compared myself endlessly with how other friends and family were parenting. There were differences and much judgment on all sides as we all did our best with our children. Friends were lost and family sometimes alienated when differences arose. As life would have it, all those I was comparing myself with now have lovely adult children, as do I. But at the time, none of us knew that our varied approaches would all turn out to be valid, and back then, one way to be comfortable with our own style was to declare it better than someone else's.

In the end, I can say that being a mother was an intense kind of spiritual practice, way more intense than setting aside an hour each day to meditate or pray. It was a twenty-four-hour commitment every day, one that asked me to find love, compassion, and wisdom inside myself on a moment's notice, whether I was personally up to it or not. The goal never left me. It was my compass point those twenty-five years, and when I got lost, I had to point myself back in the right direction once again. Time was of the essence, as I was acutely aware that I was acting in the present but creating a future, so if I was off course, I needed to right myself quickly before I did too much damage.

Mothering was also a deep study in sacrificing the needs of my own ego for the good of something larger. That was not easily done but clearly mirrored the task of any spiritual seeker. Of course, it is love that makes that kind sacrifice possible, and my love for my children is impossible to describe in a way that can do it justice. I feel it so deeply in my body, and it is so entwined with my physicality, that my mind can hardly touch it. Living with and deepening into that love is one of the greatest gifts of my lifetime.

That love is what makes being a mother a sacred task and a deeply challenging spiritual practice. It is a practice that lasts a lifetime. For me, the trickiest part is how to keep that love honest and true and coming from the higher part of me. The dedication and self-sacrifice required to parent can be carried too far, so that parenting becomes a project of the ego, rather than a reflection of our higher self. When we involve our ego too much, love can easily become contingent upon our children meeting our expectations, even our unconscious expectations; this dynamic can then cut them off from their connection to their own deepest selves. We are not perfect beings without our own needs and desires and our own wounding. Our unconditional love isn't always easily accessed, though we may imagine it so and dearly desire for it to be so. Mothering for me is ongoing work in urging my heart in that direction.

Motherhood also seems to require a constant practice of letting go. At birth, it is literal, as we allow our babies to exit the womb, begin their journey down the birth canal, and find their way into the world. We release them again as they take their first steps without holding onto our hand, and again, as we let go of the bicycle we have been supporting and find them able to balance on their own. Watching as they sit in the driver's seat and drive off in our car elicits prayers for their safety. As they reach each milestone, we let go of the young one they were just a moment ago and embrace their newfound confidence and independence in the world. Over the years, we watch with awe as they go off to school, find their own friends, identify their own interests, study, and develop their minds. We follow each step in their development, and then, before we know it, they're grown and ready to leave home. The nest that we worked so hard to build and maintain eventually begins to empty.

When my first son went off to college, I was inconsolable. It wasn't that I wanted him to stay home. He was taking his next and rightful step out into the world, and I supported that wholeheartedly. It just took my mother heart some time to be able to cope with it all. As dramatic as it might sound, I felt like a woman in the old country saying goodbye to him as he headed for the new world. Erik was headed to UC Berkeley, just three hours from my door. I had all the blessings of modern transportation, but to my mother heart, that didn't matter at all.

Considering the intensity of my emotional response, I knew it was best to say goodbye at home, so I asked John to deliver Erik to his new life. I felt lacking, like I should have been able to handle the moment differently, but the fact was, I couldn't.

The morning he was set to leave, I woke at dawn from a very moving dream, in which I was in the dining room of the home where I grew up. A bird was trapped inside and flapping up against the window, trying to get out. I rushed over to open the window so I could set the bird free. I awakened in the process. No one was stirring when I woke up from this dream. In the forest, I heard the sound of a thrush welcoming the day.

It was five thirty in the morning. When all was set to go, Erik gathered us together in the living room. He told us that as he stepped into his new life, he realized that we were all he had in the world. He thanked us for his life so far and said that it had been good. We said our goodbyes, and off he went.

I was a basket case for the next week. My tears seemed never-ending. When I managed to stop them, I was afraid to go near anyone who might mention Erik in case the flood would begin all over again. I stayed very close to home. Of course, I did see my son again, and soon after. He went on into his life, and I into mine. At the time, I saw my son as the bird I needed to free in my dream. All these years later, I see that in opening that window, I was freeing myself as well.

After Erik left, I had a new perspective on my parenting. Raising my children had felt like climbing a mountain. Now I felt like I was on the downhill side of that mountain. Time sped up. In the blink of an eye, Gabriel was leaving, and soon after that, like shooting down a waterslide, Eli flew out the door.

By the time Gabriel left, I was more accomplished at meeting the challenge. I did take him off to school. We said our good-byes, and before I drove away, I saw him riding his bike with a childhood friend from Mendocino. They were laughing and talking. Though I had some tears, they were the tears of a full heart, rather than the gut-wrenching separation I had experienced the first time.

I followed Eli through his last year of high school, marking all the endings as they came along: the last awards ceremony, the last soccer game, the last basketball game, the last this, the last that. By the end of the year, I was saying goodbye to him but also quite consciously laying down my role of active mothering. When I drove him to college, I knew he was ready, and I was, too.

Managing my own life had been one thing, but as a mother I had been in charge of the moral and psychological development of my sons. I wanted to raise open, loving, and compassionate young men. I wanted them to be independent thinkers, well-motivated, curious, and eager to move forward in their lives. Guiding others to embrace their humanity and become loving beings is no small task. I had tried my best to give them a strong base from which to fly.

My pastel drawing *Leaving the Nest* came from that time in my life. The image of freeing the bird in my dream was strongly with me as each of my sons left home. When my grief about their leaving rose, I found myself holding out my cupped hand, feeling the soft feathers of the baby bird nestled in my palm; then, raising my hand, I imagined the bird taking off into the sky. Now it was time to release them to a larger energy. I hoped they would be able to access their own inner guidance as they moved into adulthood. My main job was done.

College zoomed by, and soon my sons were sailing out into the world beyond school. They were amazingly independent. Each found his way into the working world in a role that suited his own unique style. Over time, a parade of wonderful young women passed through my life, most of whom I would have loved to have as family, but years passed by before my sons found themselves in relationships that led to marriage. I thought I had long since released each one of them but was surprised to discover that there was more letting go to be done.

The destiny of the first child is to pave the way for the siblings who follow. Erik was the first to marry. Just before his wedding, I had another dream. In it, Erik and I were hiking together in the Utah wilderness. The trail was steep, with big drop-offs. Erik was just up ahead of me, kneeling down at the edge of the trail. Suddenly, his body tipped and he dropped off the side of the cliff and fell into the canyon. I awoke with my heart pounding. Erik had been more than a little resistant about making a commitment and settling down. Now, I realize that this dream may have been about witnessing him topple off his perch up above and fall into the earthly energy of marriage and family. But, at the time, I responded to it as a mother

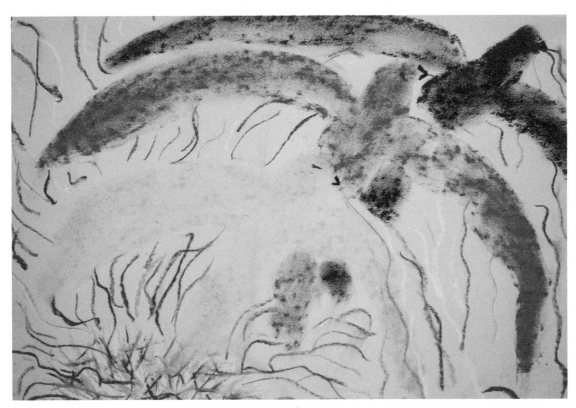

Leaving the Nest

watching her son fall off a cliff while she remained on the trail. The dream underlined the fact that, as much as our lives felt separate already, we had yet more separating to do. It also alerted me to the idea that for a mother, her son's marriage is metaphorically a kind of dying—the death of the old order—and the beginning of a new world.

My sons all married later than was typical in my generation. They had long since been on their own in the world, without any material support from me. I thought I was more than ready to say goodbye to the old order, but I have not found it easy to find footing in the new order and it hasn't happened without some painful realizations. As each son married, the intimacy of our bond shifted before my very eyes. There was now someone whom I didn't really know and someone who didn't know or trust me inside that intimate sphere. I knew that I needed to step back—one thing that was crystal clear to me was that the new alliance was between husband and wife, as it should be, and that access to my sons' lives now depended on my being in my daughters-in-laws' good graces—but the stepping-back came with all kinds of vulnerability.

My fears were exacerbated by my own experience as a daughter-in-law of Zabelle, John's mother. I believed she continued to treat John like a child, and I had no end of annoyance about that. Whenever we visited, she would immediately begin to examine John's body. "You look like you've lost weight," she would say with alarm. "You're way too thin! You must not be eating well."

In those days, I took her evaluations as a criticism of me, since wives were supposed to take care of their husbands. We were not an easy match in more ways than one. Zabelle died of a sudden heart attack early in our marriage, when Erik was just a toddler. We didn't have much time to overcome our rocky beginning. Long before I became a mother-in-law myself, I felt bad about how unwelcoming my heart had been to Zabelle. Now, I realize that I just needed to mature.

As different as my sons are from one another, so, too, are the women they married. What is right in my relationship with one seems just the wrong thing in my relationship with another. In the beginning, some of my concern may have been related to my not feeling as safe with these young women as I did with young men. I didn't have daughters, but watching friends who did had left me thankful that my sons didn't scrutinize me the same way my friends' daughters scrutinized them. *What if I annoy these young women just by being myself?* I wondered. *What if they don't like me? Maybe I'm too shy. Should I talk more or talk less? Will I be too intense for them? Will I be threatening in some way? What if I turn out to be someone they don't want to have around?* All of these questions loomed large as I worried about how I might alienate and thus find myself distanced from my sons.

I celebrate with my whole heart that my sons have found wonderful women to spend their lives with. I love each of these women myself. But in trying to find my new footing, I've come to realize that all of the jokes about mothers-in-law in our culture make light of the depth of the separation that is actually taking place. Despite all my desire and intention to let go, it isn't always easy. My own struggle has given me deeper respect for the challenge.

I've come to believe that the depth of that challenge is rooted in the physicality of the connection I feel with my sons. A woman's womb is the place where new life attaches itself to everything that came before. For me, it has become a sacred container and the place where the split between science and spirituality vanishes. There, mind surrenders its superior position and bows down to meet matter. There, the child resides as the growing tip of the thread that reaches back to however this miracle of creation began. Science serves as narrator. Matter is the great experiment itself.

In my life, my womb was the container that nurtured my sons until they could survive on their own in the world outside. From the moment they were born, my children were growing away from the biological root of my mothering. They are still growing away and will continue to do so as they inhabit their own lives and become more of who they are to become. This is the most natural process in the world. I know that my mothering energy is less and less relevant and that I am at risk of getting in the way of my own development and theirs if I'm not careful to understand that, even amid the sting of the separation. The tide is going out and will continue to go out until one of us—and I pray it is I—dies.

I can only reflect on what it might mean to feel that final separation from my place as a daughter. I was intimately involved with my own mother's care in the final years of her life. In quiet moments, I found myself looking at her body and imagining how I grew inside her womb. Even though I know the facts, it seems the most unlikely thing in the world that that was so. But somewhere beneath the place where words arise, perhaps my body remembers the physical connection to her body. The root of my biological existence lives inside her, and, though we have walked separately in the world for years now, her body will forever be my first home.

❦ *Reflection*

We all mother in one way or another. Whether you have mothered children, family members, friends, pets, work, the planet, or yourself, write your own chapter about this part of your life. What does mothering mean to you? What does it ask of you?

Chapter 8:

Give These Clay Feet Wings to Fly

Music gives wings to the mind, a soul to the universe,
flight to the imagination, a charm to sadness, a life to everything.
—PLATO

Transitions from one phase of life to another are often difficult. The enchantment of pregnancy and giving birth was hard for me to let go of, but I was now thirty-two years old and our family was complete. My life going forward was fully dedicated to being a mother, but as a stay-at-home mom, I found the demands of caring for three little boys daunting. It was hard to find a balance that sustained me. In fact, it seemed impossible.

When I think about what my life was like then, I often recall the morning I jumped into our big orange van with the kids, trying to get the older ones off to school on time. In that era before car safety restraints for children, I often carried Eli around in a little wicker cradle that had handles. I placed the cradle between the two front seats of the van, and off we went. I was a few miles down the road, when the thought struck me that I had the cradle but couldn't remember if I had put the baby in it. Fortunately, I had, and all was well, but the story is indicative of how frantic I really was.

On top of everything else, when Eli was six weeks old, we moved to a new house on a ten-acre property. There was a beautiful flower garden, lots of berries, a vegetable garden, and a mature orchard. It was just the property we had been searching for, but we weren't there long before I realized that for me, this Garden of Eden had turned into a living hell. Soon after we moved in, deer trampled the fence and ate three hundred strawberry plants to the ground. Meanwhile, the raspberry plants were producing fifty baskets each day, and then the apples started coming in. I laugh now to realize how unrealistic I was to think I could care for three kids and that massive garden all by myself. Our move is a marker of how invested I was in my earth-mother image at that time.

I did give it a good try, but I was alone and sinking. When winter came, we hadn't put in enough firewood, and when we bought more, it was still green. I remember sitting in the living room, nursing Eli the next Christmas morning, in the freezing cold. The wood was sizzling and popping in the stove, giving out no heat at all. It mirrored the way I felt, as my inner fire was indeed sputtering. There wasn't much time for any kind of adult life, no husband to have one with, and absolutely no time to feed my own soul. I was on empty.

Against this backdrop, a piano came into my life, and with it the gift of music offered itself to me. It was like a beautiful bird flying down from the heavens and calling for my earth-mother self to look skyward once again.

I hadn't played the piano for years, but music had always sustained me. Now the beauty of a Chopin nocturne floating around me captured my heart, and, like a child following the Pied Piper, I wanted to go wherever that music wanted to take me. To me it seemed that classical-music composers took all the trials and tribulations of being human and transformed our suffering into a thing of beauty. Not unlike our lives, music was a beautiful dream—it was there in all its compelling reality, and then it was gone, the vibrations that made those sounds now floating off somewhere into the universe. I wanted to make those beautiful sounds myself. I had embedded myself in the energies of the earth, and the strains of music falling around me were like manna from Heaven. I was starving, and I wanted to eat.

I found a teacher and signed up for lessons. I knew that while I could play the piano, I was not particularly gifted as a musician. Clearly, I had absorbed the cultural message that music was for the few who were born with a natural talent. However, there was no question about how much I loved it, and so, in spite of all my doubts, I went off to my first lesson. I wondered what I might be able to accomplish now as an adult, highly motivated and wanting to play for my own pleasure.

I focused on learning classical music. I thrived on the challenge of practicing my Brahms, my Beethoven, and my Chopin. All those beautiful sounds awakened me from a deep slumber. I felt as if I had new eyes and new ears. I began to notice that the music lived inside me even when I wasn't playing it. It was there in the back of my mind, supporting the flow of my daily life. It seemed to be the thing that made everything else possible. Smiles and laughter came more easily to me when dealing with my children's antics. I found myself working in the garden with pleasure. When Gabe and Erik were in school and Eli was sleeping, I went straight to the piano, leaving the breakfast dishes on the table and the beds unmade. In the evening, after the bedtime stories had been read and the children were asleep, I played into the night. I played as if my life depended on it—and maybe it did. I desperately wanted to be able to give the music full expression. Back then, I heard all its beauty externally, but now I understand that what I wanted was to convey the beauty in the depths of my own soul.

For the first time in my life, I had found a place where I could explore my intensely emotional nature and experience it as a gift. Music lifted me out of the small frame of my personal life and placed my feelings in a much larger context. Whether deep sadness, passionate anger, or great joy, all was transformed by the music into an exquisite world. In my childhood spirituality, I had felt myself held in the loving embrace of God in Heaven. Now, it was music that held me and lifted my experience of being human to a higher plane.

It seemed impossible that the majesty of what I was hearing could ever have been encoded into the notes on the black-and-white page in front of me. But as time went on, it seemed even less possible that I would be able to express the music in the way in which it deserved to be expressed. I was faced with a terrible dilemma: how to bring my small, imperfect human self into relationship with the awesome beauty that those timeless musical creations held. Not understanding my predicament as a spiritual dilemma, I didn't see that I was like Moses standing before the burning bush. My human capacity to behold what I saw was blinding. What I had glimpsed left me feeling inadequate. *Who am I in relation to this energy?* I wondered.

My wondering was quickly met by a more ominous energy. *Who do you think you are?* boomed the voice of a powerful judge inside me, clearly appalled that I even thought I could participate in any way with what I had glimpsed. Now I understand that voice as my ego rearing its ugly head, wanting to maintain its stature, rather than surrender to the passionate fire of this larger energy I was sensing. Regretfully, instead of dismissing it, I colluded with it. Thus began a battle of many years between my felt sense of divine beauty and my self-worth.

It wasn't long before I came to see that what was holding me back in my music was rooted in what was holding me back in my life. I suffered from a lack of confidence and poor self-esteem. Growing up in a family in which I was invisible in many ways had left me more comfortable hiding in the shadows than taking the risk of being seen. This was a problem in my marriage, as I had difficulty taking my own needs seriously, much less asking for what I wanted and needed emotionally. John's absence was troubling, but my own invisibility made me absent in a different way.

Now, my desire not to be seen was in conflict with my desire to express myself through music by letting others hear me play, including my teacher. In my lessons, my hands would shake and my pieces would be riddled with errors. Memory lapses left me disoriented. Distances on the keyboard seemed distorted, and section after section of what I had practiced for hours fell apart. When I came home from one of those lessons, I slammed the door as I entered my house, walked over to the piano, and closed the lid, covering the keyboard. I was never going to play again! I cried, cursing myself and the injustice it all. I planned to cancel my lessons and sell the piano. But, in the end, this turned out to be just one more skirmish in my struggle to let my creative self have a life. The next week I trudged off to my lesson, ready to give it another try.

My pastel drawing *Oh My! Can I Let This In?* marks my struggle over many years. It expresses the colorful, creative world that was entering my being. The expression on my face captures the concern and confusion I experienced. *Do I dare let all of this enter and make a home inside me?*

I entered therapy because I wanted to free myself from the dark voice inside me that questioned my right to express myself creatively. It seems odd now that I wasn't more concerned about being held back in life itself, but I evidently wasn't yet ready to look at those issues head-on, especially as they related to my marriage. My therapy was aimed at helping me to live my life more spontaneously and thus more creatively, so, as I had hoped, it was very useful.

Oh My! Can I Let This In?

I knew my music was good for my family, but, in hindsight, I think it was a challenge for John. He didn't understand where my newfound passion was coming from or where it was taking me. As my dedication increased, he questioned me. "Where is this all going?" he asked, like a parent concerned that his college-age daughter was considering majoring in music. "What are you going to do with it?"

One day when he was home, I asked if he could watch the kids while I practiced. "What are you going to do, go off on tour? Travel the world?" he asked. I thought he was being facetious, but now I think his question marked his own realization that I was changing and that the power dynamic between us was being realigned. Perhaps all my feminist rhetoric was finally going to manifest itself, as I stepped into my own being in a way I hadn't before in our marriage. He must have felt my allegiance shifting because it was.

My piano teacher had a grand piano, and, as I improved, I could hear the difference between what I could express on his piano and what I could express on my own old upright. I began to yearn for my own grand piano.

When I first brought it up with John, he protested. "What? A grand piano? Isn't that like buying an airplane? Totally unrealistic for people in our circumstances!" But I persisted, and when we built our new house, we planned the living room around the placement of my new, beautiful, seven-foot instrument. My wildest fantasy was to build a removable wall so I could play it with only the forest around me. Remembering that now, I see portents of the relationship I would have with nature in my future, but back then I settled for a skylight above and well-placed windows all around.

For as long as it remained on center stage in my life, music was my guiding light. Whether I was reveling in the light or struggling in the shadows, it did give me an existence of my own, and that was vital to me at the time. As I emerged out of the cocoon of early mothering, playing the piano was just a first step in that direction.

Some years later, I started accepting piano students at my studio, which I named, "For the Joy of It!" I rebelled against the way piano was usually taught. I wanted to teach that we are all musicians, that it comes with being human. I taught that music was a language beneath our words, a way for us to give expression to our inner lives, to express what we feel, to learn more about who we really are.

Because what I was offering was so personal, I wanted further grounding in the psychological aspect of my work. I enrolled in a master's program in psychology at Sonoma State University. My mentor, Nina Menrath, was an art therapist. Her teaching enticed me to combine art with what I was already doing with music. At first I was intimidated, but I quickly discovered the same spirit of rebellion I had found earlier in my life. In fact, unlike playing the piano, I had zero expectations about what I might make. It was a miracle to me that I could draw anything at all and a surprise to see what presented itself.

I began to see that it didn't matter whether I knew what I was doing or liked what I saw. In fact, my lack of skill often allowed my art to emerge more directly from my unconscious mind. Far more valuable than how my art looked, it told stories about my life, stories that came from a level deeper than my words. They were surprising and enlightening and put me directly in touch with a gut-level truth about my life.

Music stepped aside and made room for artmaking. Art flung open the doors to my wild self in a more concrete way than my music had. While nurturing to my soul and expressive in the moment, music disappears into the air soon after it is played. A piece of art stays around. I came to see my creations as waking dreams. It was as if they were living things. I kept them near me after I made them so I could reflect on their messages, often in my journal. Sometimes I took my art to the piano and turned what I saw there into sound. Often, my dreams picked up the themes of my artistic expressions and offered their comment on the matter. In turn, I painted my stories of the night. It became a magical circle of exploration of this deep pool inside me from which they all arose. This intuitive process taught me an important lesson: All of the different art forms available to us feed one another. All of them feed our dreams. And all of them hold great potential for healing.

This idea is the very root of expressive arts therapy. It was giving birth to itself in me, around the same time others started writing about it. Shaun McNiff wrote his seminal book, *The Arts and Psychotherapy*, in 1981. Until that time, art therapy, music therapy, and dance therapy were their own separate disciplines. The idea that mixing these modalities enhanced their therapeutic possibilities opened a whole new world of exploration in the field.

Graduate school was a time of learning to honor my expanding imagination. The magic circle of music, my art, and my dreams reenchanted my inner world. Now I had many ways to explore that territory. I studied psychological theories, but the theoretical aspects of what I learned paled in comparison with the expanding depths of my own personal process at the time. My rich inner life nourished me deeply, gave me a dimension that I had only glimpsed before, and fed my future work.

As my life filled to overflowing with all that I was learning, I was eager to share with others. My piano teaching continued, and I increasingly brought art, writing, and movement into the process. I wanted to help my students keep their creative innocence alive. That little girl inside me, the one I had tucked safely away, became an important ally. She had been waiting for a long time to come out and play once again. She wanted to press keys on the piano just to hear their sound. She wanted to twirl her body this way and that, simply for the pleasure it gave her. She wanted to watch her brush smear brightly colored paint on white paper just to see it happen. Inside her, she held the key I needed for free exploration in my life. With her at my side, I discovered that many things I didn't think could ever happen were possible. I wanted to share my excitement about reconnecting with that exuberant child inside me so that my clients could reawaken that young energy in their own lives through their creative practice.

My focus had shifted. My own involvement in the arts had become a ritual of learning to dance with the unexpected and to surrender to my own inner leadings. I wanted to obliterate the idea of looking at the arts, and at ourselves, as product and performance, and to teach that the arts are basic ways of exploring and expressing ourselves through a wellspring of spontaneity and freedom. Most important of all, I wanted to focus on finding a new way of looking at life itself as a creative flow. Then and now, the words of the potter M. C. Richards serve as my guide: "All the arts we practice are apprenticeship. The big art is our life."

✤ Reflection

What in your life lifts you out of your small, ego-focused self and brings you into relationship with a higher/deeper energy, a beauty, a flow? Life is too short to let much time go by without allowing ourselves to pursue our passionate interests. Make appointments with yourself. Mark them in your calendar. Don't let time slip away.

Chapter 9:

Finding My Sacred Body

As above, so below, as within, so without, as the universe, so the soul.
—HERMES TRISMEGISTUS

Opening to my music and finding my life's work could have been a good thing for John and me if we had been able to navigate all the changes, but we had difficulty managing that transition. The times were roiling with an alteration in the power dynamic between men and women, and we acted out that struggle on a personal level in our marriage. Standing more fully inside myself and challenging the way in which our life together had centered on John's needs caused serious problems. As I moved out into the world, childcare, housework, and money issues all became more fodder for tension between us.

As the years went by, we made our way through many storms, managing to stay in the same boat—or at least climb back in when we fell out. When it looked like our boat would capsize, I dragged John into couples' therapy.

That is how we found our way to Keith and Monique's door. They were marriage and family therapists, and we consulted them many times over the years when things became dire between us.

When we first took our troubles to them, I wanted nothing more than to come to some peace within my marriage. I didn't know I was opening a door that would lead to profound change in my life. If I had known that at that time, I'm certain that I would have walked out that door and run as fast as I could in the opposite direction.

In fact, at first, that's pretty much what I did do. Keith and Monique worked together in couples' therapy. They had a very confrontational style that kept the sessions on a creative edge. They weren't all that interested in the words we used to describe our issues; they wanted us to experience our problems with our bodies. They believed that our deepest learning comes from the body and that what we learn in that way will not be easily forgotten. For instance, in one session they asked us to align ourselves, using our bodies, in a way that symbolized how we wanted to move together in the world. We managed to turn the exercise into a power struggle as we tried to force each other into attempting different positions. At one point, John grabbed me into an embrace. I surrendered, but moving around locked in that way was not possible. Eventually we settled on facing forward, standing next to each other and putting our arms behind each other's backs at the waist. But even that was more than awkward, especially when we tried to walk through a door. Clearly, we needed to find a more flexible and dynamic relationship, one in which we could each move with more freedom and grace.

There was a feeling of aliveness in those sessions, but that scared me. I could see that that much aliveness was connected to freedom. However, at that point in my life, I had a huge investment in keeping everything, and probably everyone, under control, especially myself. As challenging as the sessions were, Keith and Monique exuded a depth of compassion that drew me toward them as much as my fear pushed me away.

We stayed in therapy for about six months. I left with deep respect for them as therapists. I trusted them as deeply as I could trust anyone at that time in my life. But when I think of it now, it seems as if I were peering at them through a tiny pinhole in a huge shield that surrounded me. Still, John and I felt good about what we had accomplished. The therapy must have helped us find a place of balance, as we remained together.

Sometimes our marriage was peaceful; other times our power struggles took center stage. Our kids were growing up and in school by then. After leaving therapy, I found myself replaying many of Keith and Monique's words inside my own head, especially in regard to going after things I wanted and claiming my own power. In one session, Keith had said to me, "It's like there's a huge banquet table before you and you're refusing to eat." That image stayed with me. I watched myself continually refuse things that I knew I wanted and needed. Gradually, with careful and nonjudgmental observation, I tired of that process and started to claim those things for myself more and more. In addition, I had indeed learned something about going into my body experience and trusting the messages that were there for me. For instance, if I was uncomfortable with something that happened between John and me, I would ask very specific questions of my body: *What are the sensations in my body right now? Heat? Tingling? Vibration? Cold? Where is my energy centered?* If I noticed my energy centered in my arms and legs, I would ask what my arms and legs felt like doing. These attempts to reclaim my body put the power of my mind into a more balanced perspective. As I began to nurture myself in this way, I felt lighter in my being, as if a weight I had been carrying for a long time was dropping away.

Then, when I was thirty-eight years old, my grandmother died. I loved her with all my heart. The reality of her death catapulted me out of my youthful fantasy that I might live forever. Of course, I knew that wasn't true, but I realized I was living as if it were.

I heard the story of her last day at home from her neighbor Georgia. Grandma had been in her garden and was heading back inside, carrying a peace rose in her hand. She paused on the landing just outside her back door and spoke to Georgia. "Isn't this the most beautiful rose you've ever seen?" she said, as she held out the flower so that Georgia could share in its splendor. Those were the last words anyone heard her speak. A short while later, she was found unconscious in her living room, and an ambulance whisked her off to the hospital. She had had a major stroke and remained in the hospital for several weeks before she died.

I went to visit her during that time. She hadn't shown any sign of being conscious or understanding where she was. As I walked into her room, I saw my devastated parents sitting with her and heard the rhythmic sound of the machine that was breathing for her. The machine's pulse was so dominant in the room that I immediately had trouble maintaining the rhythm of my own breath. I could hardly keep my tears at bay when I moved to Grandma's bedside and took her hand. To the amazement of all of us in the room, she squeezed my hand, letting me know she knew I was there. I heard my parents gasp, and I couldn't stop my tears. It was the first and only movement my grandmother made from the time of her stroke until she died. I can still feel her hand squeezing mine.

A few weeks after my visit, I had a dream that she came to visit me in Mendocino. I was so happy to see her. We walked into the living room, and she took a seat in the old oak rocking chair that I had used when I was nursing my babies. There, before my very eyes, she turned into a cat, curled up in that old chair, and went to sleep. Then the phone rang, waking me from that dream. It was my parents calling to tell me that Grandma had died.

In the midst of my deep grief, I committed myself to living in the fullest way possible. One morning, I had just awakened and could hear my kids teasing each other as they made their lunches for school. As I lay there feeling blue and not yet ready to start my day, I looked out the window at the forest around me. The sky was full of dark clouds, but the sun was still peeking through. The tops of the trees were swirling in the wind, foretelling a storm. Then a voice inside me said, *You have only one life. This is it. This one you are living is yours. Take hold of it!* These words came from my gut and sent chills up my spine. There was a sense of absolute finality in the message. I made no attempt to argue. I knew what it meant.

I instantly understood that I needed to step away from my exhaustive, single-minded attention on my relationship with John. Life was temporary and very short. It was time to let myself grow into the more alive version of myself that I had intuited was possible. *Away with the road blocks before it's too late!* I thought. I realized I was ready for change, no matter what the consequences. As for my life with John, I needed to let the chips fall as they might. *Perhaps*, I thought, *if I step back, he'll come forward more. If not, so be it.* I felt like a potted plant in too small of a container when my true home was in the forest, growing wild and free, part of a much larger ecosystem. I knew I needed help to manifest all that I was intuiting. A logical first step was to go back into therapy. I knew where I wanted to go, and this time I didn't want to let anything stop me. I called Keith. Thus began many years of intense involvement in my own therapeutic process.

I can state without hesitation that had I not chosen Keith as my therapist, I would not be who I am today. I cannot imagine how the changes I've made would have come about. But in no way do I want to suggest that he made the changes happen. *I* made them happen with my own stubborn determination to live my life more fully, more freely, more spontaneously, and more compassionately. The transformation that took place required courage that I didn't know I had. It was a special kind of courage—not the kind we need to face danger in the outer world, but rather the courage to look deep inside, face head-on what we find there, and make dramatic changes in the way we are living.

I owe a world of gratitude to Keith. As the years went on, the intensity of our connection became extreme. This was not quick-fix, "just get me through this crisis" therapy. It was an in-depth exploration of my psyche. I experienced the most ecstatic, God-like parts of myself with this man, and I experienced the darkest, most demonic parts of myself in my work with him as well. I had to give up identifying only with the goodness and light inside me. I needed to take into account that we all have a shadow side, and it behooves us to know it is there. Before my years in therapy, the idea that the greatest light casts the darkest shadow was just a thought. My work with Keith led me to understand, on a personal level, that the light and the dark cannot be separated. They are intricately bound. In the end, I'm left asking, "Would I have been better off had we never met?" There is no part of me that would answer yes.

Much of Keith's work was done with hypnotherapy in what seemed to me to be magical states. I discovered that I was a natural at letting go in order to enter into these altered states of consciousness. In my very first session, Keith led me into a deep trance. I had a profound spiritual awakening that changed my life and sent me in a direction that I spent years integrating. I wrote about it later in my journal.

In my imagination, I am floating in total blackness, my body filled with pleasure. Suddenly I come up against something that will not allow me to move further. I cannot see anything, only blackness, but, as I feel with my hands, I find an edge. With that discovery, the chunk of blackness begins to move with me holding onto it. Moving quickly now, it carries me toward a spot of light that is getting larger and larger. Soon I am in the center of this light. Energy is swirling around me like a whirlwind, and I cannot stand the brightness any longer. I close my eyes in fear and everything stops. I am in the blackness again, and now I cannot breathe. It is as if everything, even me, is coming to a stop. I can feel myself withering away. I know that I am making a choice to close myself off and that if only I opened my eyes I would be able to change this state in which I find myself. Finally, at Keith's suggestion, I do that. Eyes open, I find myself floating in the most peaceful state imaginable. I am completely surrounded by pure white light. It is as if I am being bathed in the light, taking it in through every pore. The feeling in my body is like nothing I have experienced ever before. It is hard to find words to describe it.

It was time for the session to come to a close, and I slowly came back to conscious awareness. I felt energy pouring through my head, moving down through my body with great force. My first words were "What was *that?*" Keith assured me that I had just experienced myself at a very deep level.

When I left that session, my world was not the same. My life had been catapulted into a larger context. As with the feelings I had when I gave birth, I knew my insights were real and true. I knew they were connected to religious experience—but there was nothing to doubt. I wasn't being asked to believe in something outside myself. What had happened had taken place inside me. It carried its own story and its own meaning. The fact that I hadn't asked for it—wouldn't even have known to ask for it—led me to trust it even more deeply.

In the days that followed, my life began to realign itself. There was a huge letting go as I watched myself from somewhere outside and could laugh at the ridiculousness of any thought that my little ego was the center of the universe. I began to see that I did not have control over many things that I thought I could and should be controlling. At the same time, I also realized that I mattered as an integral part of the whole. I wrote in my journal, "If that light is at my source, there is no longer any need to question my self-worth. It is not an issue."

It was only a matter of days, however, before the darkness that is bound to that much light began to cast its long shadow in my life. The inkling I'd gleaned about the real position of my ego self in the big picture of the universe left me thinking, *Wait a minute. I thought I was in charge—now what?*

Our ego does not take kindly to being displaced. It thinks it runs the show. *Oh, so you want to let go of control, do you?* a voice inside me taunted. *We'll see about that. It's not as easy as you think. Just try it.* Then the old, familiar judge that I knew so well from my relationship with my music chimed in: *Who do you think you are? All that light? I'll show you what you're made of.* Not since my early college classes had I reflected so much on my ultimate existential aloneness. There was much writing in my journal about darkness and despair.

When I reflect on the vision that came to me that day, it seems clear that it mapped precisely the journey I had embarked on. This was going to be an adventure into the wild terrain of my unconscious mind. It would require that I look into my own darkness, and through that exploration, I would grow more fully into my own light.

I was to learn that lurking in our unconscious minds live parts of us that we don't recognize and haven't yet owned. Those parts create no end of complicated behaviors. They put up road blocks to our growth and are invested in keeping those obstacles in place. For instance, that little girl who felt so unseen and unloved by her father? I came to see that she was not only sad but also full of rage. She had learned subtle and manipulative, though invisible, ways of trying to get what she wanted in the world. We don't like to face these dark parts of ourselves. We would rather see them outside us, so we project our own darkness onto others, judging and setting up no end of confusing and unloving behaviors. On a societal level, wars are fought in just this sort of process.

However, we can learn to develop a relationship with these parts of us. At heart, they are trying to tell us something important. Rather than making them go away, we need to embrace them when they appear. *Hello, old friend. I see that you're here. What are you wanting?* When we don't listen, their voices only get louder and their energies become more disruptive in our lives. When we listen, we can negotiate our way through our dilemmas, taking more of ourselves along with us. Owning our own shadow side is vital to our healing.

Surprisingly, I've learned that we also shy away from our lightest side, seeing it out there in those we admire or even idolize. We yearn for the very best of ourselves to come forward, but our highest potential can be as threatening to the status quo in our lives as our darker side is. Radical change is often not far behind as we grow in that direction. We quiver when we imagine what living into our highest selves might ask of us. It often brings tumultuous change to the structure of our lives. It might even mean changing our careers, where we live, or who we live with.

Experiencing the light of consciousness may be our greatest wish, but when it happens, it can be very intense. On this journey, if we are committed to our growth, we will eventually experience our closed eyes as a movement toward death, not toward life. We feel the experience of turning our back on life in our bodies. Observing this without judgment, no matter how long we try not to see, not to know, not to understand, we will eventually open our eyes again and, dancing between the light and the darkness inside us, will continually re-create our own newest self. This is what deep personal change looks like and, ultimately, what it means to live life creatively.

Over the next several years of my therapy, that is exactly what took place. I began to live more fully into the pledge I had made to myself. Over time, the trance states I entered in my sessions led me to see myself and the world as very fluid. I mean that in a physical sense, but the image extends psychologically as well. If I didn't turn away, I could move through the wild landscape of my unconscious mind to a place of peace, acceptance, and healing. It was a place of great beauty and was familiar to me in some vague way, recalling those early childhood experiences when I tumbled into the magical other world in my consciousness. I have come to know that place as my true home.

The art I made at the time reflected my new fluidity and openness to change. My drawings speak to a world of millions of tiny molecules in constant motion. My body and other solid matter seemed only a coming together of these molecules in some tighter space.

In *Swimming with Change as I Hold My Center*, I express the enormous possibility for change that I experienced at that time. I had clearly moved away from a stuck place of having a single image of myself with firm boundaries around me. The possibilities for my life were vast. In my drawing, I see myself undersea, holding my center like a seed buried deep inside me. I am in communication with energies from above and below. The undersea imagery speaks to my new relation to the unconscious realms. My boundaries are porous. I am a shape shifter.

I felt empowered, like I had really come into my own and more so. I was turning into someone I had never dreamed I could be. I wasn't the only one experiencing my blossoming; my friends and family were noticing as well. Many liked what they saw, but my changes were not always met with glee. I lost some friends, and I remember my brother telling me that he had never known anyone who had changed as much as I had. It wasn't a compliment but rather said with confusion and, I'm guessing, a good measure of discomfort as my place in my family of origin began to shift.

John was struggling with my transformation as well. He would have had every right to struggle, as the meek woman who had centered her life on him had long ago left the scene. He tried to put the brakes on my changes by invoking our power struggle over money, announcing regularly, "We can't afford all this money you're spending on your therapy." He also had

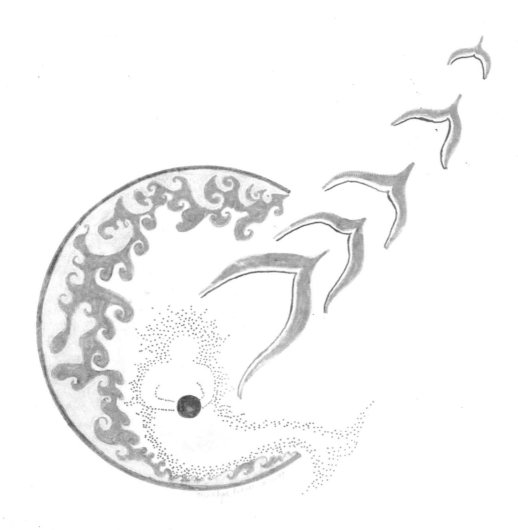

Swimming with Change as I Hold My Center

little tolerance when I wanted to bring a more spiritual perspective to our family life. When I tried to introduce a small ceremony at our dinner table by lighting a candle and asking each of us to speak about what we were grateful for that day, he ridiculed. As time went on, our worst clashes may have been his attempts to pull my chain and remind me that I belonged to him.

After several years, as I made my way through many life issues in my therapy, I finally had the courage to ask for help with my sexuality and the ways in which it expressed itself in our marriage. The sexual connection that John and I had was a strong one. Without it, I am certain we would have been unable to remain together. It has always seemed particularly sad that over the years we allowed the power struggles between us to be acted out in this arena, but that is what happened. As time went on, I tired of my role in the conflict. I felt as if my entire sexual life had existed in a world dominated by the masculine viewpoint—a view that, of course, dominated my culture. Inside me, something was awry because of it. The changes I had been making in my life were so exciting and such a relief, I wanted to see if I could alter this area of my life as well.

It was clear to me from early on that I didn't have the personality or the body that my culture considered sexy. I didn't have the foggiest idea how to play that role and felt like an impostor when I tried, which I did on occasion over the years. Take the negligees I tried to wear, for example. My small breasts were never adequate to fill the spot large tits were meant to occupy. My tall body never allowed those lacy teddies to snap at the crotch. For a young woman, being sexy was all about image, and to me these were symbols of things a sexy woman wore to please her husband. My husband wanted to be pleased in that way. My natural shyness and my more direct, "what you see is what you get" manner never allowed me to learn to be coy or flirt. So, all in all, I entered the world of young adulthood without much knowledge about how to fit the feminine mold or project any kind of sexy image into the world.

Yet, despite my failure to play the role, starting early in my teens, I always felt quite alive sexually. What I experienced inside me couldn't find expression on the outside, so I basically just felt like a terrible misfit. Later, when the findings of Masters and Johnson and feminist writers sifted down into the culture, I began to hear reference to a more "feminine sexuality." I had no idea what it might be, and I wanted to know. I wanted to figure out who I was sexually and how to inhabit that part of myself more fully in my world. What I learned over the next several years about the power of my very own feminine sexuality left the negligees, the teddies, and the kitten-like coyness I had thought were expected of me seeming like child's play.

I remember clearly the day I went into a session and announced that I was ready to look into my sexuality. In the trickster style to which I had become accustomed, Keith laughed uproariously and told me he was certain that would scare the "bejesus" out of me. When I didn't back away, he responded to my request by intensifying the bodywork aspect of my sessions.

Keith's bodywork was rooted in bioenergetics. The goal of the work was for me to learn to recognize the subtle energy in my body as a basic manifestation of my own life force. As a woman who was focused on taking care of others, I needed to be reminded that my feminine body was made to be receptive. In order to increase my receptivity, I learned to let the energy that I usually thought of as sexual energy expand throughout my whole body. Through breathing and movement, I let myself fill with increasing amounts of pleasure and learned to contain it and enjoy it. As I came to be comfortable with being really alive energetically, it changed my physical reality. I was reembodying myself, becoming more open to all the ways in which my body was trying to communicate with me, and all of this related directly to my sexuality.

As I came to own this receptive power that was distinctly part of my feminine nature, the piece of me that had always felt somewhat awry suddenly felt aligned. My body, and, therefore, my sexuality, finally began to feel as if it were my own, rather than someone else's. It belonged not to John specifically, not to men in general, and not to the culture I lived in. Rather, it was very much my own.

My new relationship with my own body energy as life energy transformed my sexuality from a very pleasurable worldly adventure into a spiritual, sacred one. It had always been clear to me that making love was a transcendent experience. In the giving and receiving of touch, bodies blended, becoming one. Embodied in this new way, I felt myself becoming one, not just with my partner but with everything.

Bringing sexual energy into the realm of what we consider sacred heals a rift that we women have lived with for centuries. Since the time when the patriarchy began replacing matriarchal societies, the power of our feminine sexuality has been eclipsed.

Anne Baring, in *The Dream of the Cosmos*, explains that as we humans began to develop our individual consciousness, we became engaged in a great struggle against the power of nature. Thus began our centuries-long attempt to control the matrix from which we have emerged. In this battle, spirit was separated from nature, mind from body, and light from darkness, and all of these separations opened the possibility for one of the two to became more valued than the other. With the rise of the patriarchy, "spirit, light, order, and the rational mind" were connected to the masculine. They were deemed superior to the feminine, which was thought to be connected with "nature, darkness, chaos, and body." As humanity's rational minds became ascendant, and with the support of the patriarchal religions, we women and our bodies began to be seen as threatening—a sexual temptation. Men thought to control our bodies in the same way they needed to master and control nature.

In our Western culture, we women live with the reverberations of that split to this day, struggling with the archetypal energies of the virgin and the whore. If we stay safely within our virginal aspect, we are ridiculed for not being sexual enough, but when we bring our sexuality to the forefront, we are accused of being out-of-control sluts. Because men are not free from this dilemma when they respond to us, this dynamic gets acted out in our relationships. It is an impossible circumstance, as both how we see ourselves and how we are seen are at play. Earlier in my life, I knew something was awry, but the words to describe the problem were not yet speech-ripe inside me. Once I was able to place my sexual nature in a sacred context, this either/or dichotomy became both/and, and in that circle I found deep healing.

To my great surprise, as I opened in this way, I found myself in ecstatic body experiences. In one session with Keith, I experienced my body becoming one with the earth. I wept as I came to understand from the inside out the abundance of life on this planet. As I experienced with heightened sensitivity the life energy that Mother Nature pours forth in every moment, I was overwhelmed by Her enormous generosity.

Following this experience, I drew *The Earth and I Are One*. Here, I am one with the landscape of the living Earth. My body curves with the rolling hills. My hair becomes a river. This experience is beyond the awareness of my individual consciousness, so I have no face. One arm reaches out to touch the rising full moon, reflecting the fact that in this experience I am experiencing the energy of the divine feminine, of the night, of the body, of sacred physicality, in the very depths of my womanhood. I am embracing my deep feminine energy, calling it to me.

I loved the change I was experiencing. It was reflected in a deeper presence and increasing confidence in most every area of my life. I felt like I was personally experiencing spirit as life energy infusing my body. When body, mind, and spirit connect inside us, it is extremely empowering. In *Sacred Body Dancing*, I am celebrating spiritual energy coming into form and owning my body as sacred at last.

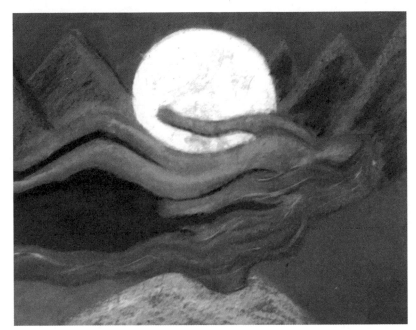

The Earth and I Are One

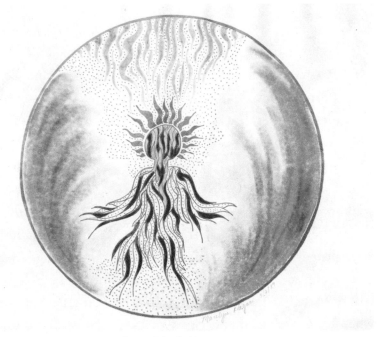

Sacred Body Dancing

Sacred Connection

Images of snakes began appearing in my dreams and my art. *Sacred Connection* emerged. At the time, I saw the snake, with its ability to shed its skin, as a symbol of the transformation that was taking place in my life. Only later, when I researched the meaning of the snake in matriarchal cultures, did I see that I was intuiting through my art something I hadn't yet learned with my mind. In *The Alphabet Versus the Goddess*, Leonard Shlain notes that early Egyptians saw the snake as "beneficent" and "vital" and associated it with female sexuality. In *The Language of the Goddess*, Marija Gimbutas writes, "[T]he vertically winding snake symbolized ascending life force." In Karen Tate's anthology, *Goddess 2.0: Advancing a New Path Forward*, Amy Peck notes the characteristics the snake shares with the human umbilical cord: "Both the serpent and the umbilical cord are pulsating, spiraling, sinuous forms emerging from a dark womb place." She suggests that we look at the serpent as "our life supplying umbilical cord to the womb of the Great Mother." All of these reflections capture what I was experiencing when I was coming to understand that my body belonged to the Earth and all was sacred.

I became aware that everything around me was expressing its essential nature—the trees, the flowers, the forest, the ocean, the heavens above me, and the earth below me. I wanted to join in by communicating my own authentic nature, and I wanted to guide others to do that as well. What I was learning in my therapy had immediate application in my work as an expressive arts therapist. Exploring the wildness of our unconscious and expressing what we discover there in art, music, movement, or writing is how we humans originally used the arts. Our words tell us only so much. With imagery and metaphor, we see both our darkness and our light in a new way. Amazingly, I have found that at the very moment we are grasping a particularly dark process inside us through the arts, our natural compassion comes to the fore. Often, humor is not far behind. When we can laugh at ourselves in a loving and accepting way, it's a sure sign that healing is at hand. Seeing ourselves through the arts offers us a path through the wilderness of the unconscious, and as we traverse that path step by step, we find ourselves living with greater authenticity.

In the end, through my therapy, my own life process and in my role as an expressive arts therapist, I've come to believe that a full and creative life asks that we find love and acceptance for all that we are. It asks that we find a compassionate place inside us where the best and the worst of us get a place at the table. As we achieve those objectives, we become more loving and accepting of those around us. But finding that place requires a strong, warm witness inside us who is not afraid to look. I have come to call that witness the Loving Mother. She watches without judging as the landscapes and characters of our inner lives reveal themselves. She lives inside each one of us. While our own mothers and even we ourselves as parents may have fallen short of delivering her perfect message to our children, it doesn't mean that she isn't inside us, offering her unconditional love in each and every moment. All we need do is quiet our self-judgment and listen. She is our guidepost and our birthright.

Eventually, Keith and Monique moved away. During our final time together, I was a sea of mixed emotions. There was the terrible grief of ending what had been a profoundly important time in my life. Consciously allowing my body to be a vehicle for receiving life energy was a deep teaching and changed things for me in myriad ways, both personally and professionally. It was life-giving to experience this marriage between the heaven and earth inside my own body. The pleasure that resulted left me with nothing but a sense of the profound beauty at the core of our existence, which continues to nourish me to this day.

Balancing Between Heaven and Earth

I know I would not have found all these parts of myself if I hadn't made a pledge to look so deeply inside. That jewel, now woven into the golden thread of my experience, leaves me knowing that my spiritual life will never again slip into unconsciousness. It exists as a deep river running through me, with its own twists and turns, dancing in and out of shadow and light. It is grounded in my body and is mirrored by the world all around me. It was up to me to decide whether I wanted to enter that river and experience these expanded parts of being human. It is not a decision to take lightly. For whatever reason, I needed to find my sacred truth at the root of my own existence. When my grandmother died, I made a conscious decision to step into those unknown waters and swim for my life. I am grateful that I did.

🌿 *Reflection*

Sit quietly and just notice your breath. When you feel ready, direct it lower and lower in your body until you are breathing from your pelvic area. On the breath in, open that area of your body as if you were opening a door outward, and on the breath out, contract as if you were closing that door. Continue for as long as you are comfortable, feeling the sensations in your body. Let this become a practice. Make an energy drawing on a large piece of paper, picking colors that call to you. Just let your hand spread color however it likes. Chalk pastels are wonderful for this exercise.

Chapter 10:

Like a Deer Caught in Headlights

*To be fully alive, fully human, and completely awake
is to be continually thrown out of the nest.*
—PEMA CHÖDRÖN

I had hoped that exploring my personal issues in therapy would help me to come to some kind of peace with John. If I could change what I was doing that contributed to our problems, I thought it might help right things between us. But in the end, my expanding life only created a greater divide between us. The more alive I became, the more John distanced himself. That was when I learned that the dynamic in a relationship is far more important than a particular stance taken. Our defining dynamic had been connection through opposition, while I was seeking closeness through emotional intimacy. The more I removed myself from our power struggles, the more uncomfortable John became.

When I say John distanced himself, I mean that literally and figuratively. For some years, he had been growing increasingly disenchanted with his life as a physician. The call schedule was grueling, but, more important, he didn't feel adequately compensated for the time he put in. The first hint I had about his disillusionment came when we moved into our new house. Finding the land on which it would stand and then building it had been one of the major events of our family life. We helped design it, served as our own contractors, and hired friends who were carpenters to construct it. On the first day we came to visit the worksite, our friends had purchased three little toolboxes, each set up with a few tools and some screws and nails. Every time we visited, they found some little job the kids could do to help. We were all part of the dream.

When the house was done and we moved in, it seemed like we now had the perfect place to raise our family and live out our lives together. However, it stands out to me now that within the first days of stepping into our dream, John was unhappy. He suddenly felt weighted by his work and began questioning whether he wanted to continue to do it. When we were building our house, he was also in charge of the construction of a new office building for his practice, something I had been opposed to because of the timing. He must have been exhausted. But it also became clear to me that perhaps his building frenzy was more about manifesting things in the world than actually immersing himself in what was manifested after it was there. With this realization, I felt the ground beneath me rumbling. I was planting myself in my new home. *Is it safe to let my roots sink down here if John isn't doing that also?* I wondered. At the time, this was just a passing thought. There was nothing to do about it right then. The house was built. We were living in it.

But over the years, the financial burden of what we had created had become increasingly heavy for John. Money was often the battleground of our disagreements. As our children grew and my work developed, I began to contribute to our life financially, but for John, we never had enough. I offered again and again to let go of all we had created and find a simpler life, hoping that would make things better for him and between us. He was never willing to take me up on that until he was ready to walk away from it all, including me.

When John attended a conference related to public health issues, he came home with a surprise announcement. "I want to leave my practice, move to Berkeley, and get a master's degree in public health," he told me.

My stomach flipped. The protective mother and defender of our family life leaped to the fore. "What about us?" I asked. "Are you thinking we'll move, that we'll all go with you?" *He can't mean that,* I thought. *Gabriel is a junior in high school and Eli is in eighth grade. It would be so disruptive for them. . . . And what about my practice?* a voice shrieked. *I've worked so hard to get it established.*

"I want to support you if this is something you really want and need," I told him. "But how is this going to work?" It seemed like a shot in the dark. *Is a career change really going to make him happy? Is he seriously going to do this?* A cascade of questions continued to tumble through my mind.

John hadn't yet thought through all the details, but he was unbending in his desire to do it. Weeks of talking and planning ensued. As we worked our way through it all, I eventually relaxed into the idea and saw it as a change that might be enlivening for all of us. It was worth a try.

Over the next few months, John ironed out the details with the doctors in his group practice. We decided that I would stay in Mendocino with our children and he would come home on the weekends. We got loans to finance his adventure. When he was finished with school and could see what he wanted to do next, we would reevaluate our family plan. I came to see John's going back to school as a first step toward some kind of restructuring the way we were living our lives. But even at the time, I had inklings that I was seeing the first card in a house of cards tumbling. I knew more would fall, and I feared the whole house would collapse. I think somewhere deep inside I knew this would be the end of our marriage, but I bravely held onto the hope that there was some way we could make it through all these changes.

John applied to graduate school, was accepted, and moved away. Once he was gone, it became clear that that house of cards I had imagined was indeed going to tumble. No amount of trying this or trying that was going to make our marriage better. John was moving on, and I was giving up. In one of our last attempts to remain together, we went away for a weekend to try to get clarity about what we needed and wanted in a relationship at this point in our lives. I was hoping to determine that we could remain together. In recent years, John had traveled to Armenia, the country of his family's origins. When he told me that one of the problems for him was that I wasn't Armenian, I felt hopeless. Although that was a clear sign that no matter what I did or didn't do, my marriage was over, it was hard for me to face that reality.

Once again, I turned to art. I did this self-portrait, *How Did I Get Here?*, during that time. My sadness, my wounding, and my confusion are all expressed here. I felt like a lost soul. If the art could speak, the woman would be asking, "How did I get here? Why me? Why now? Can I go on?"

How Did I Get Here?

When John finished his program, he looked for a job in the public health field. There was an opening for a director of public health in our county, but John was not interested, as it would have required a long commute and didn't pay enough. Money became an issue everywhere he turned. Actually, I think he began to miss his old image as a practicing pediatrician. Very soon, he abandoned his search for an interesting position in his new field and returned to pediatrics, choosing not to return to Mendocino but rather to work for Kaiser in the Bay Area.

There was so much distance between us at this point in time. John didn't actually say out loud that he wanted to leave our marriage, but all the choices he was making in his life were shouting, "I'm out!" I finally had to come to terms with the fact that my marriage was indeed ending. Still, I was unable to step up and make the decision to shatter my family. I still wanted to go forward and make it through this difficult time, even though there was no hope left for us as far as I could see. However, feeling as I did, I was violating my own integrity by staying married. It is clear to me now that it was easier for me to be the one left than to be the one leaving.

One weekend when John was home, I couldn't stand the tension of living in our tangled reality any longer. Waking up one morning with this person who had become like a stranger in my bed, I finally had the nerve to speak. "John," I said, "It seems to me that you're making every choice to separate from our life here. You aren't saying that you want a divorce, but that's what it looks and feels like to me. If that's really true, will you please leave now so we can move on from all this?"

He acknowledged the truth of what I was saying, and that was the day we decided to separate. Not long after, he pressed for divorce. I again tried to slow things down, in spite of my despair that anything would get better, but to no avail. We divorced.

I have often reflected on why I stayed in such a painful situation for so long. There were some peaceful times, but we just couldn't stop reenacting our negative patterns. I don't think I saw our marriage as abnormal; I just thought it was how marriages were and that making it through painful struggles was the hard work of staying married. Though I watched divorces happening all around me, until mine happened, it was unthinkable to me.

I have often wondered if I needed an adversary to stand against in order to find myself. Given all of our differences, it was easy for John to be that adversary. From this perspective, I see that the struggles in our marriage were the labor pains that eventually led to the birth of who I am today. In this way, our union became one long and often torturous adventure in self-discovery.

John and I couldn't find a way to treat each other with respect in our differing perceptions of what brought meaning and purpose to our lives. I was not content to sail along the surface of my life. I wanted to follow my natural inclinations and dive more deeply into my inner and outer realities. I wanted to understand my motivations and explore everything that was keeping me from living more fully. I was always looking for the larger context in which my life was held. I wanted John to join me in that deeper exploration of our lives together, because I saw it as the only way we would be able to bridge the differences between us

Tossed Out

and find a way to real intimacy. In the end, that was the irreconcilable difference between us. I couldn't live on the surface of my life, and he couldn't dive down into his.

When it finally happened, divorce felt like a gigantic volcano erupting after years of rumbling from its fiery depths. In the explosion, what had been our family unit was shattered into a million tiny pieces. The five of us were tossed into midair and left floating in space, now five separate beings, each with our own direction. None of us knew what would happen next. My pastel drawing *Tossed Out* portrays this explosion. I entered a time of great darkness. I was convinced that my survival was at stake if I remained married to John, because I was betraying my own integrity, but I wasn't certain that I could live alone, be a single parent, and take care of myself in the world. It was devastating to think about the effect this ending would have on my sons. For me, it was a time of sadness, terror, and rage.

Once we separated, life moved forward so rapidly that it was hard for me to keep up with it all. Though some friends congratulated me on my newfound freedom, I didn't experience what was happening to me as such; instead, it felt like a strange kind of death—as if John himself had died. But when death comes to take someone we love, we tend to remember all the best parts of that person. The difficult parts become humorous, minimized, or even forgotten. With divorce, the opposite seemed to be true. All the very hardest parts of John were magnified, as if under a microscope. My positive feelings faded silently into the background.

The change in my life was so encompassing that I hardly knew who I was. I felt as if perhaps I had died as well. The image of myself as a married woman was perishing, and because I had invested so much of my life energy trying to exist inside that image, it was an ego death of the highest degree. When it fell away, it was dizzying. Only later did I see that this death and my new beginning were happening simultaneously—it simply took some time to recognize the new me. When I drew *Tossed Out*, I thought I was painting a sunset, but now it looks to me more like the dawn. I had imagined the figure doing the tossing to be fate, but that figure may well be me, emerging into the light. At the time, I simply felt myself to be drowning in the blackness, but perhaps it was more like the darkness a baby experiences inside the womb. With time I would grow and mature and eventually would be delivered from that dark place. In my new life, I would find myself living a life that had much greater integrity than the one I had before. I would stand more in my own power and find myself better able to express my true self in the world. I might have found my way to a profound spiritual connection while remaining married, but, as it turned out, my divorce was the portal through which I would find greater access to a much deeper part of me.

My art became a major way of processing all I was experiencing as I tried to cope with my new reality. In *Shedding My Skin*, the snake appears as the healing symbol for my struggle at the time. The drawing gave me faith that as I shed my old way of being, the essential part of me would live on. The energy of the divine feminine is present, and the full moon, witness to this process, sends an important message of wholeness. In this drawing, my letting go and the promise of my new life are brought together as one.

Shedding My Skin

John clearly needed to find a whole new life. He was willing to leave his work, his marriage, his children, who had not yet flown the nest, and the home we had built in Mendocino. The fact that I, too, needed a new life wasn't as clear to me yet. I knew I was miserable, but my thoughts were focused on trying to find a way to make things better within the life I had. Because John's need for change was overwhelming, it was easier for me to see his needs in this regard than my own. In fact, I remember reading Murray Stein's book *In Midlife* and making endless notes in the margins about John's life. Years later, I returned to the book as the newly independent me and saw my very own midlife journey clearly portrayed there. I hadn't seen that at the time, though it was glaring when I revisited it.

In the early days after our separation, I marveled at the roller coaster of my emotions. I would find myself in the deepest pain I had ever felt and then, just a short while later, experiencing moments of exquisite beauty. I often talked to my clients about our emotional lives being like a river flowing through many different landscapes. Rather than attaching to any one place along the journey—the serene, sunny meadow or the roiling, angry canyon—we can find solace and trust in the fact that the water is always moving, always flowing, and the landscape is always changing. During this time, I had much practice in remembering my own words. I just needed to surrender to a wild ride.

The truest statement I can make about myself in the wake of my divorce is that I was enraged. My anger was a smoldering fire that would jump into flame at the least provocation. I couldn't escape it or pretend it wasn't there. The collapse of the dream I had put so much of my life energy into manifesting was hard for me to accept. However, I didn't act on my rage in dramatic ways. There were just a few moments when my fiery truth about the dark side of our union spewed out after years of having been repressed. *Spewing My Fiery Truth* represents one of those moments. A whole series of angry drawings followed. Sometimes I just filled the pages of my art journal with angry scribbles.

It was hard for me to stay with that much anger, but there didn't seem to be any way to escape it. I can see now that my rage is what helped me to survive it all. My dreams were crushed. Without that fiery protection for my wounded heart, I'm not sure I would have

Spewing My Fiery Truth

Art Journal

made it through. I fear I would have drowned in a puddle of sorrow. I needed to stay erect, stand for myself, fight for my rights, and state what I wanted from the settlement we were trying to agree upon.

In waking up to the practical, earth-plane part of my existence, I felt a bit like a woman coming out of a deep sleep into very bright light. There was so much to see outside my coupling that I had been blind to while I'd been in it. All those parts that I had unconsciously relinquished to John were conspicuous in their absence. I desperately needed to call them home, and quickly. My terror centered on the fact that, for most of our marriage, I had pretty much dedicated my life to home and family. I had eventually gone back to school and found my work in the world, but I had not supported myself with my own income. Now, I needed to focus on managing my own economic life, being a single parent, realigning my social network, and learning to take care of my home and property. In order to carry on, I needed to grow quickly, but I wasn't sure I could.

At this time, I drew another self-portrait. In *Emerging from the Darkness,* I used gesso to paint the background black as night. Still wounded and sad, using oil pastels I drew myself, emerging from the blackness and into the light. The large yellow circle connects to a matching circle inside me; an arrow pointing from outside to inside connects the two. I was not conscious of what I was expressing except some feeling that I had experienced a very bright light and needed to remember that it existed inside me as well. Looking at this drawing over the years, I've realized that it expresses my intuition about the connection between what is inside me and what is outside me. I was on the cusp of opening to a new worldview that would teach me more about that, but it would be some time before I grasped the full meaning of what I sensed then.

Emerging From the Darkness

In the midst of my mourning, my doubts about myself, and my struggle to find my new relationship to the world, an uncanny event occurred. One morning while I was washing dishes, I looked out my window and saw a little fawn lying in a heap in the meadow. I had seen it out there a couple of days before. It was not walking with full strength, and its coat looked terribly mangy. I knew it wasn't healthy. So, when I looked out that morning and saw it lying there, I knew it was gone. I felt like I was walking into a waking dream as I went out the door to assess the situation. My tears came as I approached its still body and gazed into its lifeless eyes. As the death of this innocent animal reverberated inside me, I started to cry. I saw my own lost innocence lying there at my feet.

In that moment, I knew on a gut level that the death of this creature was connected symbolically to the death of all my youthful hopes and dreams for my marriage and my family. But this flash of recognition didn't last long, as I was quickly confronted with the fact that I had to take care of this situation. I had to bury the fawn, and I had to do it myself.

I dragged it to the edge of the meadow and into the forest. It was incredibly heavy. I started to dig the hole but soon realized that I was on the outer edge of what I was capable of doing. The soil was hard as a rock. I needed to use a pick to break through the dirt before I could even begin to shovel it out. When I thought I had dug deeply enough, I dragged the fawn into the hole, only to discover that it had to be twice that size. Tears streamed down my face. I had to pause in my work when my sobs came. My crushed hopes and dreams and all my fears tumbled to the forefront of my mind. At times, my emotions threatened to defeat me, but I kept digging and eventually managed to make a hole big enough for the fawn and a few inches of dirt to cover it.

I felt like I was undergoing a rite of passage that would take me from my old life to my new one. My grief over both the dead fawn and the end of my marriage had become one. All those years before, I had stepped out into the world holding big dreams in my heart. They were born of the innocence of my youth, and now, all these years later, those dreams were dead and gone with the dissolution of my nest. I hoped that releasing my grief when I buried the fawn would help me let go of all my old desires for what my marriage could have been. What was important now was fully embracing its ending.

My dreams supported me through this time as well. Soon after I buried the fawn, in that same spirit of death and dissolution, I dreamed that I drove down my forest lane one evening at sunset, only to find my house and the surrounding forest burned to the ground. Nothing remained but a few stumps. Everything was ash and rubble. I woke up sobbing.

My dream image, as horrifying as it was, helped me to face reality. The life I had been living was over. It had been chopped down and burned to the ground. I had to fully embrace the impact of the dissolution before I could even catch a glimpse of my future. My dream gave me the perfect image to clarify what I was experiencing, beautifully portraying the fiery transformation that was taking place at that time. I expressed this fiery landscape in *Axed and Burned*. With clearer eyes, I might have seen the promise of the phoenix rising from those ashes, but at the time, I remained in the darkness.

Axed and Burned

After much heartbreaking tumult, John and I did eventually reach our settlement. It was cold and stormy the morning my lawyer called and told me that all the papers had been filed with the county and that my divorce was final. I hung up the phone and walked into the bathroom to get ready for the day. I looked into the mirror, and just then, a huge clap of thunder boomed outside. It felt like a fitting soundtrack for all that I was experiencing inside me at that moment.

🌿 *Reflection*

As our years accumulate, we all have dreams that shatter. Was there a big dream you had early in your life that didn't turn out as you hoped? Express that dream with color and shape on a large piece of paper. Reflect on all your feelings. Then tear your drawing into many tiny pieces, crumple them, and put them in a large envelope titled "In Process." Decorate it and save it for the next reflection.

Chapter 11:

Dark Energies Unleashed

Those who contemplate the beauty of the earth find reserves of strength that will endure as long as life lasts. There is something infinitely healing in the repeated refrains of nature—the assurance that dawn comes after night, and spring after winter.
—Rachel Carson

As I made my way through the early days after my divorce, my encounter with the dead fawn turned out to be the first of many synchronous events in which the state of my inner world coincided with unusual circumstances unfolding in wild nature. I found myself in awe as I experienced each one of these. There was no explanation for why these things happened or why they aligned in a meaningful way with my inner state. But, over time, as the events multiplied, I would have to have been blind not to have seen the connections.

A few months after John and I separated but before our divorce was final, I had an astonishing experience in nature. On his spring break, Gabriel offered to take Eli and me on a short backpacking trip along part of the Lost Coast in Northern California. Arriving in the late afternoon, we walked only a short distance from the car to set up camp for our first night. We planned on a longer hike the next day. We found a beautiful spot in an open area overlooking the ocean. Forested hills stood behind us. As we cooked our dinner, we watched an elk herd grazing peacefully in the distance.

As night fell, I got a little jumpy, as I usually did when camping. I knew there were bears in this area, and my lifelong unease kicked in. The guys had hung our food, and we had made our camp as safe as possible. Soon we had all drifted off to sleep.

I was soon awakened by a scratching sound on the roof of the tent. Confused and coming out of a deep slumber, I said, "What's that?" The sound stopped, and my kids, who hadn't heard it, responded, "Aw, Mom, it's nothing. Just go back to sleep." I did, but sometime later the same sound woke me up again.

This scene repeated itself several times over the night. The guys, not hearing what I was hearing, were getting increasingly frustrated with me. My mind was spinning as I tried to imagine what the sound could be. I knew there were no trees or bushes near our tent. I don't know how many times I was awakened, but by the final time, when I opened my eyes, it was early morning. There was enough light for me to see that the roof of the tent was indenting as the scratching sound was happening. "I hear it and I see it and it is real!" I shouted out. This time, my sons took me seriously and Gabriel unzipped the tent door. We saw the herd of elk scattered around our campsite. "It's just the elk," Gabe said, and we all got back in our sleeping bags.

But moments later there was a ruckus outside the tent, and we unzipped it again. One young male elk was tossing our empty backpacks around with his antlers. We shouted and banged things around to try to get him to stop. Remembering the night before, when the elk had been nearby but not bothering us, I made a suggestion. "Let's get up and start cooking breakfast," I said. "Maybe they'll just wander off." We all agreed to give that a try.

While I was terrified of bears, I was not at all afraid of these elk. They just seemed like larger versions of the deer that frequented our meadow at home. I was pretty sure that once we were moving around the campsite, they would move on, and they did. But soon one of them parted from the herd and walked over toward our tent. "I'll just go over there and show him who the tent belongs to," I said, heading in that direction. But the elk continued toward the tent, and when I approached, he lowered his head and started pawing the ground. "OK, I get it!" I said, backing away with an uncomfortable laugh.

We grabbed our packs off the picnic table and put them on our backs. After we had walked about a hundred yards, we heard the sound of fabric tearing behind us. Turning around, we saw the elk using his antlers and hooves to go after our tent. He didn't stop until the tent had collapsed and sat in a tangled heap on the ground. He was satisfied then and wandered back over to the herd. We waited until they were a good distance away before we returned to our campsite. Examining the tent, we found the rain fly shredded. One of the poles had bent, but, other than that, the tent had survived. Quickly gathering our things, we packed up and headed to the car to regroup.

We decided to change our plan and just go on a day hike, rather than try to camp again for another night, as we had planned. As we hiked along, I think we were all reliving what had happened. The memory started to seem like a movie or a dream. As I watched the elk tackling our tent over and over again in my mind's eye, I couldn't help but see a connection between our jumbled heap of a tent and what felt like the jumbled heap of our family. I commented on this to my sons. Eli thought about what I had said for a moment, and then, in one of his laser-focused assessments, said, "Look at it this way, Mom: He only got the rain fly."

I have thought of the elk and of Eli's comment many times over the years. Its meaning has continued to grow and expand. I don't want to personalize the elk's actions. I believe that he took down the tent for his own reasons. But what I found in our experience with the elk was a meaningful coincidence. Carl Jung coined the word "synchronicity" to describe this phenomenon. We can't make it happen. It always comes as a complete surprise and surpasses our wildest imagination of what is possible. Jung saw these kinds of events as proof that mind and matter are not as separate as we have been led to believe. After my experiences with the fawn and the elk, I was beginning to understand what he meant in a whole new way.

To me, when these kinds of uncanny events happen, they seem like dreams. But because they occur outside us, instead of inside, when they happen, it can feel as if the world is somehow dreaming with us. From there, it is only a small step to begin looking at the symbolic meaning of waking-life experiences, just as we look to our dreams. That is what I started to do. When we inhabit our symbolic landscape in this way, life itself begins to present itself to our imagination. Looking at our lives, our art, and our dreams through a symbolic lens opens the door to our becoming conversant in a language that is deeper than our words. Once in that realm, we have hope of learning much more about who we are and our place in the big picture of things.

It was true that with my divorce, a protective covering had been removed from my life. The structure had collapsed and fallen into disarray. Parts were broken. But the protection I missed and thought I needed was being replaced by something much more substantial and real. The barrier between the world and me was dissolving, or at least becoming much more permeable. In moments like the one with the fawn and with the elk, I seemed to be asked to make sense of a whole new world. My experiences in nature began to point to the fact that I would find my new sense of belonging and safety in a realm much larger than the small circle of comfort my marriage and family had provided. The way I perceived my place in the natural world had been called into question. This was an opening as life-changing as the experience I had had giving birth.

As much as my marriage teetered on the brink of disaster over many years, I don't think I ever really believed it would end. In the years following my divorce, my fears were constellated around the survival level of my existence. I bravely continued on, functioning in my life as I had before, but inside I was in great turmoil. I don't know if many knew the extent of my chaos, because, with the exception of a couple of close friends, I tried very hard to keep it together when I was with others. When I was alone, I had a basket full of fears and regularly collapsed into a river of sadness. It was as if the ground had disappeared from under my feet.

In my self-portrait *Two Sides of Me*, painted at the time, I am filled with fire; one side of my body reflects the darkness I was experiencing, the other side, my desperate attempt to bring the world my light.

In time, I came to look at my divorce as a radical pruning. The structure of my life was altered so dramatically that I had to dig deeply into my roots to remember my essential nature. I understand now what a fertile time it is when the images we hold of ourselves fall away. In the heat of that much change, we have the opportunity to let ourselves melt into the fluidity of new possibility. But at the time I was struggling to live with the fallout of so much change. In the wake of my divorce, all the insight I had gained in my therapy would be tested in the crucible of my life, now lived alone.

My marriage to John and my therapy with Keith were the two most influential relationships I had had with men in my adult life. I was married to John for twenty-seven years, and, though not continuously, I was connected to Keith over twenty-three years. The relationship I

Two Sides of Me

had with each one was distinctly different. With John, I was embedded in personality, family, and worldly concerns. In my therapy with Keith, it was about something else entirely—all movement and vibration, nothing to hold onto but rather learning to flow with my new, ever-changing, naturally evolving self. After my divorce, my deepest desire was to bring those two kinds of experiences together in one person. I didn't see myself living the remainder of my life as a single woman. I wanted a relationship that manifested spirit in an earthbound connection, but, as much as I hated the thought of it, I knew there was something I needed to learn about living alone. I wasn't able to welcome my new circumstance. Instead, I found myself kicking and screaming as life carried me to a different destination than the one I had intended.

Call the Cops!

At this time in my life, the energies of grief, fear, and rage were overwhelming. They were emerging from my primitive core as gut-level feelings that surpassed my mental abilities to tame them. There was no pretending they weren't there or that I could just let them take care of themselves. Turning to art, I found *Call the Cops!* falling onto the paper. I see the policeman in me trying desperately to control the wild, angry, snake-haired Medusa that I was at the time. He looks small, ineffectual, and unsure of himself in the face of her power.

I knew I needed to find some kind of container for these strong emotions, or they would indeed destroy me. Emotions amplified have that power if we let them. Coming out of such heartbreak, I've known women who curse men and swear off relationships entirely. Our wiser selves know there is a better way. I didn't want to become a bitter cynical shell of a person; I had to take charge of this situation. Since my very survival in the world was my great fear and my great problem, it occurred to me that I needed to take myself out into the world quite literally, out into nature, where my survival was indeed at stake. Maybe there I could make myself face my fears head-on, walk myself through them, and find my way to a new life.

Rachel Carson has written, "Those who contemplate the beauty of the earth find reserves of strength that will endure as long as life lasts. There is something infinitely healing in the repeated refrains of nature—the assurance that dawn comes after night, and spring after winter." Pruned by my divorce, I felt as if I were living in darkness in the middle of winter. I did not fully trust that there would be another spring. A memory from years before offered comfort. I had been to visit the area around Mount St. Helens a few years after it had erupted. In the desolation for miles around the core of the explosion, little green shrubs, mosses, and brambles, had already started growing. Remembering this, I found hope that something green and growing would emerge from this fiery explosion in my life as well.

I had certainly turned to Mother Nature to help me in times of transition many times before in my life. When I divorced, it was natural for me to do so once again. I was seeking the solace of nature, but I knew I needed to embrace more than her natural beauty—I needed to come to terms with her ferocity as well. I sensed that the only energy big enough to hold and contain the dark energies coursing through me at the time was in Mother Nature herself.

Supported by Mother Earth

I knew I needed to transform these dark energies inside me into something useful, something healing, but that doesn't just happen without our taking hold of them, owning them, and working to transform them. I committed myself to that process. Erik and Gabriel had gone off to college. Eli was home for just a couple of years before he went out the door. My active mothering was coming to an end. I felt lost, to my family and to my own soul. Fortunately, I had a career that I loved, but family had given my life deep grounding for many years. I knew that I needed to find new ground.

My art helped me to understand that I was in a death-rebirth cycle. Images arrived on the paper. In *Supported by Mother Earth*, I'm in a birthing position, the element of fire spewing from my mouth and the element of water flowing from my vagina, along with drops of blood. I see the blood as menstrual blood, which holds the promise of the fertile situation in which I found myself, a promise that birth, or, in my case, rebirth, is always possible. I am sitting on the top of the world, the energy of the heavens behind me, earth, fire, water, and air all there, supporting me as I tried to cope with the powerful emotions I was experiencing and give birth to a new me.

╰╮∿

Looking back, I see the years immediately following my divorce as nothing short of heroic. Moving out into the world as a single woman unwrapped from the cocoon of marriage and family, I felt exposed and vulnerable. I knew I needed to find tougher skin. I had to call on my inner masculine energy and develop the muscle I needed to find my own way in the world. At the same time, as a woman alone, I heard my intuition calling me to sink more deeply into the roots of my feminine consciousness.

Finding My Way was drawn to the music Des pas sur la neige (Footprints in the Snow) by Claude Debussy. I walk alone through a snowy landscape in the far north, guided by the moon, the stars, and the aurora. I hold my own candle as a symbol of the light of my own consciousness. I am in touch with the deep feminine energy inside me. Walking through the snow-covered landscape in the dark of night, I am finding my way. I am seeking belonging.

Finding My Way

Trusting into My True Home

This time of my life attested to how completely I had given up looking to an outer masculine energy for support and belonging, whether that be a Father God in Heaven, my own father, my husband, or my beloved mentors. Now I sought support from Mother Earth herself. This was not simply an idea but a physical calling. I yearned for a direct connection between the earth and my own body. It wasn't just a matter of sinking my hands into the soil but a need to stretch my body out on the ground and feel the literal support of Mother Earth. One whole summer, I slept outside in my meadow more often than I did in my own bed. It was the only thing that comforted me. My pastel drawing *Trusting into My True Home* shows me lying on the forest floor, tired and vulnerable, surrendering to the ways of the wild world around me, the night sky above me, Mother Earth below me, the trees sheltering me. In order to make such a surrender, I needed to call forth a radical trust.

The stories and the art that follow chronicle how I took myself out into nature, seeking healing, and what I discovered about myself in the process. I went alone, learning to fly fish, hike, and camp by myself, trying to trust wild nature to teach me what I needed to know.

❦ *Reflection*

New dreams are often born out of old ones. Take your ripped and crumpled dream out of the envelope where it has been incubating. On a big, colorful piece of paper, glue those little pieces into some new shape or form. Do you need all the pieces, or can some be thrown away or burned? Do you need to add something new? Does your creation or the process of making it give you any hints about new directions? Write in your journal.

Part II

Entering Midlife

Nature is an incomparable guide if you know how to follow her
—CARL JUNG

Chapter 12:

Cast Out There

The water you touch in a river is the last of that which has passed,
and the first of that which is coming. . . .
—Leonardo da Vinci

I can't remember when my awareness of the natural world wasn't a big part of my life. Like the little one I was, so taken with those shadowy leaves fluttering above me, we are all born mesmerized by the wild outdoors, but being with my father in nature let me witness its power to heal. As a child, I didn't have the word "depression" to define my dad's moodiness, but that is what it was. Amazingly, in the beauty of nature, all that gloom fell away. There, he was open and in awe. I can still hear the deep resonance of his voice marveling at the beauty of a waterfall in Yosemite Valley, a high mountain lake in the Sierras, or a beautiful sunset over the Nevada desert.

In nature, it seemed like a door to my father's heart opened, a door that was normally closed. As a tiny child, I felt a rush of warmth move through me as I realized this was my chance to walk through that door and find my place in my father's heart. He wanted me to see what he was seeing, and I wanted to see it. It was like finding a hidden spring coming out of a crack in solid rock—I was thirsty, and I wanted to drink. His love, gushing forth in this way, was contagious. I figured that anything that could bring about such a transformation in my father must indeed be very powerful. It made me take note, and from him I learned that nature can change us. It heals.

My childhood was filled with family camping and fishing adventures. Most often, my grandparents came along with us. I spent many hours sitting by clear blue mountain lakes, listening to the gentle lapping of the water on the shore and breathing in the muddy smells. I watched the birds fly overhead and was lulled by the sound of the wind in the pine trees. I had endless patience and could sit for hours clutching my fishing pole in my little hands, waiting. What joy and excitement I felt if a fish interrupted my reverie by finding its way to my line. While I reeled it in, my dad and my grandfather whooped and hollered. Then, there it was, that shiny, silvery creature from the depths. Most often, it had an iridescent rainbow on its side, but I was particularly thrilled when I caught an eastern brook trout with its beautiful orange spots and its delicious orange flesh. There was always a competition to see who could catch the most fish, and on occasion I was the winner. My eyes widened as we measured each fish and admired one another's catches. Our mouths watered, as we knew they were headed for the frying pan. I always got to eat the fish I caught and would watch carefully while my mom was cooking to be sure mine didn't get mixed up with someone else's.

If we weren't sitting by a lake, we were fishing in small streams all over Nevada and eastern California. I was sent out on my own and told to stay by the stream, something I bet doesn't happen often today. I would make my way through heavy underbrush, sneaking up on quiet pools where I had learned the fish would be waiting for their food. I knew just where to cast to make it seem as if my bait were just like all the other food coming downstream. I loved using my knowledge and skill to catch my own food. Once I caught them, I kept my fish in my father's old willow creel. My heart burst with pride when I pulled them out and showed them off at the end of the day. I never shied away from slitting a fish open with a knife, examining its contents, wiping out its guts, washing all the blood away, and getting it ready for the frying pan.

"Look at her," my dad would say to my grandfather. "She doesn't mind this at all!"

"Yeah, she's not squeamish, I guess," he would reply.

In those moments, I knew I belonged to these two men.

"Here look at this one, Kay. It's a female—see all these eggs?" my grandfather would say, holding out his fish so I could see. Looking at all those little orange beads in her belly, I felt a kinship, a kind of pride in her ability to make these precious jewels, something I knew my body did, too. I felt like I was peeking into the mysteries of life.

I see now that in those moments I was holding life and death in my very own hands. In those days, I was easy with that kind of power. It was very straightforward: I caught the fish. I needed food. The fish would nourish me. It was that simple. But as we grow and face more nuanced situations, most of us find ourselves much more comfortable encouraging life than ending it. When we can't do both, we lose our place in the oneness of things.

My mother and my grandmother didn't fish, though I heard stories about what a good fisher my grandmother was in her younger years. "Grandma, why don't you like to fish anymore?" I'd ask. "You used to. Grandpa says you were really good at it."

"Oh, I don't know," she'd say. "I guess now your mom and I are the camp chefs." And they were. They cooked the fish over the open fire they had tended just for that purpose. We left our fish with heads and tails and cooked them that way, eyes and all. Gathered around the camp picnic table, we ate them with our hands, using the heads and tails as handles so we could nibble down the top, exposing the spine. Then we gently peeled away the skin and flesh from the sides with our teeth and lips, tasting the tender meat and leaving the bones. It was a wild taste, flavored by the water the fish had come from. When we camped, we ate fish for breakfast, lunch, and dinner. Those were the best of family times for me and the best of times with my father.

There were darker shadows as well. I was aware that the connection I had with my father through fishing was fragile. I knew I was being allowed to hang out on the fringes of his world, but what we were doing was centered on him and not on me. He was the king in our family, and we were his subjects. My mother reminded us often that he worked hard to support us and that our vacations were planned so that he could relax and enjoy himself. Fishing was serious business for him, and my brother and I weren't always allowed to accompany him. When I did get to go, it was clear that he had a single focus. He wanted to catch fish. He always rigged his gear and got it in the water first, and then helped me with mine. If he got snagged, he grumbled. If I got snagged, it was my fault. If one of his fish got away, I was sure to hear, "Goddamn son of a bitch," followed by some stomping around and loud clangs of his gear while he fixed his line for the next cast. Sometimes, sitting next to him, I felt like he was a time bomb waiting to go off.

Whatever darkness may have been attached to those adventures, I learned to love fishing. My parents were amazed at the patience I had with it all. "She's a natural," they would say, and I would bask in all the attention I received. Fishing was our family tradition; so much of our lore centered on that topic. I often felt like an outsider in my family, but when it came to fishing, I belonged. I couldn't wait for our next adventure.

I felt a great sense of expansion in wild places and, like my father, a great sense of awe. Being in nature and moving at its pace supported my natural introversion. There, it was easy to find and be with a deeper place inside me. Though I was very young, memories of these wild places remain with me in my whole body—the sights, the sounds, the smells, the tastes, and the textures, all there. With just a moment's reflection, I can sense the young one I was then, as if she were alive in this moment.

Outdoors, I felt nurtured by a power much larger than I and stronger than all of us, even the adults in my life. I found a deep peace in nature and a sense of my belonging that was harder to find at home, at school, or even with my friends.

Years later, I taught John to fish. When our kids came along, we camped and fished on most of our family vacations. When I was newly divorced, I knew I had to keep taking myself out there, but I was frightened about doing that alone. Soon after my divorce was final, I heard an interview on the radio with a woman who specialized in teaching women to fly fish. As I listened, memories of fishing with my dad and my grandfather flooded to the fore. I wasn't allowed to fish with a fly as a child, but I always wanted to give it a try. I remembered those times, usually late in the evening, when my father would notice the fish rising to feed on the surface. He would get out his bamboo fly rod with its thick orange line and begin casting. I was mesmerized watching the line fly back and forth over his head. I don't actually remember his catching fish but rather the grace of watching him try. As I listened to this woman on the radio, I decided then and there that I was going to sign up for one of her classes. I contacted her school, only to learn that she was booked years in advance. Still, I needed a big adventure. I needed to go somewhere I had never been before and learn to fly fish. I did some investigating and signed up for a class at a fly fishing store in Jackson, Wyoming.

I had realized by now that my divorce was asking me to come into a better relationship with my own masculine energy. I knew that men dominated the world of fly fishing. I felt an inner challenge to enter that world as a woman and see what I might learn there. It seemed that learning to fly fish might help me find something of that spunky young girl I used to be. That kind of energy would very be useful for me now.

I planned my trip, allowing enough time for the class and some camping and fishing by myself afterward. I had never camped alone and wasn't at all sure it was a wise thing to do, but I knew that finding the spark to do what we love can save us when our lives have fallen apart. If we can't find the will to fire our passions, we're at risk of just withering away. I wasn't going to let my divorce do that to me. This trip would be the first of many solo outdoor adventures that became a vital part of my healing from the immediate trauma of my divorce. Doing what I loved to do, no matter what, helped me to forge a powerful new trust in myself.

I borrowed my son's fly rod and bought enough flies to get me started. When I got off the plane in Jackson, I was trying very hard to look cool, but my heart was pounding. A voice quivered inside me: *What have I done?*

Waiting in line to pick up my rental car, I clutched my fly rod in its aluminum case as if it were my badge of courage. I found my hotel, got some sleep, and arrived at my class early the next morning. The class took place in an Orvis store. I knew when I walked in the door that I was walking into a man's world—all the equipment, clothes, and everything else was made for the male body and aimed at a masculine sensitivity. I imagined that the way I felt in this environment must have been how a man might feel walking into a fabric store to pursue his new interest in quilting.

Our teacher turned out to be a Marlboro man who looked like he'd ridden into town right off the billboard. He was friendly and informative. He taught us how to tie knots, showed us slides of bugs, took us to the local park to practice casting, and played the part of the fish, holding onto our lines so we could reel him in. He encouraged us all to practice catch-and-release fishing. To do this, the barb on the hook is pinched down so it can be removed easily. No more catching fish for dinner. They are quickly released back to their life in the water in order to preserve wild trout populations.

All went well, except it was clear that the men in the class were the "real" students; when we introduced ourselves, each of the wives said they were interested in learning to fly fish because they wanted to be able to fish with their husbands. It was hard to tell whether the fishing or the husbands were their real interest. That left me in a funny position, since I was not there with a man. I spoke of my dad and my grandfather and my longing to give fly fishing a try. Though they all listened to me, they seemed surprised by what I was doing—the travel, the fishing, the camping, all of it. They gasped audibly when they heard that I was doing it alone. The whole environment was so oriented toward men that I wouldn't have been surprised if they had surmised from my story that my real motivation was to use fishing as bait to catch a man. That wasn't true, but I was there to take a peek into their worldview and see what I could learn.

"Well, that looks easy for you," the teacher told me, as he watched me practice tying the knots. When he saw that my casting was coming along, he looked surprised. "I can see you're catching on. You're a natural at this." His comments made me feel like maybe I had succeeded in proving myself worthy of being there and was earning his respect.

The last day of class, we went streamside. The teacher led us about, looking at fish and explaining to us that this little stream was a place for experts, not beginners. We would not catch fish. We beat the water in the hot midday sun, trying out dry flies, nymphs, and streamers and learning the techniques for fishing with them. When I mentioned that I was going to go fishing there that evening, the teacher looked horrified. He discouraged me by telling me that if I did, I risked being attacked by badgers and weasels. I think he was just trying to keep me out of the way; evening is prime fishing time, because that's when the fish like to feed, and he might have been concerned that my ineptitude as a beginner would disturb the area for those who came along to fish after me or that I might not understand fishing etiquette. Fly fishermen can be terribly snobby, and at that time they were just beginning to welcome women. Discouraged by his comment, I didn't fish there that evening.

I decided to extend my learning period by going out with a guide on the first day after class. He was a big, burly guy with dark, curly hair and a hard-living kind of lifestyle. We had so little in common, it was hard to talk about much of anything, and it was a bit of a drive to our destination.

"What do you think of our local bars?" he asked, making an attempt to break through my silence. "Have you checked out the Million Dollar Cowboy Bar? They have saddles for stools!"

"No," I said, "I haven't been in any of them. I'm not much of a drinker."

"Well, whether you drink or not, go in there and sit in one of those stools. It's an experience you won't forget."

"OK, I will," I said, knowing full well that wasn't going to happen. The conversation fell back into an uncomfortable silence.

"Well, if you aren't here for the nightlife, why'd you come?" he queried, genuinely trying to figure me out.

"I'm here to learn to fly fish," I said.

"Are you here with your husband or someone?"

"Nope, I'm here by myself," I said.

"You came all this way by yourself, just to learn to fly fish?" he asked, wide-eyed.

"Yeah, I needed an adventure," I said casually. "I'm recently divorced after a long marriage. My husband just needed to find a whole new life."

"Oh, goody!" he exclaimed, "A midlife crisis! I've been telling my wife I want one of those. I'm watching my friends sleeping all over town. They're having a ball!"

I laughed uncomfortably and tried to think of a way to change the subject, but I couldn't think of anything to say. *What am I doing here? Certainly, there's not much I'm going to learn from this guy*, I thought. Turning my head the other way, I looked out the window.

"Do you know about our trumpeter swans?" he asked. "We have some resident pairs in our wildlife refuge. They manage things better than we humans. You know, they mate for life."

"Interesting," I said. "I didn't know that."

We finally arrived at our destination and started to fish, but before long the sky darkened and a late-afternoon thunderstorm began. Lightning flashed in the sky, loud claps of thunder boomed almost simultaneously, and rain poured down. We stood in the middle of the river and, pointing, the guide yelled, "Cast out there."

Standing there in the water and holding my graphite rod, I was more than a little concerned for my safety. "Should we really be out here in this?" I asked.

He looked at me, thrust his arms out wide, and shouted, "Aw, hell, if we get struck by lightning, we won't be the ones who care!"

We went on with our fishing in the pouring rain. Clearly, I was learning to fly fish, but I was also getting a crash course on this man's male perspective. Would I ever be able to throw caution to the wind like he did? The overly cautious Marilyn didn't think so, but his words have stayed with me and urged me on.

I was surprised at the end of the day when he offered to let me to borrow the waders I had used that day, as long as I returned them when I came back to Jackson to catch my flight home. I hadn't yet invested in waders, and this was a wonderful offer. *Gruff but generous*, I thought as I accepted, thanking him profusely.

After that adventure, it was time to set out on my own and find a place to camp in the big, wild world. *What were you thinking?* a voice screamed inside me. Suddenly I couldn't even imagine myself out there camping alone. *Did you lose your mind when you made this plan, Marilyn? What about the bears?*

All my earlier bravado was gone. But the next day I gathered up my nerve and headed south, because someone had told me I had less chance of running into grizzly bears in that direction. I found a camp spot in a hilly area along the Green River. It was open country, not forested, and I was the only one there. I fished until sunset, having no luck at all. I ate my dinner and climbed into my tent early, as I was spooked by nightfall.

All was well until the middle of the night, when some creature, I don't know what it was, began circling my tent and rubbing up against the sides. I moved to the center of the tent and stayed awake the rest of the night, emerging only when I saw the early-morning light. I decided that camping there was too big a challenge, so I packed up and moved my camp that day to a more populated campground in the forest a few miles away.

I found a perfect little stream nearby. I had it all to myself and knew exactly what to do. By the time I sat down to eat my picnic lunch, I had caught so many fish, I'd lost count. I couldn't believe my good luck! Sitting there enjoying my sandwich, I realized there was nothing in my mind but the sound of the rushing water. It was as if it had carried all my worries and concerns with it as it tumbled downstream. This was just what I had hoped for.

My confidence plummeted when I drove north and arrived in West Yellowstone. I was tired and overwhelmed by the bigness of everything. Somehow, I just couldn't see myself walking out onto one of those rivers and starting to fish. Where to begin? I decided to spend money I didn't have and hire another guide. This one was a very young man, about the same age as my twenty-something sons. He was professional but a little aloof. His standoffishness, combined with my shyness, led to a lot of silence between us. Our long, quiet drive up to the Gallatin River was interrupted by only a few words—until a huge black bear almost ran right into our car, causing both of us to shout wildly. That relaxed things a bit.

When we arrived at our appointed spot along the river, my guide got out and began putting on his waders. I followed suit. He set off down to the river at quite a pace, as I struggled to keep up. Then, he charged across it.

I swallowed hard and stepped out into the river. I tried to step sideways, as the Marlboro man had instructed, but I was slipping and sliding and the current was way too strong for me as I neared the middle. My guide was on the other side and already heading upstream before he finally looked back to see where I was. Fighting back tears of mortification, I struggled the rest of the way across. When I finally caught up to him, he managed to apologize, saying, "I didn't realize . . ."

He didn't finish his sentence, but I filled it in for myself: *He didn't realize that I was really this old and decrepit.*

Looking back on this scene, I see how it mirrored the challenge I was experiencing in my life at the time. Crossing that river, fighting against the current, almost losing my balance, not trusting my own strength to carry me forward, feeling too old to meet the challenge my life was giving me—all were right there in front of me in concrete physical form.

Once I made it across the river that day, we started fishing. Those fish were really big and really quick. I didn't know what I was doing and missed several good chances to catch a fish. I saw my guide's jaw tense and his upper body tighten. He looked like he wanted to grab my rod and catch the fish for me. Instead, he just stared out into the river, motioning for me to try again. I was sorry I was missing the fish, too, but I thought he might explode. I had told him that I was just beginning and that what I wanted was good instruction. He tried to give me that over the roar of the river, in as few words as possible through his clenched jaw. After I had exhausted this hole with my ineptitude, he said we'd return to the other side. The look of horror on my face probably caused him to offer me his arm, and we both made it back across.

There I finally hooked one that did not let go, and it was a wild struggle to bring it in. Three times it leaped into the air. I was laughing and crying at the same time. Never had I experienced anything like that before. This fish was big! Who knows how big—all I knew was that it was beautiful and the first big fish I had ever caught on a fly, probably the biggest fish I had ever caught in my entire life.

We released the fish quickly. I was in shock. The guide blew off my fly and handed me my rod, indicating that I should cast again. I thought he was kidding. He gestured again. I had been trying to do things his way, but I just couldn't move on so quickly. I stood there, my body shaking. I could still feel the tension in my arms from reeling in the fish. My eyes kept seeing it jump. My ears kept hearing the splash as it fell back into the water. And then my hands—oh, that moment of ecstasy, freeing the fish, letting it go, watching as it darted back into the shadowy depths. My emotions were wild and all over the place. I wanted to savor this moment, to honor its magic. This was a total-body experience, and my body needed time to calm itself down. I sat giving thanks for my life and the beauty all around me. My guide got only that something important was happening, something he surrendered to, and we both sat, watching the river.

It was dusk when we took off our waders and climbed back into his car for the long drive back to the fly fishing store.

"Well, this is my last day of guiding for the summer," he told me, as we drove into the darkness. "I'm headed back to school in Bozeman tomorrow."

"Was it a good summer for you?" I asked.

"To tell you the truth, I'm glad it's over. You deal with all kinds of people when you're guiding. So many of them don't really care about fishing at all. They just want a picture with their trophy fish so they can take it home and brag about it."

"Yeah, I bet," I said.

After a bit of silence, he spoke again: "You know, I want to thank you for being such a genuine person. I have a lot of respect for your being out here, giving this a try. I can see that it means something to you. Keep it up, because I think you could be a really good fly fisher."

"Thank you!" I said. I hadn't expected this kind of softness from him. "I will keep doing it, because I love it. Fishing is part of me. I don't see it going away anytime soon."

I could hardly move when I fell into bed that night at the lodge at Old Faithful, but what a day it had been. My mind couldn't let go of my experience of catching that big fish. I relived it again and again. I began to see all that had just happened as a metaphor for how I might reengage when I returned home to Mendocino. My divorce, which had caused me so much pain, began to recede into the past. As I started to fill in my life with these colors, I was imbued with new hope. I realized that, for the first time, whole days had gone by and I hadn't thought about my divorce even once. I was ready to return home.

When I was a little girl, the most important question asked about angling was, "How many?" When I began to fly fish, the question became, "How big?" As I made fishing my own, I realized that those questions were too small and the answers irrelevant. I fished because fishing was a great practice for living life itself. When we cast into those mysterious waters and feel that wild tugging on our line, we are practicing receiving life, holding it long enough to experience its beauty, and then, yes, letting it go, trusting that life is full, abundant, and just waiting to send new energy our way. I couldn't have asked for a better teacher or a more important lesson as I began to heal from the breakup of my marriage.

Some years later, I brought my fly fishing gear along while vacationing with a friend in New Mexico. After a long day of sightseeing, we arrived late at our campsite along the Rio de los Pinos. The next morning, I was up early to fish at sunrise. It was a beautiful day, and there wasn't another fisherman in sight. As I was tying on my fly, I looked out at the water, thinking how much my grandpa liked fishing similar streams before he got too old to navigate the rough terrain. This river was just my size. I knew where to fish and where to place my fly.

I cast into the current and let the fly drift into a quiet pool. *Bam!* There it was, a trout—a huge one for this tiny river. It swam downstream, taking my line with it. I brought the fish in, received its blessing, and felt my hand open to let that life return to the water from which it had come. As I released the fish, I knew I was setting myself free as well. There was so much beauty in that moment of letting go. As I sat on the grassy bank, I couldn't help but feel my grandfather's presence beside me. This time, I'd brought with me a different kind of guide, one who had been inside me all this time, gently encouraging me, winking at my blunders, urging me to try again, and, in this moment of grand celebration, beaming his radiant smile in my direction.

Fly fishing was the bridge that carried me back out into the flow of my life after my divorce. As odd as it seemed to my circle of friends, I was glad I had listened when that quiet voice inside called me back to those shimmering waters of my childhood fishing adventures. In my encounters with those male guides, I found a glimpse of what I was seeking. It did help me begin to reconnect with my positive masculine energy. Traveling alone, camping by myself—all of it made me stronger. I felt like I could take my life in hand. I was finding my footing in my new world and better able to face living alone. But, most important of all, those fishing adventures made me ever more consciously aware of nature as an important guide and a powerful teacher.

As the years went on, I began to see my relationship to fishing change and transform. When I began, I wanted to catch fish but was equally captivated by the ecstatic joy I found in letting the fish go. This mirrored the major task of my life at that time. I was letting go of being a wife, letting go of John as my husband, and letting go of my children as they moved on. Kneeling by the river's edge, removing the hook from the fish's mouth, feeling its powerful energy struggling to be free—all were exact metaphors for my life process at the time.

Later, as my new life began to take shape, I came to see that if we want to live in our own creative flow, each moment is kind of like stepping out into a river, casting into the current, and waiting to see what might connect with us. The fact is, we never know what is going to happen from one moment to the next, despite all of our planning, so it's better to surrender to life's flow. I find I don't want to control my life as much as I did when I was younger. That was way too limiting and only allowed my life energy to flow in a proscribed and narrow channel, like the cement-walled drainage ditch that we called the "wash" in the town where I grew up. If we can just learn to let go of control, our lives can flow like wild rivers through natural landscapes, surprises around every corner, always moving, always changing, making their way to the sea.

In my painting *Fishing for Life with Heart Bait*, I depict myself as a cosmic fisherwoman, casting into life with my open heart as bait. I stand in the water, riding the waves. Life energy swirls all around me. The day sky reveals the nighttime stars still visible—a symbol that I am bringing the gifts from my night world into my waking reality. I stand with my rod, casting out into the universe to see what new life energy might want to come my way.

Life has carried me downstream, and it has been some years now since I've fished. In one of my last adventures, I was out with a guide along the north fork of the Yuba River in California. I was hooking a lot of fish, but they were releasing themselves as they neared the shore. I was not discouraged; I was having fun. But guides feel as if they're getting paid to produce fish for their clients. They're probably more used to hearing a string of profanity when a fish gets away, so my reaction was surprising for my guide.

About halfway through the afternoon, after yet another fish released itself from my line and I joyfully watched it go, the man looked at me and said, "I think I can relax here. You seem

Fishing for Life With Heart Bait

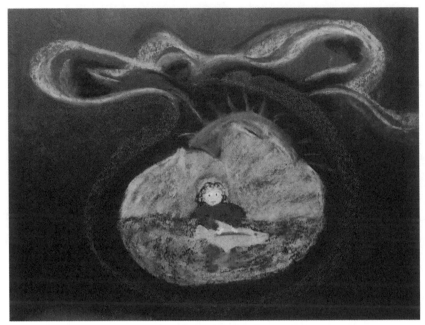

Touching the Rainbow

just as happy to see the fish as you are to land them." I hadn't been so aware of that but when he said it, I knew it was so. I loved feeling my connection with the fish when it tugged on my line. Reeling it in and seeing that silvery sparkle appear in the dark water seemed like a kind of magic. At that time, it was all I really wanted.

That sparkle appearing from the depths was not unlike the rich new life I was discovering as I explored the wild landscape inside me. It is not in my nature to see only what is on the surface; I want to explore what isn't visible, what is hiding, what lies underneath what I see and know about myself. In *Touching the Rainbow*, I have joined the fish in the water. No longer so afraid, I've jumped right in. I touch the fish's rainbow, and the aurora borealis swoops down to embrace me, the sky world and the undersea world supporting me as I learn to stand more solidly in the river of life.

Fly fishing let me know that a river teems with life underneath. Connecting to that life, like connecting with our unconscious minds, is a kind of magic. In *Fisherwoman Dances with the Fish*, I see that my rod has completely disappeared. My skin is scaly like the fish, my dress covered with plants from the watery depths. A wormlike creature becomes my hair, and I wear

Fisherwoman Dances with the Fish

rainbows on my body. It looks like I'm just conjuring the fish out the darkness. We belong to each other, and we dance.

Now, rather than casting my line into the deep pools of my childhood streams or into those clear blue mountain lakes, I send it out into the watery depths of the wild landscape inside me through art, music, writing, movement, and remembering my dreams each night. When I catch a glimpse of the abundant life energy that lives there, I feel blessed. And, like the fish I caught so long ago, what I find down there feeds me. All we need is a glimpse, a quick flash, like rainbow colors on iridescent skin appearing out of the depths, and the surface of our life holds new possibility. Just a glimpse of it affirms us and can lead us in new directions.

❧ *Reflection*

Take yourself on a hike in a wild place or go for a walk in a park. Sit by a tree; spend time by a stream, a lake, or the ocean. Make it a practice. Reflect in art and writing on who you are when you're out there.

Chapter 13:

The Bear in the Apple Tree

Once upon a time, there was a little girl named Goldilocks.
She went for a walk in the forest. Pretty soon, she came upon a house.
She knocked, and when no one answered, she walked right in. . . .
—From the folk tale "Goldilocks and the Three Bears"

W hen I started going out into nature by myself, I knew I had to get a handle on my fear of bears or I would have to leave a vital part of my life behind. Ever since my early dream, the little girl in me had kept that fear alive and regularly fed it with her wild imagination. As I matured, my fear was well buried, except in my dreams, but when I went into wilder spaces, it jumped to the fore in all its irrationality. No matter what my age, it was as if I were still three years old.

When I divorced, confronting my fears directly became a personal challenge. I began to look at my irrational fears as waking dreams, messages from my unconscious mind that were so powerful, they could break through the armor of my rational mind and speak to me. So I suspected that I had much to learn by facing my irrational fear of bears, rather than trying to flee from it. All that fear didn't just vanish but rather gave way over a period of time when, along with many more bear dreams, I had several encounters with actual bears in the wilderness. To my amazement, the bear took center stage in my symbolic landscape and led me toward the next important phase of my life.

I'm certain that my little-girl fear of bears all started with the story of "Goldilocks and the Three Bears." In fact, when I was helping my elderly parents move from their home, I came upon the very book my mother had read to me when I was small. As I thumbed through the familiar pages, there it was: a picture of the bears coming through the door as they returned home from their morning walk. I'm pretty sure it was that picture that set the scene for my childhood dream.

From The Mother's Home Book, *1914*

Certainly, every child who saw those bears didn't latch on to them the way I did, but they made their den in my unconscious and have stayed there over my lifetime. As a child, I didn't live where I would have seen bears in my waking life, but in my mind, they were everywhere. Though I never saw them, I also never knew when they might appear. Like Goldilocks, I might just stumble into the wrong place, at the wrong time, and there I would be, face-to-face with one. I was certain that the bear would have only one intention, and that was to devour me.

Then, in my early fifties, I started encountering bears in the wild. The first of these incidents happened in the Angelo Preserve, a Nature Conservancy property just north of my home in Mendocino. It was a beautiful, hot, sunny day when I stepped onto the trail for an eight-mile hike. I had brought lunch and lots of water, and I planned to eat and rest at an old homestead cabin before I began my return. My trail guide had told me that I would come down the hill into an old apple orchard and, just beyond it, would find the old house.

The trail meandered through the forest for some time, then narrowed as it moved away from the river. Soon I was walking through the lush green grass at the edge of a meadow. I saw the orchard, and, sure enough, there was the little house just beyond. I was hot and tired and ready for a rest.

As I walked underneath the branches of an old apple tree, thinking about my lunch, I heard a rustling sound above me. It wasn't a large rustle; I thought it was a squirrel as I turned to look up over my shoulder. Imagine my surprise when I saw a bear's head about six feet from mine. *Oh my God! Now what?* I knew I was supposed to stop and then slowly back away, but stopping that close did not make sense. Because I had just walked underneath the bear, I did not want to retrace my steps. I did manage to move slowly, stepping sideways toward the old house. The trail ended there. I remember having the overly dramatic thought, *If I die here, at least it will happen in a beautiful place.*

I tried to get into the house, but the door was locked and the windows were boarded up. I could see the bear in the tree, happily munching small green apples. I was amazed at how little interest it had in me. I, on the other hand, was consumed by its presence. After gathering my wits about me, I decided to cut across the meadow in front of me and climb the hill back up to the trail. I moved fast—too fast—in the 105-degree heat. I realized I needed water and sat down right on the trail, facing the direction of the bear. I was sure it was coming after me, though it had made no move to get down out of the tree. I sat thinking, *All right, Bear, if you're coming, you're coming. I guess if you want to eat me, you will!* The bear never came.

In the days that followed, flashbacks of the experience kept arising. In one, when I watched myself trying to get into the house, rattling the door, pulling on the boarded-up windows, I was struck with the memory of my old dream. There were the house and the bear, and there was me. This time, rather than being inside, I was outside, and, though I desperately wanted to be in what I imagined to be the safety of the house, that wasn't possible. It was as if my waking life were living my childhood dream forward, collapsing the years in between and rearranging the story.

Thinking of my experience as a waking dream, I realized the truth of this new juxtaposition. Now, in my fifties and living alone, I lived in a world quite different from that of friends who remained coupled. I seemed to have a more feral existence, to be living a wilder version of my old self. But did that mean that I belonged outside in the forest with the bear?

I began to think that maybe that little girl who hadn't yet learned to separate her dream world from waking life was right, though not in the literal way she thought of it at the time. Perhaps our dreams and our waking reality aren't really as separate as we have come to believe. I wondered if there could really be a continuous thread of symbolism linking my three-year-old self with the fifty-year-old woman I am today. Could that thread cross the boundary from my childhood dream world into my waking adult reality? I started to think that maybe we *do* each develop a unique symbolic language that spans our lifetime.

That was when I started to realize that in all my explorations of the unconscious realms—through my dreams, my art, and my metaphorical take on waking life—I was actually witnessing my own symbolic landscape. I was learning the language that my own wild voice uses to communicate with me. I was seeing that if we pay attention, we can trace threads and follow patterns from that realm and disparate pieces will begin to fit together, as in a puzzle. As we get a sense of this landscape and the images and symbols that are born of it, we can become conversant in a language deeper than our words. That language is wilder than the language our more rational selves speak, because it comes from a deeper place in our consciousness. Learning to listen to our wild voice gives us access to the profound wisdom we each carry inside us. Listening to that wisdom and letting it guide us does require discernment, commitment, and dedication, but it is the pathway to greater authenticity.

What I took from my experience with the bear in the apple tree opened my mind to new possibility. I thought of the closet in my early dream where those bananas were left to ripen. Perhaps I was indeed ripening and maturing in my relationship with the unconscious realm out of which our waking life arises. It seemed as if I was now ready to peek out of that dark, protected space and take another look around. The older me wanted to take that little girl's hand, open the door, and let her lead me out into a world where more things than I knew might be possible. We both seemed ripe for exploring.

🌿 *Reflection*

Pay attention to your irrational fears. To begin a relationship with a fear, draw some representation of it. It can be big or small, in a box or a frame—just represent it in a way that feels safe. Stand back and look at it. Then create a soft blanket of colors all around it. Begin a conversation with it in your journal.

Chapter 14:

The Bear in the Elwha

To exist is to change, to change is to mature,
to mature is to go on creating oneself endlessly.
—Henri Bergson

In the end, the most important thing I learned that day in the Angelo Preserve was how disinterested the bear was in me. It tolerated my intrusion without much response and then returned to its main interest: eating apples. But when the child in me jumped forward, she was unable to imagine that the bear could have interest in anything but devouring me, its prey. I saw the bear as a predator—and not just any predator, but my own personal one.

It's laughable to me now, but I don't think I'm alone in this kind of response. We have a way of projecting specific and unreasonable ferocity on large animals above us on the food chain. In fact, throughout our history, we have gone all-out to eliminate them. In California, we have a grizzly bear on our state flag but the last grizzly bear in our state was hunted and killed in the 1920s. These animals have the power to make us feel very small. They are meant to be respected, as they are wild and ferocious. Our demonization of them says more about their place in our psyches than it does about any true definition of the animals themselves.

Thankfully, my experience with the bear in the apple tree allowed me to see that this animal much preferred fresh fruit to my human flesh. Something in me relaxed with that knowing, and a huge portion of my irrational fear dropped away. This was a first step in coming home to an honest relationship with what the bear actually symbolized in my psyche.

A Dark Presence

The image of the bear appeared regularly in my artwork. It wasn't a conscious thing; I would just sense a big, dark presence, and when I painted it in, there was the bear. In my pastel drawing, *A Dark Presence*, the bear, standing on two legs, looms menacingly in the forest looking at me. Given that this image occupied my psyche, it's no wonder I was so afraid when I set out into the wilderness alone.

My father used to tell a story of having come upon a hunting camp when he was out fishing in the Ruby Mountains as a young man. The hunters had killed a bear. It was hanging where they had skinned it. I can still see my father's exaggerated shiver when he said, "It looked an awful lot like a human!" *How could that be?* I wondered. *We are so very different from the bears.* But the story has stayed with me. I see the camp, tents and all, young men from another time, a few scrawny trees, and the bear/human, hanging there. I can see how, without all that fur, the bear might have represented what my father said it did.

Looking now at the bear in *A Dark Presence*, I think it was addressing me, as if to say, "Here I am. Look at me. I'm standing on two legs like a human. You are not separate from me. I am the ferocious part of Mother Nature, in charge of endings, death, and dissolution. If you want to belong here, you must accept my important place in the circle of life."

At the time, I wasn't ready to listen, but I soon began to accept that the bear's appearances in my waking life, in my dreams, and in my art were bringing me closer to a great fierceness that both creates and destroys.

Eastern philosophy, as exemplified by the goddess Kali, does a better job of holding the circle of life than we do in the West. We attach more to beginnings, birth, and the newness of life than to life's endings, dissolution, and death, and thus we render ourselves poorly equipped to deal with life's waning phase. But over time we are asked to turn our attention to loss and dissolution again and again. If we allow that, each time we grieve an important loss, the lessons we learn are carved a little more deeply into our being and we find ourselves more able to accept our place in the wild process of living and dying that holds us all.

Because the bear was so present in my psyche, I did some research. I learned that the bear was an original symbol of the Great Mother. The Great Mother was credited with the creation of all life, everything, but she was also seen as the bringer of death.

In cultures the world over, the divine feminine is seen in three phases: the Maiden, the Mother, and the Crone. In US society, we are enamored with the youthful beauty of the Maiden and pay homage to the all-giving Mother, but we haven't come to terms with the death-bringing Crone. I came to see how timely it was that the bear was appearing in my waking life and symbolically in my psyche. Serving as a central image for the ferocity of nature, it was helping me move toward that next, natural phase of my life. As my marriage ended and my children left home, I was moving more deeply into middle age. I had lived the Maiden and the Mother; now, it seemed, my psyche was grooming me to accept the awesome power and responsibility of the Crone.

My divorce had awakened me from an immature innocence about life. Turning away from the innocence and embracing the fierceness, I was developing a new relationship with that hard fact that things are created and indeed things are destroyed, even something as precious as my family life. A new level of grief was being carved into my being.

In *Opening to the Feminine*, my vagina is spotlighted in the middle of my body where my heart should be. The bear as Great Mother energy is opening this deeply feminine part of me. I painted a body floating near her mouth. I thought the bear was eating the person, but as I continued painting, I realized that it was spitting the person out. In my painting, I am surrendering to this process, like a woman giving birth. Near the bottom, I see that what I have given birth to is a bright fuchsia heart. This painting lets me know that love is as present in death and dissolution as it is in birth and creation.

Opening to the Feminine

Clarissa Pinkola Estés begins her book, *Women Who Run with the Wolves*, with the story of La Loba, the bone collector. La Loba wanders the landscape, collecting bones. When she has assembled a full skeleton, she sings over it, bringing the creature back to life. In many shamanic rituals, the initiates are symbolically taken back to their skeletons and reformed as healers. Our bones are the indestructible force in the structure of our bodies. Returning to our bones is a way to start over and to let new life rise out of the ashes of our skeletal remains.

During this time when I was trying to place myself more peacefully within this cycle of death and rebirth, I painted what I later titled, *My Divorce: A Shamanic Perspective*. I believed that my divorce had taken me down to my bones, to my basic structure. I had only the image of myself as a skeleton when I began the painting. The rest of the picture filled itself in from there, the meanings revealing themselves only after the fact.

The bear appears behind my skeletal self and embraces me. He carries a black satchel on each arm. Like the grim reaper, he is collecting people. On one side of his bag, he has me, as my former self; John is on the other side. Like smoking volcanoes, our hearts are still burning from the aftermath of our separation. Up above, my heart appears amid my skeletal remains. It is cracked down the middle but shows that a passionate fire can still burn from its center. With that new fire, many colors begin to fill my chest area. The color green is predominant and speaks of rebirth. My ribs are rainbow-like; light emanates from my body and out the top of my head, indicating my embodied spirituality. For me, this painting marks my divorce as a healing journey of a shamanic nature.

Meanwhile, my adventures with bears in my waking life continued. My son Gabriel was a backcountry ranger whose post was twelve miles in on the Elwha River Trail in Olympic National Park. I had visited him once before. On that trip, he had hiked out the twelve miles and then hiked back in with me. This time, I thought I could make the trip in on my own. The trail was well marked, so there was no way to get lost. The only problem was that with a pack, I couldn't make the twelve-mile trek in one day, so I needed to spend one night alone, at a camp along the way.

My Divorce:
A Shamanic Perspective

At that time in my life, the question haunting me was, "Can I make it in the world on my own?" This hike represented a way to face some of my fears. It all seems concrete and literal to me now. But on the edge of my consciousness at the time was a sense that I needed to address my question on a very basic level. I hoped that taking myself out into this wild landscape would help me find trust in life anew.

The morning I was to head for the trail, I treated myself to breakfast at my favorite café in Port Angeles. I frittered away the morning with last-minute preparations before I finally realized that I was procrastinating because I was scared to death, so, stomach fluttering, I got in my car and off I went.

I pulled into the trailhead parking area, managed to get my pack on my back, and set off down the trail. I hadn't gone far before I started to question my sanity. *What made you think you could pull this off? Your kids are in their twenties. You're in your fifties! What are you doing out here?* Though I had trimmed my pack to the barest essentials, it felt very heavy. Filled with self-doubt, I walked on. That inner voice working so hard to sabotage my confidence was winning, though I was struggling hard not to listen. Lost inside myself, I remember finally thinking, *I can't do this. I'm not going to make it!* I was only twenty-five minutes into my hike.

Coming around a curve in the trail, I heard crashing sounds in the brush just up ahead. Then I saw a big, furry black back rear up out of the greenery. Startled, it began to run toward me. It was about fifteen feet in front of me. I froze, heart pounding. It hurried past me, thankfully keeping to the side of the trail. I didn't exactly run, but I started moving forward quickly. Since we had passed each other, my back was now to the bear. *Don't look, whatever you do!* an untrustworthy voice inside me advised.

My natural reaction was somewhat childlike. It was as if I were thinking, *If I don't see the bear, it doesn't exist.* Denial in the physical world is a dangerous thing. When I heard the clamoring of claws on wood and then a big hiss that sounded like a giant fireplace bellows, I knew I had to turn around and look.

The bear had climbed up a tree. It was clinging to the trunk about twelve feet up, looking over its shoulder at me as if I were the scariest creature on Earth. The feeling was mutual. Finally, my survival instincts clicked in. *Cubs?* flashed through my mind. I didn't see any, so I slowly backed away, going around a curve and moving quickly down the trail. I could no longer see the bear, but my ears were cocked in its direction.

Filled now with adrenaline and knowing that the bear was somewhere between me and my car, I had nowhere to go but onward. My steps were quick, my pack was light, and my heart was still pounding. It was as if I had been jarred into another reality.

After I had traveled some distance, the trail slanted uphill. I realized I needed to slow down and parse my energy. I stopped for a drink of water. Even though I had been advised of the silliness of such a thing, I attached a little bell to my pack hoping its jingle would make my presence known to all the creatures in the forest. Clearly, I had forgotten the first lesson of being out in the wilderness: Pay attention! As I hiked on, I lectured myself. I needed to sharpen my senses and stay tuned to the world around me. This was no place for wallowing in self-doubt—an important lesson I took note of for my life as well.

My encounter with the bear remains with me like a moment outside time. The sight of its black back rising from the bushes and the sound of the crashing brush as we scurried in our opposite directions are seared into my mind. It was the second time in a year that I had found myself way too close to a bear—for a moment, in fact, within arm's reach. If my meetings with the bears had been dreams, I might have felt as if I had been given the gift of brushing up against a great wildness. But experiencing this encounter in waking life was more threatening. I knew that by being in the wilderness alone, I was seeking belonging, but I had no idea that this much wildness was what I belonged to.

I have made much of this encounter over the years, but I sense that the most important thing that happened that day was my participation in that moment. My presence there, facing Bear, and Bear's presence, facing me, shattered the walls that our culture builds around us. When those walls fall, we are left free to sense the wild universe of which we are a part and are given a startling chance to come home to the world in which we belong. But, as with all amazing moments of insight and mystical beauty, it can take years before the gifts we receive are integrated into our beings. Now, this wild moment marks what was true for me at that time: owning my personal wildness was terrifying.

I hiked on and arrived at my camp in good time. I quickly hung my food and personal items on the bear wire, as Gabe had taught me to do. This camp was located on the Lillian River, a beautiful, roaring stream that obliterated all the other sounds in the forest. My eyes became my protectors as they darted about nervously, scanning the forest. We most often orient to the world in front of us, but out there, what was behind me seemed rife with possibility. I found myself turning around every few minutes to be sure all was well.

I had sacrificed my tent to make my pack lighter, bringing only the rain fly in case of bad weather. I set it up and arranged my sleeping bag under its shelter. Then I went down to the river to filter my water. Having completed everything I needed to do to set up my camp, I sat down and watched the river. Before I knew it, the light was fading. I got my food and ate a quick dinner, then carefully hung everything back on the bear wire so I wouldn't have to struggle with that later.

My anxiety increased as night began to fall. I was afraid of the dark. I was afraid of creatures big and small coming in the night. I had forgotten that the camp would be overrun with mice as soon as the sun went down. The thought of them running over my sleeping body was nearly as bad as imagining a visit from a bear. In the gathering darkness, I wrote in my tiny journal. I knew I was in an exquisitely beautiful place but realized that I could not feel the beauty. I felt strangely vacant. I knew this was going to make a very good story when it was over, but in the moment, I was frozen with fear and discomfort. I realized that my ego had been overly invested in my trip, wanting me, and probably everyone else, to believe I was the "brave Marilyn." It made such a good story. I wrote:

Really, out here, it doesn't feel like I am "brave Marilyn." It feels like I am the small, fearful, somewhat empty Marilyn—not nearly as dramatic a story. I wish I at least had the safety of my whole tent. With only the rain fly, I will sleep with a crack open to this forest world all around me. I realize that I'm looking for home and terrified of my home all at the same time.

Mice began to skitter around my campsite, dashing here and there in the rapidly fading light. All my bravado from earlier in the day had completely vanished. I resorted to prayer, not to a God above but to the energies that surrounded me:

River, sing to me. Tell me what it means to let go and fall toward home. Tell me how
   it feels to let life flow freely.
Trees, sing to me. Bend with the breezes and whisper to me of time and changes and
   standing strong.
Night, fall gently around me. May I be soothed by your darkness. Twinkle your stars
   to remind me that morning will come and light will once again fill the world.

While I sleep, let my soul wander with this wild world around me. Let me sleep with
   dreams deep and clear, so my life is fed by that deep source inside me.
Old Man Bear, watch over me as I sleep. Keep all harm from coming my way. Lend
   me your strength and your protection. Let me be your child tonight. Guard me.
Forest, love me and let me feel loved. Let me know I belong.

I climbed into my sleeping bag before it was completely dark. Ridiculously, I placed one hiking boot on each side of my head, thinking that might discourage the mice from running over my face. I curled into a fetal position and prayed for sleep.

I was physically exhausted from my extraordinary day and, thankfully, drifted off without struggle. I slept peacefully until about 2:00 a.m., when a nightmare shattered my peaceful slumber. I woke myself up screaming, "Get out of here!" at the top of my lungs. In my dream, I was camping out in the wilds. I was startled awake in the dream by jackals snarling just outside my tent door. Still in the dream, I sat up, grabbed a broom that looked like a witch's broom, and started pounding on the fabric door of my tent, screaming at them to go away.

Awake for real now, sweating and heart pounding, I tried to calm myself, but I stayed alert for the rest of the night, listening to the river, falling back to sleep only when I saw first light.

It was bright daylight when I opened my eyes again. I got up, retrieved my undisturbed food from the bear wire, and ate breakfast. The arrangement that I had with my son was that he would be hiking toward me that morning and we would meet somewhere on the trail. If I didn't feel like I could go on alone, he would meet me at this camp. I ate some breakfast and sat, trying to decide what I wanted to do. Loving the roar of the river for itself but not liking that I couldn't hear anything else, I decided I would be much better off getting on the trail and moving forward.

I had more confidence than I'd had the day before and was determined to keep aware of the world around me, rather than falling so deeply inside myself. But I wasn't without fear. I was more than a little jumpy. Every little sound made my heart stop. When I was a child, I used to sing when I walked into my empty house. I figured if there were burglars, it would let them know that I was coming and perhaps they would run away. On this day, I found myself singing to the bears. The words and melody came spontaneously. "Good morning, Bear, I'm coming. Let me walk in peace. Lend me your spirit. Protect me on my path. Good morning, Bear, I'm coming. Let me walk in peace." I sang really loudly when the fear was big, and the act calmed me. Just when I began to feel like I might belong in the forest with all the other creatures, I heard human voices off in the distance. As I came around a bend, there was Gabriel and a fellow ranger heading toward me on the trail. With a big smile, I waved enthusiastically. My body relaxed as that smile spread from my head to my toes. *I did it!* I thought. *I actually did it!*

When we reached one another, there were hugs all around. My story of the bear poured out, our laughter echoing through the forest.

I spent the rest of the trip with my son, but that day and night when I had only myself to count on left me marked by the wildness of my adventure. I returned home stronger than I had been when I'd left.

During the remainder of that month, I saw seven more bears—one a mother who sent her cubs up a tree to safety while my friend and I retreated, and six more from a safe distance in Glacier National Park when I was traveling with my eighty-two-year-old parents.

I had taken my parents on vacation the summer before, but I was surprised at the toll one year had taken on them. This trip was harder for them in every way. The big energy of the mountains seemed too much for their spirits. Where just a few years before they would have been swooning at the rugged, awesome beauty of the landscape, they now preferred to sit around the fire in the big, old lobbies of our hotels, watching the world go by.

Sitting in a dining room overlooking a deep blue lake surrounded by dense green forest with snowcapped peaks rising abruptly behind it, my mother saw a large, dead tree framed by the window in the foreground.

"Look at that old, dead tree," she said. "I wonder what killed it. I guess it's just there to remind you that old Mother Nature can come along and take a whap at you whenever she pleases."

Over the days that followed, I saw the world through eyes much older than my own. I returned from my travels filled with the intensity of my adventures. My experiences with the bears and with my aging parents seemed a part of the same story. Their failing strength made visible the great fierceness of life. My child heart missed the parents I used to know.

I found myself singing my bear song on my morning walks in the forest at home. I was surprised at my sadness that there were no bears around to hear me. I felt as if I had stepped back into a tamer environment and in doing so had reverted to a less wild version of myself. All those bears had awakened something in me, and I didn't want that part of me to go back to sleep.

The morning I was to return to work, I was awakened by a dream in which I came face-to-face with a huge black horse the size of a dinosaur. Its head was a big black skull. I gazed deeply into its eye sockets, where there were no eyes. I faced this monster, stared right back at him, and made him back away. On my morning walk, I sang my bear song. As I sang to the bear, I realized I was singing for my parents, for myself, and even to death itself. I opened my mouth to sing again, when a voice took charge of mine. I spoke out loud: "Marilyn, you are here to walk in the mouth of the bear. You will do this over and over again in your life. Sometimes the bear just spits you out. Sometimes he chews you up and then spits you out. In the end, you will be devoured."

Goldilocks Moves in with the Three Bears, At Last!

As I surrendered to all my feelings, a deep sense of peace rose in me. It wrapped around me like the softness of my favorite blanket when I was a tiny child. I had a glimpse of what being in the arms of the Great Mother energy feels like, and I let myself be held. Like Goldilocks fleeing the house of the three bears, my youthful innocence had been running away from the acceptance of an important part of being human: embracing our own dissolution and eventually our own death. In my art, I drew myself surrounded by bears. Only later did I realize there were three bears and that I had made my hair golden. I titled the drawing, *Goldilocks Moves in with the Three Bears, At Last!*

It was as if the bear in my childhood dream had taken off his overalls and what I saw in that naked revelation was not masculine at all, but a feminine energy powerful beyond all measure. My little-girl body had grown into adulthood. I had become a wife, been pregnant, and given birth. I had learned to take charge of my feminine body in a culture that thinks women's bodies belong to men. I had experienced the rigors of being a mother, and now these experiences with Mother Nature were strengthening my connection to the deep feminine. Life's lessons have a way of multiplying inside us. The power of recognizing and beginning to surrender to the fierceness of wild nature fortified me.

I came away knowing that I did have what it would take to move through all the endings I was experiencing at the time, and I had increasing confidence that I could face other important endings that were coming my way. I realized for the first time that helping my parents at the end of their lives and accompanying them to their eventual deaths was lurking there in my future. I was preparing to meet that task.

Life has a way of bringing us full circle. My encounter with Bear began with the story of "Goldilocks and the Three Bears," which brought to life the dream that has remained with me and unfolded in mystical ways over many years. As I healed from my divorce, the bear became my teacher. *Teacher and Student, Now Forest Friends* portrays my new sense of belonging. My bones have been collected and reassembled. My new body is now fleshed out. I portray myself naked, like a newborn baby, as I begin to accept my place in this wilderness that is my new home.

Teacher and Student, Now Forest Friends

Bear's energy is never far away from me now. She can be a good teacher for all of us. She teaches us about the cycles that flow through our lives. She tells us when to enter our caves for winter and when to burst through the snowy door in early spring. She tells us when the berries are ripe and where to find them. She shows us how to protect what we give birth to. She teaches us how to go after what we want and need.

In my life, she has helped me trust my solitary nature. Her ferocity is in me now, and I pray each day that I will use it wisely. I am learning that the more I can surrender to the circle of life that she embodies, the richer and more substantial my own existence will become.

Not long after my series of waking encounters with the bears, my mother heard me telling the story to my sons. I was saying that before those adventures, I had seen only two bears in my whole life. Seeing so many in one summer was amazing. "No, Marilyn," she interrupted. "That's not right. You saw three bears. Remember?"

I looked at her, searching my memory.

"Remember when you were three—the one in the overalls when you hid in the closet?"

The adult in me laughed out loud, but the little one inside me crawled up into her mother's lap, comforted at last.

🌱 *Reflection*

How do you relate to life's waning phases? Cut some 6"x6" squares of fabric. With colored markers, use words and art to create prayer flags commemorating major times of loss in your life. String them together and hang them somewhere you will see them. Reflect in your journal about what new parts of you grew from these losses.

Chapter 15:

The Denali Bear

Take this as a gift from a crone to a maiden, and know there is not
so much difference between the two. For even a tottering granddam keeps a portion
of girlish heart, and the youngest maiden a thread of old woman's wisdom.
—LLOYD ALEXANDER, *The Chronicles of Prydain*

Life carried me forward, and before I knew it, my sixties were looming in the not-too-distant future. In my circle of women friends, it was all the fad to celebrate turning sixty with a ceremony, accepting our new place in society as Crones. *What will that be like?* I wondered, trying to imagine myself stepping into the final phase of my life. Now, I think we were rushing things a bit with our Crone celebrations, but those birthdays did mark the time when we felt the tide beginning to turn.

As it does for all of us as we age, life's inevitable ending was increasingly appearing on my radar screen. My friends and mentors began to die in increasing numbers. I watched my parents, now in their mideighties, still managing on their own, but it was increasingly clear that that would soon come to an end.

What will we do then? I wondered. *Am I going to be able to help when that time comes?* I hoped so.

I was acutely aware that elders in our society are pushed off to the corners of our busy world, not valued when their productive years conclude and not at all honored for what they might still have to offer. *Why don't we seem able to embrace this phase of life for its positive potential?* I wondered.

In *The Crone: Woman of Age, Wisdom, and Power*, Barbara Walker comments about why we have such trouble embracing this final stage. She notes that because we are so dependent on our parents in our infancy, they take on god-like proportions and live in the depths of our psyches as our divine parents. In this deep place, we recognize the Mother as the most import-ant. "She is everything necessary to life. . . . To be rejected by her is to die," Walker explains, so abandonment by the caretaking Mother is difficult for us to imagine. But the Mother as the giver of life is also the bringer of death, because as each life comes into being, it holds within it the promise of its end. Walker writes:

> Just as a seed developed into ripening fruit, then withered away, so growing up would pass through maturity into growing old. . . . As the birth-giving Virgin and the death-dealing Crone were part of one another, death and life together were like the new seed within the withered fruit.

In Western culture, we live outside this comforting circle where aging and death remain a part of the whole. We chose the Father in Heaven over the Mother goddess. Unable to face the negative aspect of the life-giving Mother and to hold a place for the Crone phase of life, the patri-archal religions created a plan for a different kind of eternal life, one that was much more linear than circular. When we shed our bodies, which on some level we have always scorned, judging them inferior to our spirits, we hope for a better life in Heaven. In the patriarchal imagination, an old man in the sky sits on high and rewards or punishes the dead, offering the virtuous an eternal life in Heaven and condemning the sinners to an endless life of suffering in hell. That is the end of the story, on into eternity. There is no circle, no movement, no recycling of life as the old pass away and the new are born. Without this circle, we can only imagine aging and our eventual deaths as our bodies, and therefore Mother Nature, ultimately betraying and abandoning us.

The damage from our collective fear and denial of the Crone archetype has caused enormous suffering. Sexism, racism, ageism, the burning of the witches, the destruction of our planet, and the violence of war are all part of the fallout. But, as Jung said, an archetype cannot disappear; it simply goes underground until it is called forth once again by crisis in a culture that desperately needs it to find balance.

Listening inside as I aged, I found the Crone archetype trying to come alive in me. My dreams continued to bring wild animals marauding through landscapes in the night, and my art continued to portray those creatures. Musically, I was drawn to the piano sonatas that Beethoven wrote late in his life. And my waking encounters with bears continued.

In my early sixties, I traveled through Alaska. As I rode in a van with others, returning to our lodge after a day of hiking, our driver spotted a large grizzly bear up ahead and pulled to a stop. The bear was right at the edge of the road. I was sitting in the front passenger seat of the van and had a close-up look at it. It was digging for grubs and paid no attention to us. Its claws were easily six inches long. When it pawed seemingly effortlessly at the ground, a deep hole opened up. *Raw power*, I thought as I watched. *Unbelievable in its effortlessness.* Then these words filled my mind: *Marilyn, if you are ever attacked and killed by a bear, it will be nothing personal. It will just be a power greater than all of us claiming you as its own.*

After a lifetime of imaging my own death as completely personal, I found great liberation in that thought. The power I saw in this bear's paw had jarred me awake. I immediately knew in my body that what creates us will also destroy us. In the grand scheme of things, we are simply small specks in the magnificent sweep of time.

We had been watching the bear for some time when a man sitting behind me asked if I would be willing to roll down the window so he could take a photograph. I looked at our guide to see whether that was a safe thing to do. He assured me that if we didn't speak, it was fine. The sound of the bear's digging spilled into the car as I lowered the window. The passenger took the photo, and we drove on.

As we moved down the road, we were all stunned into silence. Sitting with my own thoughts, I heard the words, "Would you be willing to roll down the window?" echo inside me. I knew they applied to far more than the moment I had just experienced. It felt like a much bigger question from a much larger source. I had been witnessing the barrier between who I thought I was and my wilder nature begin to crumble. That request seemed to be asking me to take another step in that direction.

Alaska was the wildest place I had visited, and I returned home filled with that wild energy. One morning, I awoke with a numinous dream that I knew was directly connected to my experience with that grizzly bear. In my dream, it was night. I was sitting in my car, deep in the wilderness. I was in the driver's seat, looking through the windshield into the night sky. Suddenly, the aurora came into view, and as I watched, I sensed a powerful, loving energy enveloping my car. A mountain lion appeared outside, floating near the passenger side of the windshield. I watched as it reached toward me, now about to touch the glass. I mimicked its movement, moving my hand to the inside of the windshield. Imagine my surprise when the glass disappeared and I felt my flesh touch fur.

Waking with tears, I could feel that touch as if it had actually happened. As I lay there, bathed in love, these words floated into my consciousness: *I am animal. There is no barrier between flesh and fur. My wildness is embedded in deep and abiding love.*

I marveled at the wisdom of this dream, which seemed a choice to reimagine Michelangelo's painting, *The Creation of Adam*. In the Father God scenario, the divine figure and the human reach for contact, but they do not touch. That tiny space that separates the two remains a chasm that can't quite be crossed. In my dream, that space was no longer there. The glass, separating what I saw and thought from what I knew in my body, was gone. My dream offered the possibility that I had moved beyond an intellectual understanding of my place in the circle of life to embodying it. The overwhelming love in the dream left me with a sense of ultimate compassion. In my art, I began to depict bears as fierce guardians, holding the Earth and all of suffering humanity in their arms.

In my art quilt, *The Great Mother*, the bear holds the world with both her heart and her claws. Looking at that watery planet in her arms, I know we are somewhere there, invisible now, like minute grains of sand in this larger perspective. Yet inside our own skin, we are here on this green, growing planet, a tiny but vital piece of the whole. My original drawing did not include the vines growing outside the frame, but as I worked on the quilt, I saw them there and began the laborious process of hand-appliquéing each little leaf into place. As I worked, I was reminded of those shadowy leaves in my earliest childhood memory. The fact that those leaves found their way into my quilt just when I was integrating the life-giving Mother with

The Great Mother

the death-bringing Crone attests to the way in which our wild voice speaks to us continuously over our entire lifetime.

I've come to believe that our dreams are our own wild voice speaking to us in the night. Art is a way of engaging with that voice and allowing it to find expression in our world. Over time, my waking life joined this conversation as the creatures from all my outdoor adventures chimed in. My inner life and my outer world became not one or the other but a meeting that took place in a circle, each nurturing the other. Once I accepted this connection, I could no longer imagine human life existing within the limits of our personal psyche alone. Once again, I found myself understanding that all questions about believing or not believing in a larger energy are both too small and irrelevant. We have the ability to directly experience that energy inside us, because we embody it and are therefore an integral part of this much greater story. There is no separation between us and it.

🌿 *Reflection*

Write a fairy tale. You are the main character, but, instead of being human, you are an animal, real or imagined. With colored construction paper and glue, make a mask representing your animal self. Let the mask speak to you in your journal.

Chapter 16:

The Bear and the Yurt

[Alice] said: "One can't believe impossible things."
"I daresay you haven't had much practice." said the Queen.
"When I was your age, I always did it for half-an-hour a day.
Why, sometimes I've believed as many as six impossible things before breakfast."
—LEWIS CARROLL, *Alice's Adventures in Wonderland*

The evolving story of my relationship with the bears seemed like it had come full circle. In my collage titled, *My Life with Bears,* I try to capture something about the long story of my experiences with the bears and my relationship to the inner wildness they seem to represent in my psyche.

The story is told in a circle, going counterclockwise, starting at the bottom left. There, eggs sit in a nest, waiting to hatch. The young child sleeps with the bears and dreams. To the right, the young woman at the bottom center who is holding the bear in front of her is posing a question: *What do I do with this?* Her wildness is externalized, as she is busy becoming educated, busy learning to be civilized. Behind her, the somewhat older blond woman in the right-hand corner is a slightly older Goldilocks struggling to incorporate her own wildness.

175

My Life with Bears

She has a taste of it, but she's not sure she likes it, as she senses it may cause serious disruption in the way she's living her life. Above, snakes, a pile of skulls, and a mother bear and her cub stand by, watching as death comes closer with the passage of the woman's beloveds—grandmothers and grandfathers, precious great-aunts and uncles. The older woman at the top is dancing in the mouth of the bear, finally accepting and celebrating her rightful place in the order of things, completing the circle. This is where I saw my life at the time; though I was perhaps not yet celebrating, I did have a glimpse of that possibility.

I didn't ever finish this collage and might have been unconsciously leaving room for an unknown future, but I was certain that my story with the bears had come to a graceful and blessed ending. As it turned out, that was not to be so. The most amazing part was yet to come. What happened next took me to the edge of what I thought possible.

It all began with my dream of building an art studio on my property that would serve as the home of For the Joy of It!, my expressive arts practice. I had spent many years exploring the power of mandalas and often chose to draw inside circles, instead of rectangles or squares. I came to wonder what it would be like to do my work inside a circle, and I fell in love with the idea of housing my studio in a yurt. I held that dream in my heart for many years. When I saw a yurt for the first time, made with lattice walls and canvas siding, I realized that I could indeed have something like this of my very own.

Actually making it happen was a challenge. The skills I needed were not in my normal bag of tricks so there was a steep learning curve for me, but I finally purchased a yurt and the construction of the foundation began. The workers dug five holes where the posts and piers would be placed to support the structure. The next day, they would pour the concrete. In addition to all the masculine energy I was channeling to make the yurt happen, I wanted to consciously bring some of my feminine energy to the project. I felt called to do a ritual. I wanted to dedicate to a sacred purpose the work I would be doing in the yurt.

The next day at sunrise, I stood in the center of a circle drawn on the forest floor and asked that the yurt be a place of health and healing, for me and for all who came to do their personal work there. More than believing I was in touch with energies outside myself, except metaphorically, I saw it as a way to focus my inner intentions. Because the image of the bear was so deeply connected to my own healing by then, I placed a small brown bear figure in each of the holes on the periphery of the foundation and a small white bear in the hole in the center. I asked for the bears' strength and protection to be with me in my work there. Then I returned to my house, and the foundation was poured later that morning.

The foundation and floor took a couple of weeks to build. The yurt itself went up in just a day and a half. The next morning, I awoke from a powerful dream. It was about 5:30 a.m. I recorded the dream in my journal, got up, and went downstairs to have my breakfast. It was going to be a busy day. I needed to select carpeting for the yurt floor. I grabbed my carpet sample book and started out the door. It was just a short walk across my meadow to the circle of redwoods where my yurt now stood. As I approached, I gasped when I saw a giant tear in the side of the yurt, just to the left of the door, and mud smeared all over the fabric. I walked around the yurt and saw more tears, more mud, and mangled plastic on the windows. It was hard to make any sense of what I was seeing. *Who would have done such a thing?* As I continued to circle the yurt, I realized that amid the muddy smears were clearly defined prints that looked like bear paws.

The shock of it made me crazy—quite literally crazy, in fact. Though by this time there were occasional sightings of bears in my area, they were by no means common. I just didn't believe this was really the work of a bear. I thought the yurt had been vandalized. Some strange people had been hanging out in the forest recently, so this wasn't a completely illogical leap, but it was mostly crazy and then got worse. A story started to form in my mind in my desperate attempt to make sense of what I was seeing. I decided that whoever had done this knew of my experiences with bears and had actually gone to the trouble of making it look as if a bear had done the damage. I even imagined someone making a board with a raised bear print on it and stamping it around the yurt, then smearing mud and tearing the fabric.

After I surveyed the damage all around, I ran back to the house to call a friend. Through my frantic babble, we must have decided that calling the police was a good idea. I did that and then ran back out to the yurt. As I hurried down the path, a worker who was helping erect the yurt came running toward me.

"Marilyn, a bear attacked the yurt! It's torn all around!" he shouted.

"I know, I saw it. It wasn't a bear; it couldn't have possibly been a bear. I think someone vandalized it. I just called the police," I assured him. It seems laughable now, but I had thoroughly convinced myself that this was so. He looked at me as if I had gone mad, which, I'm afraid, was true.

It was easier for me to believe my fantastical story than to face the fact that I had in effect called the bear energy to this very spot just a few days before, though I had been speaking metaphorically. Rather than opening my mind to the idea that the bear had somehow responded to my call, I found it easier to stay with my own view of what was possible and what was not; thus, my paranoid story evolved.

The policeman arrived. I explained to him what I thought had happened. He listened patiently and then walked around the yurt, inspecting the damage. After a careful inspection, he turned to me and said, "Ma'am, I think it really was a bear." He patiently showed me the prints, pointed out the wet saliva on the windows around the bitten areas, and showed me where the bear's claws had made clear indentations in the foil insulation underneath the fabric tears.

At that point, I had to accept that a bear had indeed visited the yurt, though allowing that reality to sink in remained difficult. Later that morning, I called some of my dream-group friends. They had heard many dreams about bears trying to break into my house, as, in addition to my childhood dream, this had become a frequent theme in my dream life, but they were all as surprised as I was that it had actually happened. One of my friends contacted a man who knew a lot about bears to see if he might have some input. He stopped by and, after he investigated, said he thought the bear had just been curious, looking here and looking there, tasting this and tasting that, as bears do. "It's their way of discovering the world," he said. "If the bear had wanted to get into the yurt, it would have had no trouble doing that." That comment was reassuring and not reassuring all at the same time.

Throughout the afternoon, I recognized a small, young, persistent voice inside me. It kept repeating, *You see, bears* do *come to houses. It's really true! Look what happened!*

I spent much of the day just trying to integrate this amazing turn of events. It seemed magical, really, but definitely more magical than I was prepared for or comfortable with. I fell into bed that night filled with wonder and feeling blessed by this truly mysterious event. My place in it all was confusing. *Could I have made such a thing happen?* I asked myself. *No*, I insisted. *I'm just an ordinary person; that couldn't be.* As I went to pull the covers over me, I found my dream journal lying open on the bed. I picked it up, glancing at what I had written that morning. In the flurry of it all, I had forgotten about my dream. As if I weren't already awed, what I read put me over the top.

In my dream, I was in a yurt-like structure with lattice walls. I had just entered after being outside. I was talking with a man. I decided to go outside again, but when I opened the door,

I heard a terrible, loud growling sound. I knew it was a grizzly bear. I panicked and rushed to close the door and quickly bolt it. I thought of trying to hide, but I realized if the bear wanted to get in, there was no escaping. I went over to the window and looked out. It was like looking out the windows of the yurt. I saw a jester-looking guy out there, dressed in brilliant colors. He had a bear on a leash. The bear had a hump on its neck. It was a grizzly bear.

As I lay there, recalling my powerful dream, the mystery surrounding this incredible day was amplified tenfold. It was hard to go to sleep that night. I tossed and turned in my bed for many hours.

Some days later, I did a series of paintings about the event. This one, *The Opening Between the Worlds*, shows the bear and the jester finding a colorful passageway from my dream world into my waking life. There is humor in this drawing. The jester as a trickster figure is the energy behind the bear; they look like partners in crime. In my dream, he has control of the bear, walking him like a dog as they head for my front door. This image makes them seem harmless enough as they walk through my forest. But the roar that I heard in my dream was loud enough to reverberate throughout the universe, announcing the true power of the one on the leash.

I did feel the energy of the trickster as I tried to make sense of all that had happened. It began to feel like a cosmic joke, and the joke was clearly on me. I had asked, and the world had produced. So there! Turning to art helped me find some perspective.

I was able to replace the damaged parts of the yurt though I left a muddy paw print on the door. The remnants of that print are there to this day. When I led my first event there, I handed the women in my creativity group drums and rhythm instruments and we danced our way along the forest path to the yurt door. My desire to work inside a circle had finally become manifest. I drew *Dreams Held in the Heart Really Do Come True*.

In the months that followed, my mind spun with thoughts and questions. *Enough with all these bears!* I told myself. *I know my inner life and my outer world are connected, but I didn't know this much connection was possible. An actual bear came? How can that be? Who am I if that is possible? Who is the bear?*

It took years for me to find peace with the bear's visit. Initially, I responded like a small child who had touched fire and been surprised by the heat. I jumped back, way back. I knew that what had happened was a powerful synchronicity, but it was too destabilizing for me to get very close to it.

The Opening Between the Worlds

Dreams Held in the Heart Really Do Come True

I adamantly didn't want to put the experience in any kind of box. I didn't want to pin it down with my intellectual mind. I didn't want it described in a way that categorized it. For instance, many saw it as a shamanic experience; therefore, I was a shaman. However, I was certain that it had nothing to do with my ego. I didn't want to use it that way myself, and I certainly didn't want anyone else projecting specialness on to me.

As time passed, "I'm just an ordinary person" was my mantra whenever I thought about the bear's visit. Sometimes it was insistent, sometimes defiant. In spite of my not having wanted my ego involved, in hindsight I'm suspicious that it was—that despite all my protestations, my ego wanted to think that it had the power to make such a thing happen. Our egos always seem ready to take credit for something that belongs to a larger part of who we are. Though I revolted against the thought, perhaps I was protesting too much. My denial was just the other side of the coin of bragging about what happened. I needed to get off that ego coin entirely, but it was hard to find my way.

I was willing to consider that the bear had come, like a waking dream, to show me something. The words of the man who told me the bear was just curious stayed with me. *Who would I be if my curiosity was like the bear's curiosity?* I wondered. It had sniffed, chewed, and pawed. *Perhaps I wouldn't think so much before taking action; I'd simply jump in and do things.* The bear just went for what it wanted and certainly wasn't afraid to leave its mark. *Who would I be if I approached the world with that kind of energy?* Now, *that* was a question worth spending some time with.

Time passed as I lived with all my inquiries. The only thing I knew for certain was that I felt blessed by the experience, whether I knew what to do with it or not. The synchronicity of the bear's visit had cracked my world open. I was unable to pretend it hadn't happened and unable to put things back together as they had been before. Instead, I chose to sit with the shattering. I understood more deeply the words from Rilke that I had carried in my heart for many years: "Be patient toward all that is unsolved in your heart and try to love the questions themselves, like locked rooms and like books that are now written in a very foreign tongue. Do not now seek the answers, which cannot be given you because you would not be able to live them. And the point is, to live everything. Live the questions now. Perhaps you will then gradually, without noticing it, live along some distant day into the answer."

This time in my life reminded me of when I realized that I could no longer believe in my childhood religion. At that time, it was the energy above me that had shifted. The Father God watching over me was no longer real for me. That shifted my perception of the world and my place in the cosmos. Now, the ground under my feet was not as solid, not as impenetrable, as I had believed it to be.

We use the word "awe" to describe something so powerful and so vast that we cannot easily explain it. When we are in awe, we find ourselves surprised by a mixture of reverence, wonder, and fear. Pure wonder is something different. That tinge of fear that comes with awe and is related to reverence marks our awareness that we are standing in the presence of something so grand that it might challenge us to redefine our world. As I had come to follow all of these synchronistic moments, I had begun to suspect that there is more to life on the material plane than we usually imagine. The bear that came to the yurt convinced me and engendered a radical change in how I looked at Mother Earth and at what it means to be human.

Some years later, I read David Abrams's book *Becoming Animal*. In his introduction, entitled "Between the Body and the Breathing Earth," he writes:

Owning up to being an animal, a creature of earth. Tuning our animal senses to the sensible terrain. . . . Feeling the polyrhythmic pulse of this place—this huge wind-swept body of water and stone. This vexed being in whose flesh we're entangled.

Becoming earth. Becoming animal. Becoming, in this manner, fully human.

As I turned the pages of his book, my sense that I am somehow separate from this planet that nurtures me quickly began to disappear. The images he conjures with his poetic language carry the reader deeper and deeper into the reality of our "inter-being with the earth." For me, it was a sensuous read. Though our minds must process the words on the page, they are meant as direct communication with our physicality. Somewhere near the end of the book, I felt my body let go of any feeling of fear or strangeness or uncomfortableness about my ritual and the bear's response. After ten years of pondering, I found myself suddenly able to accept all of it as simply the way things are.

I began to hear my old words in response to the bear's visit in a new way. Before, I had taken the words "I am just an ordinary person" to mean I couldn't have this inner and outer world blending with the bear, because ordinary people can't do that. We don't live in the world like that. But after I had held my experience in a dark, unknowing place in my heart, Abrams's words revealed to me that my definition of an ordinary person had changed and evolved. Something had shifted inside me, and, with great calmness, the conversation about my ordinariness began to sound like this: "Yes, I am just an ordinary person. Who I am now is what that means. Life has presented me with experiences that have led me to remember that I am part of and deeply connected to the energy of wild nature. I am wild inside. We all are—it is just something we have forgotten."

In my art, my bears started having wings. In *The Flying Bear*, my animal body, infused with the vibrant energy of spirit, crystalized in the form of this magical creature who is equipped to live life on many levels. She can hibernate inside the earth, walk her forest landscape, and fly into the heavens. That is an expanded reality!

The Flying Bear

My life experience had awakened me from a deep cultural sleep. I know now that what happened with the bear and the yurt is indeed possible and very, very real. Did I make it happen? Not in the usual way we think of causing things to happen, as in cause and effect. Just as I did in those moments when I was a tiny child slipping into a special feeling of oneness, the morning I did the ritual in that circle in the forest, I opened myself to an energetic oneness with the earth energy that is our birthright. In that place, the boundary between what is inside us and what is outside us aligns in a different way.

I believe now that that place of belonging to Mother Earth is the truth of our human existence. I *am* an ordinary person. This is what being an ordinary person looks like. We can learn to re-own this essential part of what it means to be human.

At times like the ones when the fawn died in the meadow just as I was experiencing the death of my youthful innocence, when the elk shredded our tent just as my family was disintegrating, and when my adventures with the bears guided me toward the revelation of the Crone phase of my existence, we have a brief glimpse of the wisdom, inner and outer, that is just waiting to reveal itself to us once we are open enough to receive it. In my lighter moments, I sometimes have the feeling that, like the jester and the bear who found the passageway between my dream world and my waking life, these energies are there. We are the ones with the closed doors. We just need to dedicate ourselves to opening so that we can let both worlds in.

Paying close attention to our imaginal world as it expresses itself through images and symbols is one way to experiment with opening those doors. Playing with that imagery, noticing synchronicities, and paying attention to our dreams are all practices that help us build a bridge between inside and outside. As we traverse that bridge again and again, the boundary between those two worlds can become much more permeable than we have ever imagined.

As I write, I'm seeing the yurt as I found it that morning, with the tears in its walls, its chewed-up windows, and mud smeared all over the fabric. In my own playful way, I wonder if that bear, in all its curiosity, was showing me that I could make more holes in the walls and open more windows. The structure underneath is strong. I don't need to worry about it. Until it is my time to cross over, the structure will stand. As I follow the Crone and walk further into old age, I can still be myself, continue to open, continue to wonder, continue to imagine. Maybe that is a big part of what our final phase of life is all about.

In my art, this picture emerged. I titled it, *Riding the White Bear Home*. I'm small on the back of this creature. We are running in the north country, the place of the aurora borealis.

Riding the White Bear Home

Here, I accept my place on the back of this great, wild energy. The story this picture represents is a far cry from the story of "Goldilocks and the Three Bears." In that, Goldilocks ran from the bears, just as I had been running from what my life experience was showing me to be true. Now, riding on the bear, my inner and outer lives are not walled off from each other. The separation between the two is much more permeable. I am riding toward an entirely new world. The Celts associated the north with the element of earth, and the Lakota believed that the north was a place of wisdom. My experiences in midlife with the bear and the other wild ones opened my eyes to Earth's wisdom. Those adventures left me with some important keys to unlock the doors to my new home in the world as a Crone.

I have never been one to believe that looking inside is an end in itself. All the insight in the world is worthless, as far as I'm concerned, if we don't find a way to use what we have learned to give back to our families and our friends, to our community, and to our larger world. I have been lucky to have my work as a way of giving back to my own community. I know I will continue it in one form or another as long as I have the strength and ability to do so.

In my personal life, as I watched my parents getting older and older, I began to feel an urge as strong as the one I had felt when I realized that I wanted to become a mother. Only this time, that urge was calling me to use all I had learned in my personal exploration to give back to my aging parents, to support them in ways large and small as they moved through the final phase of their lives. The force was as strong as gravity, pulling me downward into the earth as I contemplated what dedicating myself in that way might mean for my mother, my father, and me.

❧ *Reflection*

To explore your relationship with awe, make a triptych by folding heavy paper or paperboard into three sections. On the left, draw or collage yourself before an experience of awe; in the middle, depict yourself as the awesome event strikes; and on the right, show who you are after being awestruck. Reflect in your journal.

Chapter 17:

A Ritual for My Family

Ritual is able to hold the long-discarded shards
of our stories and make them whole again.
—FRANCIS WELLER

While all of my outdoor adventures and my animal encounters over these years helped me to heal from my divorce, my mother heart was often concerned for my sons. I know John's and my difficult marriage and its dissolution affected each of them in unique ways. I had hoped to give my children better modeling of closeness and intimacy and provide them with an intact family over my entire lifetime. Whatever my marriage itself had, I think divorce puts an exclamation point on the struggle. I know it affects children deeply, no matter what their age. Although I had realized that divorce was right for me individually, I had continued to grieve that failure for my sons.

Years passed before they found themselves in relationships that led to their own marriages. I was concerned that their parents' divorce had made them leery of committing. Having turned their lives over to the larger world and to whatever energies now guided them, I decided that that broader arena would be the best place to address my own concerns as well.

I was determined to listen to my wild voice and honor my intuition. It came to me that to focus my wish for healing for my family, I needed to take myself back to the Oregon wilderness, where, on a family camping trip, the distance and animosity between John and me had expressed itself in the worst possible way for our sons. I wanted to atone for all the darkness in our marriage and ask for forgiveness. I believed I needed to address this problem in a physical way. Sitting at home and thinking about it was not the answer. I needed to reconnect with the physical place that symbolically held that particular darkness. If for no other reason than to clearly understand the depth of my concern and my commitment to healing, I needed to go that extra mile. I knew ritual would provide the perfect space for directing that kind of intense focus.

So, all those years later, I found myself in Oregon, hiking alone to the spot where the trail to Maidu Lake crosses the Pacific Crest Trail to perform my ritual—to give thanks and to ask for mending of the past and help for my family's future. I brought a pine needle basket that I had woven myself. Inside, on little pieces of colored paper, I placed a prayer for each one of us, asking for healing in the area of relationships in each of our lives. I brought a little trowel and dug a hole just to the side of where the trails crossed, I placed my basket in the earth, watered it with some tears, and sprinkled dirt in it until it had disappeared under the soil. I placed some needles from the forest floor over the top and sat for a while in silence.

I did not have a belief system that supported what I was doing. I was simply listening to a quiet voice inside me. These were prayers from my mother heart. They belonged to Mother Earth. When I finished my ritual, I hiked back to Miller Lake and baptized myself in its icy waters.

All three of my sons have indeed found their way to marriage, as has John, twice again now. I did include a prayer for myself that day, a prayer that hasn't yet become manifest, as I remain single. The fact that I haven't found my way to a relationship is actually the deepest sadness of my life. I understand that this deep longing I feel externalizes something that I yearn for internally. I know that psychologically, if we are to continue to mature, we need to find balance between the masculine and feminine energies inside us. That work goes on, and I hope it always will, but I am stubborn and demanding. I long for the chance to live it both inside me and outside me.

Now, as my sons give marriage a try, I realize that when I see trouble in a particular exchange, I react with panic. I so want their unions to go better for them than mine did for me. My children are clearly adults now and independent of me. They are creating their own marriages as best they can, just as I did. It is beginning to occur to me that I don't have to feel as despondent as I have been all these years about handing them the legacy of divorce.

Marriage itself is always changing. Just as my parents' generation saw it differently than mine, what my generation asked of it is different than what others ask today. It is a passage in life that many of us choose to enter. We do the best we can with it. As it happened, I came out of that passage alone, before either John's or my death intervened. Others make a longer journey of it, sometimes for the better, but sometimes for the worse.

My own parents remained together for some seventy years, but their apparent lack of emotional connection and their adherence to the traditional roles that their generation espoused made their marriage a union I would not have thrived in. Looking at their relationship, I have found great compassion for the younger me, who walked down the aisle with high hopes and my parents' teachings about marriage inside me. I was ill prepared for the task. I was, however, ready and willing to bring my all to it, and I didn't leave the relationship until I had exhausted every last possible hope.

I know my mother heart wants the very best for my sons. But now is their time in that passage, and it is up to them to make the best of what they were given, just as I tried to do. It's not that I'm not willing to accept responsibility for my failures; that's just not the whole story. For each of us, resilience is also always a possibility. If I continue to carry a vision of my sons as hopelessly wounded by their parents' failures, they remain my children. That vision leaves no space for them to take responsibility for their own lives in this regard and, in my mind, to be the adults they have clearly become.

What I chose, though I kicked and screamed along the way, was the fullness of my own life. That was something that I couldn't find within the boundaries of the marriage I had. Realizing that, I rejoice that I didn't consciously choose to make myself smaller so that I would fit the mold that would have made my marriage work. Looking from the outside, I believe that my own parents did just that in order to remain together. I don't think they were conscious of making that decision. Like many of us, they simply seem to have perceived life to be that way. Thankfully, I came to perceive it differently. I was able to find and listen to the quiet voice inside me that knew living more fully, or perhaps more deeply, was possible.

❦ *Reflection*

Is something troubling you, something that feels out of your control? Are you willing to hand it over to a larger energy? Find a spot in nature that symbolizes your issue. In that place, let a ritual emerge from inside you. Give thanks and do your ritual. When you finish, plan a symbolic transition back to your normal life.

Part III

Elderhood

*Religion isn't about believing things. It's about behaving
in a way that changes you, that gives you intimations of holiness and sacredness.*
—KAREN ARMSTRONG

Chapter 18:

Death Rides Beside Me

A hundred times a day I remind myself that my inner and outer life
are based on the labors of other men, living and dead, and that I must exert myself
in order to give in the full measure I have received and am still receiving.
—ALBERT EINSTEIN

When they were eighty-six years old, my parents came to the conclusion that they shouldn't continue living by themselves, so far away from family. My father had been diagnosed with congestive heart failure. That gave us a fright, but he seemed to be living well with it. Then my mother had a medical emergency that took her on an ambulance ride to the hospital in the middle of the night. She was their mainstay, the one who was keeping their daily lives functioning. When she got to the hospital, all turned out well, but soon afterward she called to tell me about it. "On that ambulance ride, I realized that if something happened to me, your father would be left in the lurch," she said. "We need to make a change."

Internally, I had planned far ahead for this moment—I just didn't know how or when it would happen. I couldn't see myself moving to Nevada to care for them long-term, but I was prepared to invite them to relocate to Mendocino. I understood that this was a family matter involving my parents, my brother, my sister, and me. We gathered and made the decision: My mother and father would move to Mendocino and live with me.

While I busily readied my house, getting stair lifts installed and making room for them, they closed down their life in Reno, sold their house, and shed most of their possessions. The day my siblings delivered them to my door, there were balloons and signs welcoming them to their new home. Shortly thereafter, the moving van arrived and unloaded what remained of their precious belongings. It was a joyous day. But as night fell, when my brother and sister had returned home and my parents had gone to bed, I found myself sitting at my dining room table, surrounded by moving boxes, in tears. I was fully committed to the decision we had made and had no regrets, but as I sat there alone after the hustle and bustle of that day, I felt the weight of what I had just stepped into fall down around me. It was palpable—an actual physical feeling of the burden of responsibility I had just invited into my life.

It was a time of radical transition. I felt very much like I had when I'd decided to have children. There was no way I could know what would be asked of me in the years to come. I would just have to throw everything into the air and see how it came down again. But as I sat there that evening, I didn't feel like I was doing that; I felt my life sinking more deeply into the earth, heavy, ponderous, even, not light or airy but rich with materiality and all of its earthly demands. In fact, I see now that I was deepening my dedication to the Great Mother energy, feeling called to live in a manner that respected all I had learned in those years after my divorce.

In the days that followed, my parents and I began to settle into our new life together. I did this pastel drawing, *Sheltered*, to express the feeling I had about my new life. If I thought I would be funding with my own energy all that would be asked of me, this drawing told me that I was mistaken. I saw that I was being supported by the natural world around me, the forest, the meadow, the river, the full moon, and that all was held under the wings of a big black bird. This was the nest into which my life with my parents would settle. I began to breathe more deeply as I relaxed into it.

Sheltered

I loved my parents dearly, though things hadn't always been easy between us. My life had veered far from the course they had set for me, and over the years that divergence had had consequences in our relationship. As we had all aged, things had calmed between us, but I wasn't naive—I knew that without all the years I had spent in psychotherapy, I would never even have considered inviting my parents to move in with me. I said as much to friends who marveled that I had invited them. I was aware that taking this on was yet another chance to fire, in the crucible of my daily life, all the inner changes I believed I had made. If those changes were real, they should serve me well in this endeavor. I had never trusted the new-age idea that if our family of origin was too difficult, we could make friends our "chosen family." I did have friends whom I considered family, but I thought that if I couldn't find a loving place in my heart for my own family, something was amiss.

In the weeks before my parents arrived, I surprised myself when I commented to friends about how excited I was at the prospect of having someone to love in my very own home. I had navigated on my own for eight years and had found meaning and significance. While I grieved not having found someone romantically special, I certainly felt as if my loving energy was benefiting my family, friends, and clients. But, I don't think I was aware that I was missing the concrete expression of that love to dear ones who were part of the minutiae of my daily life. I was ready to welcome that back and happy that that kind of loving was part of inviting my parents to live with me. I realized the solemnity of giving away some of my freedom, but isn't that always a necessary sacrifice when we live with those we love?

As I had aged, I had come to feel a great deal of gratitude for my parents and the life they had provided for me. As I found acceptance for the light and dark parts of myself, I came to accept my parents in all their humanness and to believe that in raising me they had simply done the best they could at the time. Becoming a parent myself was certainly humbling. My ability to love had indeed matured. Now that my mother and father were vulnerable and needing help, I genuinely wanted to give back in kind the energy they had invested in raising me.

Still, I did not feel as if I was giving up my own life to help them with theirs. As much as I had committed myself to living fully and vibrantly, I did not want to turn away from life's waning phase. Earlier on, I had embraced giving birth; now, I needed to find my courage and embrace the far end of life as well. My experience with all those bears had left me pointed in that direction.

Death Rides Beside Me

In a lecture, I heard the poet David Whyte speak about the time in our lives when we begin to "apprentice ourselves to that great disappearance." That is what I believed I was doing when I invited my parents to live with me. I was, in some sense, inviting the Crone aspect of the triple goddess to make her home in my home.

In a synchronous moment a couple of months after my parents arrived, I found myself in my car, stopped for a red light at a busy intersection. It was around Halloween time. I happened to glance over at the car in the next lane. The driver had placed a skeleton-like, life-size doll in the front passenger seat. I was so struck by the image that I went straight home and drew what I had witnessed, titling it, *Death Rides Beside Me*. It was exactly how I felt about my life at the time.

I wasn't imagining that this would be easy psychologically. Just as we see our younger selves when we watch our children grow, so we see our older selves when we watch loved ones age. It's hard to look in that mirror and see the Crone stare back. Everything about our culture at large supports us in turning away. Doing otherwise requires conscious intention.

I had already felt a strong desire to turn away from it all as I had watched my parents in recent years. I remember a particular visit with them in Reno when I felt almost claustrophobic in their house. Life moved so slowly there. It was hot and stuffy. They had a grandfather clock that ticked and chimed all day and all night. On that visit, I felt as if that clock were ticking our lives away. When I got in my car to leave, I was fleeing, not just returning home. As I drove away, I recognized that underneath all that discomfort was a fear of the aging process—theirs, my own, everyone's.

In my pastel drawing *From the Beginning to the End*, I pictured myself holding my life from childhood to the present and looking into my future. My vision of the old woman in her decline is not optimistic. She has a sad expression on her face. Her life looks like a struggle. Clearly, my own vision for the future was clouded and disturbing. It was as stuffy and stultifying as I had found my parents' home on that visit to Reno. It felt important to bring this out of the shadows, shine some light on it all, and allow a new story to evolve. In a society that has little respect for our elders, I suspect that many of us attempt as much.

The first several years of living with my parents were lovely—easy, really, when I look back on it now. We enjoyed more closeness and intimacy than we had ever experienced. They were grateful to be living with me and expressed that easily and often. I used to think how tired they must have been of saying "thank you" by the end of each day.

Certain iconic moments of healing between us stood out to me. One morning, my mother was watching me clean up in the kitchen after breakfast. Out of the blue, she said to me, "You know, when you were growing up, I didn't really know what a sensitive person was."

"What do you mean, Mom?" I asked.

"I mean, I really just didn't understand it. You know, I'm not like that. I don't clue into what's going on that way. I just didn't know there was another way to be."

Before I could say more, she went on: "I understand what a sensitive person is now, and I know that you're one of them. I know that's why I'm here right now."

I turned to her and smiled. "Thanks, Mom," I said. "It's always nice to feel seen. I'm glad you are here." Inside, I was thinking, *It's nice to get something like that sooner rather than later, but later is good, too. Always good to complete a circle that you've been waiting a long time to complete.* That was a rare reflection on my mother's part.

From the Beginning to the End

A moment I hold dear with my father happened one stormy morning when a tree had blown down across my road. I got my chain saw from the garage and asked my father to go out to the tree with me. It was too far away for my father to walk, so we rode out to the tree in his golf cart. I tried and tried, but I couldn't get my saw to start.

"Darn," I said, returning to the cart, where my father was waiting for me. "I just can't get it to start."

"Do you have someone you can call?" he asked. I knew he was regretting that he couldn't fix the saw for me himself.

"Yeah. I'll take it up to the saw shop. I'm sure they'll be able to get it working. I'll have to call my neighbor to get rid of this tree."

I turned the cart around, and we drove back to the house. As I was putting the saw back in the garage, I realized that in trying to start it, I had done everything exactly right, except one thing: "Dad! I forgot to turn on the power!" We had a good laugh together as we got back into the golf cart and went off to try again. My dad stayed in the cart while I hopped out and approached the tree. The saw started easily, and I had the tree cleared from the road in no time. When I turned around and looked at my father, he was beaming his beautiful smile at me and giving me two thumbs up. It was a small gesture, but I could hardly keep my tears from coming. I took a snapshot of that moment and filed it away in my heart. Sometimes, if we are empty enough, a moment like this holds healing energy that can wash away the pain of a lifetime. *Look at that!* I thought. *Take this in and let it fill all those empty places your father should have occupied in your young life. It's never too late! Enjoy this moment!*

There were ups and downs as we went along. Six months after they moved in, my father had a serious health crisis and it looked like he might be dying. Our family gathered to say goodbye, but instead of sending him on his way, that act seemed to buoy his spirits. He recovered and life went on. This was the first of many crises. Again and again, death would come close for my parents and then recede, without any major medical interventions. It just seemed to be the natural way of things, and a way of practicing for when that final moment did arrive.

A Mythic Journey

This collage, *A Mythic Journey*, emerged early on after my parents came to live with me. I pictured us as three bears walking into the future, led and surrounded by wild forces. Behind us, fading into black and white, more primitive energies lurk. The landscape—the world above, the northern lights and the world below, the undersea world—points to the wilderness through which I believed we were traveling. The journey I had set out on was not unlike my adventures in the wild. I was coming to understand aging as a force of nature inside our own bodies, clearly a manifestation of our own inner wildness. In old, old age, that animal part that we have tried so hard to suppress comes barreling back to claim us as its own. A new story about aging was taking shape. I found a harsh kind of beauty in it.

All was not completely smooth sailing with my parents in those first years, because early on I was aware that difficult family patterns from my childhood were revealing themselves before my very eyes: my mother's nagging; the dark silence that consumed my father when he was displeased. I think our bodies remember those things from childhood before our minds catch on. I would notice an ache in my gut, a flutter in my heart, and, when I thought something unjust was happening, shock and confusion. I hadn't expected my responses to be so visceral.

In the first year after they moved in, my father bought a new car, an Avalon. A week after the car arrived, I was going away for the weekend and my brother and his wife were coming up to stay with my folks. I assumed that I would take the new car on my trip, as my dad was no longer able to drive.

"It would be nice to take the new car when I go down to the city, Dad. Is that OK with you?" I asked one evening. I was sure he would say yes, but it was his car and I wanted to ask.

"Can you take the other car?" he asked, without looking up from his crossword puzzle. "I want to show the Avalon to your brother when he comes."

"Sure." I said, my body roiling. I waited a moment and then got up to leave the room, taking my feelings upstairs with me. *Family patterns!* I shouted inside. *Watch out! You know your brother is the number-one priority in this family. This shouldn't really surprise you. Why did you think this would go otherwise?*

This small interaction triggered so much in me. It was a warning sign. I knew it was good to recognize all my feelings, but I wanted to deal with them on my own. This was no time to be working this out with my vulnerable parents. I hadn't invited them to Mendocino to do that. It seems wise for anyone caring for parents to watch out for this urge. I'm sure it's how some elder abuse happens—a need to get back at, to settle a score. I didn't want to get anywhere close to that.

My father must have taken a few things under consideration as well. "Why don't you go ahead and take the Avalon when you go to the city?" he announced a few days later over dinner. "I can always show it to your brother another time."

"Thanks. I will. I would enjoy that," I told him.

In many ways, watching those patterns emerge gave me great compassion for the young girl I had been growing up in this family. While working with family issues in therapy, I dealt with my memories of how things had been, but memories are wobbly. There was a certain validation in seeing that my memories were true and correct and happening the same way right there in front of me now. It brought the young one in me leaping to the foreground, where I could see and even feel her struggle. Those were precious moments of insight and understanding. They always ended in a feeling of deep compassion and love for that child inside me.

That love pouring back through the years did find its target in my misunderstood younger self. Years of self-judgment surrendered, and I found a softer voice: *Oh, my dear, sweet little one, of course you felt that way. How confusing this must have been for you. Of course that was how you responded. Let me comfort you.* That was the voice I heard again and again as my family's dynamic played out before my much older and wiser eyes. Although my personal work in therapy was real and valid, it went only so far; living this forward with the actual folks who did the wounding in the first place took my healing to a whole different level.

With that, taking care of my parents became a living act of forgiveness. As that compassionate stance moved through me, I was forgiving my parents and forgiving myself. That became the sacred challenge of my time as their caregiver.

In my drawing *Mother Bear Holds the Child*, I found myself as a little one held in the heart of the Great Mother Bear. As in all my art, it was unplanned, but one eye looks back, obviously pained at what it sees there. The other looks to the future. All is held in the landscape of the night sky and the full moon. Important things were coming full circle inside me.

Mother Bear Holds the Child

Inviting my parents into my home brought a surprising consequence. I can say without a doubt that I have never done anything in my life that has caused so much response, both positive and negative, from everyone around me. I've been admired and I've been cursed, deemed an angel, and told I was selfish and uncaring. I've been judged immature and unable to set boundaries, and I've been set apart as more mature than everybody and saint-like in my actions. From close family and friends to grocery-store clerks and restaurant servers, no one seems immune to having a strong opinion and wanting to express it. I didn't believe that everyone should care for their parents the way I was, but everyone seemed to be using my decision to measure their own choices. I can only guess that response came from our enormous societal discomfort with the ways in which we care for our loved ones as they age.

As time went on, whether I was being blessed or cursed, people's judgments left me feeling exposed and alienated. Friendships and family connections were rattled, my work disrupted. I received far more support for putting my parents in a facility than I did for my decision to care for them in my home. In that, I felt completely alone. As a result, this time in my life became a deep meditation in keeping my center, trusting my internal compass to guide my actions, and trying to look honestly at my own desires and motivations. In *Spiraling to My Center*, I picture the darkness and passion that were swirling around me. To stay balanced, I had to sink very deeply inside myself and find a beacon of clarity and light at my center.

In her book *Braving the Wilderness: The Quest for True Belonging and the Courage to Stand Alone*, Brené Brown talks about the times when we need to be able to stand alone in a sea of dissent. Without that ability, we have difficulty maintaining our personal integrity. It's not that we shouldn't listen to what others are saying, but that if we know deep in our gut that our own truth is calling, we need to pay attention and be willing to act on it. It's an apt description for me; it instantly took me back to my hike along the Elwha River. I was practicing my ability to be alone in the world, sharpen my instincts, and be my own guide. Back then, I was honing those qualities in order to move forward after my divorce, but the lessons I learned there paid off far into my future.

When I welcomed my parents into the intimacy of my daily life, I knew there would be challenges in our relationship, but I didn't fully realize that I was inviting my entire family and our old family dynamic to return, front and center, as well. I thought we had moved on from the worst of our issues. As it turned out, the darkest shadow in those early years of our living together came from my siblings.

Spiraling to My Center

The meeting we had to decide where my parents should live went well on the surface. As we sat around my sister's dining room table that day, my mom began our discussion. "We looked into an independent-living facility in Reno where some folks we know have moved. It's where I play bridge sometimes," she said. "It's not a great place. Your father didn't like it at all. Besides, we would like to be closer to family."

"How about finding a place like that in this area?" my brother suggested. "They cook for you and organize all kinds of classes and activities. They're great places for social interaction. You would make all kinds of new friends."

"I find those places depressing," my mom said. "There aren't any families or kids around. You're just kind of stuck with people who are all your own age. It doesn't seem natural."

My father was silent. I wondered if he was thinking what I was thinking: *That sounds like an introvert's nightmare!* I had a hard time imagining him living in a situation like that.

My sister spoke next: "We would love to have you live with us. We're moving and are looking at a house for all of us. It would be great to have you be part of our family. I'd love my kids to grow up with their grandparents. We would have three generations!"

Her husband, Chris, chimed in: "Even though you would be living with lots going on—kids, maybe a dog, the whole chaotic family experience—we'd love to have you."

Eventually, I came forward with my offer for my parents to move to Mendocino. We talked for quite a while about all the options. Only much later did it become clear that many things went unsaid. We didn't get close to talking about the emotions that lay beneath our offerings. My brother didn't bring up that fact that he was radically opposed to parents living with their adult children as a general principle. I was happy that Laura and Chris were looking for properties that could accommodate three generations. To me, that made sense, as I didn't know what the future would bring, but I didn't fully understand that they were assuming that my parents would move in with them right then. When I invited my parents to live with me instead, my sister and her husband were shocked.

I realized on the edge of my consciousness that if my parents lived near my brother or with my sister, the family dynamic that had been so difficult for me would intensify; I would continue to be on the periphery of our family at a time when I wanted to move closer. What I knew absolutely was that I wanted to participate in caring for my parents at this time in their lives. I felt called to it, and I had done the personal work necessary to actually pull that off. I was ready and willing to give back in an openhearted way. I had the physical space to accommodate them and was convinced that my small-town rural existence, with its slow pace and natural beauty, would be a great gift for them at the end of their lives. If there ever were a time not to be invisible, this was it. I stepped forward. Now, I understand that it must have seemed to my brother and sister as if I were planting a stake in the ground to claim my territory. It shouted, *I am here and I will be included!* But that was only a vague awareness at the time and crystallized into words only with this writing.

At the time, I had expected my siblings to be exceedingly grateful that I had stepped up and offered to be the main caregiver. My brother had cautioned that he and Susan knew that they would also need to care for Susan's mother at some point in the not-too-distant future, and my sister's life was already pretty complex, since her kids were still at home. My life was relatively quiet compared with both of theirs.

Though my dad commented here or there, he didn't speak much during the meeting. He sat with his head down, arms folded, resting on the table. After he had listened to all we had to say, he looked up and announced, "I think I know what we ought to do."

We all stopped and turned toward him, shocked by the sense of finality with which he spoke. There was a pause, and then he said, "I think we should move to Mendocino to live with Marilyn."

We all turned to my mother. She did not disagree. His announcement opened a door to the next part of my life, but my brother and sister experienced a door closing.

Giving up living independently made my parents feel vulnerable. I am certain that they saw moving in with me—a daughter living alone in a big house with plenty of room for them, both mentally and physically—as the choice that would be least disruptive to their children's lives. I never once thought that they made that choice because they loved me best. In fact, in our family, all evidence in that regard was to the contrary. If something else filtered into their decision, it might have been the sexism behind feeling safe in a daughter's care. Whatever their reason, the decision was made and it severely challenged our family structure, transferring the center of the family to my home in Mendocino and, increasingly, to me. My siblings experienced my father's announcement as our parents' choosing one of us over the others. Their decision to move in with me opened the gates of hell, where the sleeping dragon of sibling rivalry had lain dormant for some years. That dragon woke up breathing fire and immediately began causing serious trouble in the kingdom.

I Stepped into a Hornets' Nest

It was as if I had stepped into a hornets' nest. I felt an instant, buzzing fury all around me and painted *I Stepped into a Hornets' Nest*. It portrayed the feeling I had of being ganged up on, all these insects with their stingers pointed in my direction. My siblings' resentment about my parents' choice only festered as time went on. I believe with all my heart that it was at the bottom of all the difficulty that was to come. In a phone conversation as my parents were preparing for their move, my brother said to me, "You have made a decision that affects my life!" I could see the truth of his comment, but it seemed like that was just part of being a family at this end-of-life stage for our parents. We were all going to be affected one way or the other.

I think my brother was confused by his anger, which became harder for him to conceal as time went on. He focused it on my parents, for wanting to live with an adult child. That just wasn't right in his mind. He was critical of my parents on many fronts, not to them but to me. In the early years when my parents went to visit him, he had them stay in the independent-living facility where his mother-in-law was living. I didn't ever ask, but I wondered if he was hoping our parents would like being there and would decide to relocate. Whatever his reason, my parents went along with it all, grateful when they went to his house for a visit and never complaining.

He also expressed his resentment about the whole situation by criticizing me for how I was caring for them and for the fact that I was even doing it at all. He thought they were taking advantage of me and that I wasn't seeing that. He thought I was paying way too much attention to their needs, and delivered the underlying message that they didn't deserve that. On the other hand, in his softer moments he would say, "I don't know how you're doing what you're doing. I know I couldn't do it!" It was a terrible frustration for him. He repeated over and over to me, "You have captured the high moral ground!" In that, I think he meant there was no room for him. I attempted to explain otherwise.

I was trying to keep both my brother and my sister in the loop so they wouldn't feel excluded, but they often threw back in my face my efforts to do so. My sister was understandably busy with her own life. If I tried to talk with her about some of the adjustments our parents and I had to make in our early time together, her only response was, "If it's not working, have them come live with me."

Little to no expression of gratitude came from either my brother or my sister for the gargantuan task I had taken on. A few months after my parents moved in, my brother suggested that he, our sister, and I meet for lunch. I was happy to make the two-hour drive and thought that the situation with my parents would be a major topic of conversation. I drove home dumbfounded that the subject had never come up.

In response, I was at first compassionate and understanding but also confused. I tried to explain that I didn't think everyone should do what I was doing, but that I felt called to do it. I thought if we could just communicate clearly, all would be well. When that didn't happen, I tried to talk about sibling rivalry rearing its ugly head, to no avail—I was met with blank stares or outright denial.

My siblings lived two to three hours from my house. As time went on and my parents didn't feel comfortable being alone when I wanted to go away, I asked if my siblings could take turns coming to Mendocino for a weekend once a month to give me a break. For each of them, that would be once every two months, but it wasn't easily arranged. Rarely did they offer their time, and when I asked for it if there was something special I wanted to attend, my brother would cancel things and resent me for asking, rather than simply saying he couldn't come. I felt like I couldn't win. I had hoped that we could pull together as a team as we moved into this time of caring for our parents. As time went on, I was to discover that there was a team, all right—I just wasn't on it.

I read oodles of books, anything I could get my hands on that would help me manage it all. I did learn that I wasn't alone in my struggle with my siblings. Francine Russo's book, *They're Your Parents, Too! How Siblings Can Survive Their Parents' Aging Without Driving Each Other Crazy*, was the most helpful. She explains that after growing up together, siblings go off into their own lives. Even if they have remained close, when parents need help, they are drawn into the immediacy of one another's lives for the first time in a long time. That's a natural setup for all of the primitive feelings they had about one another to come zooming back, almost as if they had never left. In my family, our problems persisted. My brother and sister are good people, but we simply couldn't find a way to support one another at that time.

I didn't ever talk with my parents about the difficulties I was having with my siblings. I wanted to be sure they didn't end up in the middle of that struggle. But, that desire left me feeling isolated. For the most part, when we were all together, family times went on as they always had, but underneath bubbled a cauldron of bitterness and resentment.

I'm afraid I burned through friendships trying to find my way through it all, and those friends who did stay with me heard earfuls of my rage and self-righteousness. I imagined that after my parents died, I would have no connection with my brother and sister ever again. Not only were they not helping, they seemed to be trying to sabotage what I was doing. How would I, as a self-respecting person, find my way to forgiveness? I couldn't see any way out.

I did many drawings trying to express this darkness. *Exploding with Fury* was one. It clearly portrays the primitive nature of my rage. It frightened me how dark my feelings actually were. I had never experienced such radical and intense hatred—not toward my father, not toward John, never. I knew that no matter who my siblings were, I was not in right relation with who I wanted to be. I now believe that without having gazed into that abyss and felt the degree of hatred that I am actually capable of feeling, I might not have found my way out of it. It is much easier for us to project our hatred outward and see it in others. I would have loved to do that, but the mirror in my heart showed me myself, not someone else. In many regards, I believed if I stayed with that much hatred, I would be condemning myself to a personal hell.

I feel fortunate to have found my way out of that dark dungeon. An enlightened moment helped me to move forward. After one of our more difficult confrontations, when I was beyond hope for how to take care of myself in this situation, I was fantasizing about never seeing my brother again once my parents died. I know many of us choose to distance ourselves

Exploding with Fury

from our relatives at some point. In some circumstances, it's an appropriate thing to do. I had done it myself for a time. But as I was driving across the state of Nevada that day, in the bareness of that landscape and under that big sky, it occurred to me that at this point in my life, any fantasies I had in that regard were simply control fantasies on my part. Whatever I might have been imagining, what would determine when I never saw my brother again would be when death came our way and took one of us before the other. Like the sun peeking through dark clouds in the sky that day, a little sliver of my love for my brother broke through the darkness of my heart. All it took was that glimpse, and I was able to move forward. I realized that if the loving care I was giving my parents ended in my hating my brother and my sister, all would be lost. My ability to work my way out of that tight place was perhaps the greatest spiritual gift I received from that intense period.

Foolishly and with much hubris, I thought when they moved in that my mom and dad had maybe three or four years to live. What I had offered seemed doable. Those three or four years I imagined in the beginning turned into sixteen years of being intimately involved with my parents' care. The clarity I started out with was turned upside down; it tumbled and crumbled amid the reality of watching my parents decline, face health crises, become increasingly vulnerable, and eventually die. In the end, to borrow words from Zorba the Greek, I experienced the "full catastrophe" of what it means to be in a family with parents at the end of life—the light and the darkness, the love and the hate, the hope and the despair.

I did succeed in not turning away. With eyes wide open, I came out on the other end with more compassion for all of us. In my self-portrait *Eyes Wide Open*, I picture myself wide-eyed as I travel this long road.

In the spring of 2009, after my parents had lived with me for more than six years, it all came crashing to an end the evening my ninety-three-year-old mother's leg broke out from under her as she was getting ready for bed. I can still hear the loud thump of the fall and her calling

Eyes Wide Open

A Fragile Nest

for help as I ran down the stairs to see what had happened. Amazingly, she was not in terrible pain. Our volunteer fire-and-rescue people came, and the ambulance drove my mother off while I settled my father with a friend and then followed her to the hospital. There, we learned that her leg was broken. It took until four o'clock in the morning to find a hospital that would accept her case. When the fog lifted five hours later, she was flown by helicopter to the closest trauma center, where surgery repaired her leg that evening.

Just weeks before my mother's leg broke, I drew *A Fragile Nest*. The delicate nest with three little blue eggs sits on a single tree limb. It is set against the night sky and looks as if it is resting on the edge of the world, beneath the full moon. The picture speaks to me of the fragile nature of the nest I created in my home for my parents, and of the folly of trusting the nest to hold, especially when my real-life nest was filled with two now ninety-three-year-old people. The full moon represents the fullness of their lives and the possibility of their deaths bringing them full circle. When I look at the image, the nest seems like an offering I'm making to the great beyond: *Here we are, way out here. This is as far as I can take them. I can go no further. The rest of the crossing is for them alone. I will stay behind.* The truths I gleaned from my drawing were not unknown to me, but the idea that this nest was an offering was new and brought all those truths closer to my heart.

In the aftermath of my mother's fall, my picture of the nest came to life, becoming animated in my mind. In my imagination, I saw the nest falling from the tree, the little blue eggs flying through the air, certain to shatter upon hitting the hard ground. Everything was topsy-turvy.

Difficulties with my siblings reached a climax as we tried to deal with my mother's broken leg. When she was ready to leave the hospital, she needed to be in a nursing home where she could have full services for her rehabilitation. We settled on one near my brother and sister, as there weren't good options in Mendocino. In order for my father to remain closer to my mom, my sister invited him to live with her. He was happy to be welcomed into her home, rather than stay in the assisted-living part of the facility where my mother was.

My father's choice to live with family for a second time infuriated my brother. Admittedly, Dad's choice made things more complicated, but I was happy that my sister had her chance to step in with the caregiving that she had initially offered.

Our differences were highlighted at every step along the way. I felt like I needed to be my mother's advocate in the nursing home. I wanted to be sure she was being treated well and getting what she needed. My brother seemed to align with the staff, rather than my mom, and what I thought of as advocating made him uncomfortable. He was so angry with my parents that it was hard for me to think he was sincerely watching out for them. After being their sole caregiver, I tried to soothe the trauma of these big changes by being as present as possible, staying down there part-time. My sister, amid her busy life, drove my father over to stay with my mother each day and stopped in to visit briefly. One morning, she surprised me when she said, "Why are we watching over them so carefully? I think this should be like when you send your children off to kindergarten. You just kind of need to hand them over to the teacher and hope for the best."

During this time, I realized that I didn't really know who my brother and sister were, nor did they know me. Our family is terribly intellectual. For years, whenever we were together, we discussed ideas, politics, philosophies, all of which seemed irrelevant in this gut-wrenching situation. We needed to understand one another on the inside.

Of course, my brother and sister would have their own story about all of these events, and it might be very different than mine. Now, I can see that I expected too much of myself and too much of them. As I came to understand more, I backed off. I know we were all struggling inside. Each of us was concerned for our parents in our own way, and we were all in free fall.

One day, as I was returning home from the nursing home, I looked up into the rosebush that climbed the side of my house. Just below the upstairs bedroom window, the window right next to which my mother's empty chair sat, was a beautiful little bird's nest. I ran upstairs to peek through the window. The mother bird was gone. The nest was full of blue robins' eggs. It was as if my drawing really had come to life. I stared at the eggs, thinking that even when it seems as if life is shattering, there is a greater holding. Nothing could have spoken to me more profoundly. This synchronous miracle was just what I needed that day.

The deeper teaching took days to reveal itself. I kept an eye on the nest when I knew the mother bird was not there. One day, I discovered with alarm that one of the little blue eggs was missing. The mother still returned to sit on the remaining eggs, but, over the next few days, one egg after the other disappeared, until the nest was empty. I sat with these events like one sits with medicine one must take but resists. The Great Mother energy was again revealing her ferocity. Yes, there was that "great holding" that I had basked in just days before, but there was also its opposite. All of our nests will eventually be empty. All things will pass away.

My parents thanked me again and again for my help during this vulnerable time. I was touched when my father called me on the first night I was back home in Mendocino. We chatted about the day, something we rarely did. I kept waiting to hear why he was calling, but there didn't seem to be a reason. Near the end of our conversation, he said, "Well, I just wanted to call to say good night."

"Good night, Dad," I said. "I love you."

"Well, I love you, too," he said.

My father called me every night before he went to bed for the three months when my mother was in the nursing home. If I knew I would be out, I was sure to give him a call before I left. Those were the sweetest times I had with my father in my entire life. Our evening conversations showed me that love has a way of coming full circle if we can remain open enough for it to find its way.

My mother did not die. She survived this crisis by embracing her physical therapy and after three months was ready to leave the nursing home. She was in a wheelchair most of the time but could walk short distances. Her doctors recommended that she enter an assisted-living facility to complete her recovery. That brought another round of decision making and more trouble between my siblings and me. It was like we were back at square one, with my brother wanting them to be in a facility in Sonoma County, my sister wanting them to live with her, and me offering for them to return to Mendocino. My parents, who by then had made friends and a life for themselves in Mendocino, chose to return to the coast.

They relocated to the Lodge, the local assisted-living facility, seven years to the day after they had moved in with me. I was greatly relieved, because I had exhausted myself. "We never knew we would live this long," my father told me one day soon after they moved in. "You took care of us long enough. This is fine for us. I'm pleasantly surprised," he said.

"The staff come quickly when we need them, and the food is wonderful," my mom added.

Mom slowly recovered and was able to leave her wheelchair behind. I remained active in their lives, taking them out on excursions and bringing them to my house when I could, but as my mother recovered, I began to realize that I did not have it in me to ask them to live with me again. Those seven-plus years had taken a toll on me. *Running from the Fire* and *Witnessing My Burnout* speak volumes about my life as I began to realize that I was indeed burning out.

The problem with caregiving is that you don't know how long it's going to last. It was as if I had been running a race without knowing the distance I would be running. When I started, I didn't know whether it was a fifty-yard dash or a marathon. Was it a double marathon, or would I be running from coast to coast across the entire United States? By then, I definitely felt as if I were on the cross-country route. When I began, I knew I had three or four years in

Running from the Fire

Witnessing My Burnout

me. I made it through those years without serious trouble (except with my siblings), but each year after that became increasingly difficult. I kept thinking it couldn't go on forever. This new arrangement at the Lodge was exactly what I needed. My parents seemed able to deal with it, so that was how we moved forward.

Around that time, my mother shared a dream she'd had. In it, she and my father were strolling with their walkers down their road, heading to the highway that would take them to my house. They had gone quite a distance, when my father turned around to return to the Lodge, as he realized before she did that they weren't going to make it back to my home. Her dream was prescient. They didn't move in with me again. A couple of months later, my father was dead.

❦ *Reflection*

When you witness loved ones who are aging, ill, or incapacitated, what does it trigger in you about the waning phases of your own life? Make a drawing or a collage that expresses the ebb and flow of life. Place yourself, as well as your ancestors and future generations, somewhere in the midst of it. Write your thoughts and feelings in your journal.

Chapter 19:

Crossing Over

While I thought that I was learning how to live,
I have been learning how to die.
—Leonardo da Vinci

A month before my father died, he began to wake up in the night feeling as if he didn't exist. He would panic and press his button for help. The caregivers came and took his vital signs, which were normal. He was reassured, but it kept happening. We made a trip to the doctor's office, but he couldn't find anything that could be causing this problem. Things would calm down for a few days, and then it would happen all over again.

Then, late one afternoon, my phone rang. It was my mother. I heard the panic in her voice as she said, "Marilyn, your father is very upset. He says he's dying, and he wants me to ask you to come over."

"Did he press his button? Are the caregivers there with you?" I asked.

"No, not yet," she told me.

"Well, tell him to press his button. I'll stay on the line until someone is there with you."

It was just a few minutes before I heard the caregivers knock on their door. In the background, I heard my father say, "I don't think I'm going to live."

"I'll be right over, Mom," I said, hanging up the phone. I grabbed my keys and flew out the door. They lived just fifteen minutes away.

By the time I arrived, my father was feeling somewhat better. He no longer thought he was going to die and instead was stewing about "crying wolf" once again. He seemed very confused about how he could be so sure he was dying one moment and then have it all slip away.

Though my parents were now ninety-three years old, they were not philosophical about death. Many old ones I've known seem comforted by talking about it, maybe as a way of warming up to what they know is coming, but my parents weren't like that. It wasn't a topic they brought up, ever. It would have been much easier for me if they had. I wanted to be available to them in times of emergency, but I knew I couldn't keep running over every time my father had one of these scares. These events were certainly bringing up the topic of death and illustrating his fear. I didn't want to force an uncomfortable conversation, but perhaps this was an opening.

When I next visited, I tried to explore the subject. "Dad, if you're feeling like you don't exist when you wake up in the night, are you afraid about dying?" I asked.

"Well, yes, that thought has occurred to me," he said.

"You know, Dad, I will miss you terribly when you're gone. But at ninety-three, death is probably a possibility in the not-too-distant future."

"Well, of course," he said.

"Is it OK if we talk about it?" I asked. I paused for a moment, trying to figure out if it was wise to continue. It seemed like it was. "I'm wondering what kind of death you're hoping to have."

"I'd like to have a peaceful, quiet death," he told me.

"I certainly hope it will be that way for you," I assured him.

My mother was also in the room. I knew this conversation would challenge her "look on the bright side" disposition. She couldn't keep quiet any longer. "Well, when I wake up in the night," she chirped, "I don't think I'm dying. I just take three really deep breaths and fall right back to sleep."

"I know, Mom," I replied, "but you and Dad are different, and he seems to be having a different experience."

I asked again if my father could explain what he felt like in the night. He tried many ways to express his feeling of not really being there. His speech had grown difficult, and he kept searching for words. He held up both of his hands, rubbing his fingers together in the air.

"It's just like there's . . . nothing there. . . . I'm not there. . . . I, uh, can't feel anything." He continued to rub his fingers, looking puzzled, really struggling to make some sense of it so he could tell me.

My mother shook her head as my father talked about his long, sleepless nights. "Well, I hear him sleeping some of the time he thinks he's awake," she said.

I ignored her comment. "Maybe what's happening is kind of a dream, Dad," I said. "In dreams, we have a sense of not being all there sometimes. We're sort of disembodied."

"I don't think it's a dream. I don't know what it is, but I know it's something," he said. "And I don't like it."

"Well, that's for sure." I said. "Do you think we should talk to Dr. Kirkman about it again?" I knew that he liked to check things out with his doctor.

"Maybe so, but I don't think it will do any good."

I told him I'd set up an appointment and then went on, "Dad, if you think you're dying, are there things that you want to do or things you want to say before that happens? If so, we should pay attention to that."

"No, no, I can't think of anything like that," he said.

I then asked what was frightening about these experiences and what made him finally ring his pager to ask for help.

"I ring my button when I can't stand to be alone with it all," he told me.

I felt my stomach flutter as his vulnerability spilled out into the room. "Would it help if you talked to Mom?" I asked.

"I don't know if I want to do that. I don't want to frighten her, too," he said.

My mother, getting more serious now, told a story about a conversation she'd had with her beloved uncle. "I remember Uncle Dan telling me that when you're older, you don't fear dying as much as you do when you're younger. I feel that way now," she said, and then paused. "I feel much different about dying than I did when I was your age," she said to me.

"And I feel different about it at sixty-four than I did when I was in my thirties or forties," I said. "I'm sure I will feel different again if I make it to my nineties."

My mother thought for a second and said, "I don't think I thought about death at all when I was in my sixties."

"Well, I do think about it," I said. "You probably thought about it when someone died, like your friend Raleigh, or when Eleanor had breast cancer."

"Oh, yes, I suppose so," she said.

My father added, "I don't want to be afraid, but I am."

"Well, the life force is very strong," I said. "Maybe a part of us is always afraid when it comes to losing it."

My mother, now teary-eyed, said, "I remember when your grandfather was near the end. He got up out of his bed and came out into the kitchen one day and, in tears, told your grandmother that he really didn't want to leave her."

"Yes, I remember that story," I said. "It's very hard when one of a couple has to leave the other."

Neither of them responded. I imagined this was as close as they had ever gotten to talking about how that situation might be for them.

Returning to my father, I said that I didn't know much about dying but that if it was anything like giving birth, another process in which the body determines its own goal, at some point, we just need to surrender to the process.

My mother looked shocked at first, but gradually it seemed to make sense to her. "I bet that's right," she said.

"Maybe it would help in the night, Dad, as long as you're not in pain, to just let it be. Maybe that's a way to practice your way to a quiet, peaceful death. As much as I would like to be with you when you die, if I were to learn that you died peacefully in your sleep, I would be very happy for you to have gone that way." I again reassured him how much I would miss him and told him how grateful I was for the past seven years we'd had together.

It was nearing time for them to go to the dining room for lunch, and I could see my father getting anxious. "Well, I can tell you're affected by this talking," he said. "I'm sorry to lay this big thing on top of you today. It was probably the last thing you needed. I bet you're feeling really sorry for me right now."

"No, Dad, I'm not feeling sorry for you." I looked him right in the eye and said, "You know, I understand way more about life than you give me credit for."

"Well, that's probably so," he said.

"You certainly do," my mother said. "You understand so much about life, sometimes I wish I were you. I just don't think about things the way you do."

I thought for a minute and, holding back my tears, said, "And sometimes, Mom, I wish that I were like you. We're a good balance for each other." As I spoke, I felt the long journey of my relationship with my mother flash through me. It had been hard for us, as different as we were in almost every way imaginable. I felt the healing of this moment come to rest inside me.

My father pried himself from his chair, holding on to his walker, and I watched as his crooked, bent body headed out the door. I told him I would make an appointment with his doctor and placed my hand on his back as he walked by me. "I love you, Dad," I said.

"Well, I sure love you, too," he replied.

My mother didn't follow him. It was clear to me that she needed some transition time after a conversation like this. "I hope this talk helps, Mom," I said, as my dad closed the door behind him.

She pushed her walker into the bathroom, looked in the mirror, and began combing her hair. Turning to me, she said, "You know, when Uncle Mark died, Claire and I were there. His breathing got slower and slower, and then it just stopped. It was really very peaceful."

"I remember you telling me that. That whole experience was so reassuring." As we turned to go out the door, I said, "Mom, maybe in the night you just need to tell Dad how much you love him."

"I do," she said, "but he doesn't have his hearing aids in, so he can't hear me."

"Of course," I said, throwing my head back and rolling my eyes. "I forgot about that." *Oh, the complexity of getting old!* I thought, as I walked with my mother down the hall to the dining room. I hugged both of my parents, told them I loved them, and said goodbye. They each thanked me profusely.

Later, when I took my father to the doctor's office, the nurse weighed him and took his vital signs. I remember him telling her with a downcast voice, "I live at the old folks' home now." When she asked the reason for his visit, he said, "I can't get all here," trying to explain his feeling in the night that he didn't exist.

Dr. Kirkman entered the exam room and asked what he could do for us. My father told him he was having trouble adjusting to his new living situation. *What?* I thought. *Why haven't I heard anything about this before now?*

We talked for a while about his feeling as if he didn't exist in the night. The doctor was trying to get information that might be related to physical causes, but my father's vague statements about emptiness in his solar plexus, and his rubbing his fingers together in the air, led nowhere. Finally, the doctor asked him if he was depressed. "Oh, yes," my father said—he was sure of that.

Someone knocked on the door, and the doctor had to leave for a minute for an urgent telephone call. I took that moment to ask my dad about living at the Lodge. What was it in particular that was bothering him? "My life feels all cut off," he said.

"Say more," I said.

"Well, everything is all the same. Nothing exciting ever happens."

I pushed my feelings aside and took a deep breath. "I can certainly understand why you would feel that way. It *is* quite routine there, each day the same." But I couldn't resist adding, "You know, Dad, when I offer to take you out, to come over to my house or to do something different, these days you don't really feel like it."

"I guess that's true," he said.

When the doctor returned, he poked and prodded, listened, and tapped on my father's body, as is the way of Western medicine. All was normal. All looked really good, in fact, and out the door we went.

The rain pounded on the window, and the windshield wipers whipped back and forth on their highest speed as I drove Dad back to the Lodge. I knew he wouldn't hear if we talked, so I was silent. I could see him hunched over in the passenger seat, gray and still, shrunken remains of the father who had once been so much more and full of life. Many thoughts rushed through my mind. *This isn't going to be easy. I think this is the day I'm going to have to tell them that I can't have them live with me again.*

Once inside, Dad headed straight for the bathroom, while Mom asked what the doctor had said.

"He found nothing physical," I told her. "But Dad is depressed and told the doctor that he's having trouble adjusting to life here at the Lodge."

By the time Dad came out of the bathroom, evening was falling around us, the gray day turning to dark night. My mother squirmed, and I could see that she was panicked when I brought up the subject of their living situation and my father's unhappiness.

"I know you chose to move here of your own volition, but I guess the transition is rougher than you expected, Dad. I don't know what we need to do. It's taken me a while to realize it, but I know I can't have you come back to my house again. I'm just too tired. I can't do it any longer," I said, with tears in my eyes.

My father took that news calmly, as did my mother. I offered other options—living with my sister or a larger assisted-living facility in Santa Rosa—but nothing appealed, so we moved on. I felt as if I had taken a knife and cut through the bond that I had crafted carefully and lovingly in my role as their main caregiver over the last seven years, but I knew it was essential for me to do it—that was my truth.

A few days later, I felt the result of that severing come from the other side. It happened over a simple thing: the condition of my father's hearing aids. I had just gotten home after visiting with my parents, when the phone rang. It was my mom. "Your father can't hear a thing," she said.

"I just cleaned his hearing aids and replaced the batteries," I whined. "I'm sure they're functioning properly. Maybe he just doesn't have them in right!"

I heard my father's sarcastic voice in the background, disparaging me: "Well, sure, Marilyn knows," he said, meaning, *Marilyn thinks she knows everything, but she doesn't know anything at all*, and I could see him shaking his head in disgust. I knew this part of my father well, but it hadn't been directed at me in a long, long time. When I hung up the phone, I burst into tears. My body registered his disconnection before my mind. Something important had broken. When my mind caught up, I knew that I had lost my father's trust. I felt the world around me shift. I was standing on new ground.

There was nothing I could change about the situation. All I could do was stay very present for myself and for him. I didn't like it, but my stronger feeling was that it was perhaps inevitable. I prayed that I would remember this moment, as someday I might experience something similar from the other side: my own sons letting me know that they had done all they could do for me. *Perhaps this moment is necessary so we can let go, as one person moves on to their final destination and the other to what of life remains for them*, I thought. But in spite of my understanding, this moment was shattering and called forth the early wounding I carried in relation to my father.

I started to paint *My Father and I*, but Dad died before it was completed. I found myself unable to return to it. Perhaps it says all I needed to know at the time. Its meaning remained a mystery to me while I was painting it, though I knew I was expressing something important to me, and that alone was comforting.

My Father and I

Over time, what I saw was a portrayal of my life with my father from childhood to the present. On the right, as a little girl, I have climbed a ladder, trying to make myself taller in hopes of reaching him, making some connection with this shadow man who remained such a mystery to me. I am longing to be seen by him and equally longing to know him. When I reach for his arm, it disintegrates and falls off. I cannot find connection. On the left, the older me, my current self, stands with the bear, the full moon behind us, powerful, our arms raised in the universal sign of victory. My childhood experience of disconnection with my father was a tragedy beyond all measure. Yet now, in this moment, perhaps disconnection was exactly what we needed. I could accept that.

The last days of my father's life are marked by specific memories. A week or so after the doctor's appointment, Dad was feeling down and didn't want to attend the Valentine's Day party at the Lodge. I took a chocolate truffle to his room. A little later, he came to the party—probably seeking more chocolate, something he couldn't resist. A choral group had come to sing. They were performing love songs from the 1930s and '40s. I sat across the room, looking out over the sea of old faces. My parents were the only couple among them; I was sitting just behind them. I couldn't stop tears from brimming up and spilling down my cheeks as I grasped the losses present in that room in that moment. I wondered if the love songs were a good idea. Were they bringing good memories, or were they a special kind of torture these old ones didn't need? My question was answered when a woman I often visited with reached out her hand and showed me her ring. "My husband gave me this on our fiftieth wedding anniversary," she told me, with tears in her eyes and a heart full of love. *How brave these people are*, I thought. *Where do they find their courage?*

My parents still had each other, for better or for worse. They had lost many friends and family members by then. My mother had a whole address book filled with the names of deceased people. But she and my dad hadn't yet lost each other. I know they were the envy of many who lived at the Lodge, as some of the residents had told me so.

That day was the last glimpse I had of my parents in public as a couple.

The memories that are harder to be with are the ones I have of the days just before my father died. It turned out he wasn't feeling well on Valentine's Day because he was coming down with a cold. It started with a severe cough. It was something that was going around, and no one was alarmed—no one but my father. He was not an easy patient. He tended to overreact to his situation, which pulled me toward taking the opposite position, reassuring him that he was really fine; it was just a cold. He was not good at covering his mouth when he coughed, and I was concerned that my mother would get sick, too. It was claustrophobic to be in their tiny room with his complaining and coughing. Mom was frantic, and all I could think of was to get her out of there. We would go down to the fireplace room to visit while my father napped.

One day, a day or two before he died, I saw him cough right in Mom's direction. I was at my wits' end and tired of days of reassuring him. "Dad! Do you think it's important to cover your cough?" I blurted out.

"Of course I do!" he answered.

I felt bad as soon as I spoke, but there was no taking it back. "Sorry," I said. "I'm just worried about Mom getting your cold." It wasn't what I had said, but my tone of voice, that had bothered me. I had worked so hard not to be demeaning in any way to my vulnerable, old parents. In this moment, I had failed to reach my highest desire. Clearly, I was expecting way too much of myself.

The nurse at the Lodge advised me to give it a few more days, but by the fourth day, I was increasingly uncomfortable with the sound of my dad's cough and decided that we should check with the doctor. He was quite weak, although he didn't have a fever. When I picked him up to take him to his appointment, I saw that he was really wobbly, so I asked him to go in a wheelchair. He had never used one, but he didn't argue.

The doctor was concerned but not alarmed. He suggested that my father go to the hospital for a chest x-ray, explaining that he could possibly be admitted. He also told him that he had a choice: If he was comfortable, he could just go home. He gave him a prescription for an inhaler that he thought might help his cough. My father opted to go home, so we did. I will be forever grateful to the doctor for giving my father, a ninety-three-year-old man, that choice. I am certain that even if he had known the consequence of his decision, he wouldn't have decided otherwise.

Some don't want to see their loved ones after they are dead, because the living are concerned that that is the way they will remember them. I, on the other hand, am haunted by memories from when my father was still alive, especially my last encounters with him. It was evening when we left the doctor's office that day. In one of my final recollections, I see my father, who in his prime was a tall, strikingly handsome man, now small and shrunken, huddling in the passenger seat of our van as he waited in the Safeway parking lot for me to pick up his last prescription. That day, as I hurried toward the van, medication in hand, what I saw took my breath away. The man I saw there was my father and not my father. He was there but not there, alive but with hardly anything left of him. The sight of him sent a shock wave through my body, but my mind didn't know how to name it. I now think I should have known that so much contraction, so much implosion, meant death was nearby. I was glimpsing something I had never seen before. I tell myself now that if I ever see it again, I will know what's going to happen next.

We drove home in the pouring rain once again. My father was obsessing about the wheelchair and my ability to get him back into the Lodge. He kept saying I would never get him up the wheelchair ramp. I assured him over and over that it wouldn't be a problem for me.

"Dad, that's what wheelchairs and ramps are for. It won't be a problem, and besides, I'm stronger than you think I am."

He just kept saying, "What a mess! What a mess!" He repeated it over and over, all the way home.

As I left his room that night, he looked up at me from his chair and said, "Thank you so much for everything you did for me today." Those were the last words I heard my father speak. I've asked myself a million times if I told him I loved him as I closed the door and walked back into my world. For the life of me, I can't remember what I said.

Whatever my connection with my father might have been throughout my life, the morning he died, I was given the gift of a dream that let me know we were connected in ways deeper than our waking reality. That dream led me to believe that I had accompanied my dad to death's door. I myself could not cross that threshold, but I had a glimpse of the doorway through which he had passed before I knew it was so.

In my dream, I had been away from home for forty years. It felt like I was in West Covina, where I often ran around in a pack of kids from my neighborhood. Although we were still "the kids," we were adults now and had all been away, in an almost biblical sense, and were returning home for this great reunion. Entering through a sliding glass door, I walked into a large room with three rows of tables set up for the feast we would share. There were women cooking in the kitchen, off to the left. Behind the tables and up a long ramp was a door to the living room, to the right.

I knew that all the "old ones" were in the living room, and I wanted to see them. I tried to navigate the long tables so I could get up that ramp to where they were waiting to see us. I made it around the first two rows of tables, but there was no way to get around the third. I knew I would have to go all the way down and around before I could get to the ramp. Just as I turned to do that, out of the corner of my eye, I saw my great-aunt (my father's favorite aunt) and uncle standing in the living room doorway. Then I woke up.

I lay there for a moment, amazed at how real my deceased Nanty Stine and Uncle Glen seemed in the dream. I marveled that after so many years (about forty), I could actually re-create them with my own mind in a scenario that seemed so real.

I opened my dream journal and had written the first sentence of the dream when the phone rang. The nurse at the Lodge told me that my father was unresponsive. As odd as it may seem, I didn't realize that "unresponsive" meant dead. As I drove to the Lodge, I was full of surprise at this crisis. For years, I had been expecting this day to come at any moment, yet I couldn't believe it was here now. I hoped I would be able to have last words with my father.

The morning was stunningly beautiful; the sky, the clouds, the roiling waves all seemed sparkling and fresh, lit from within. I had made that drive many times, but on this morning, I had new eyes. It was all intensely alive! As I drove, I berated myself as the details of life with my father over the past week tore at my heart. I had been lost in all those small details. This morning, the big picture thrust itself into my view. Everything else seemed so small, inconsequential. *How could I have been so caught up in it all?* I made desperate and sincere promises to myself to learn from this. I uttered prayers that I not forget.

All these thoughts disappeared when I entered my parents' room and saw my father lying dead in his bed. My mother was sitting on her bed, her back to Dad, and I moved immediately to comfort her. She looked up at me and said, "Marilyn, this is when it's not good to be an optimist, because you're not prepared when something really terrible happens."

We canceled the ambulance and called the mortuary. The coroner came with his standard questions for my mother. As her story poured out, dark pictures of the night before took shape in my mind. In the dim glow of the nightlight, I saw my father getting up to use his commode and toppling over in the process. I saw him there on the floor by the door, curled up, waiting for someone to help him back into his bed. He was confused, despairing, helpless, and abandoned. I wondered if he had found his tears. I was sorry I wasn't there to comfort him. Then help did arrive, and he was safely back in his bed, apparently unharmed by his fall.

My mother told the staff not to call me. I would have liked to have been called. I would have liked to have been by his side when he died. But that wasn't how it happened. He died in his sleep, a death most ninety-three-year-olds hope and pray for.

As the day unfolded, my dream gave me great comfort. I believed that I had accompanied my father right up to the passage between this world and whatever happens next. All the old ones who had already crossed over were waiting in the "living" room—an odd twist, since, from this side of life, they are the dead ones. The great homecoming was not for me but for my father. My dream made it clear that I could go only so far; there was more life for me to live. I had to go down and around before I could access that great doorway. My father had been right the day before, when he'd been so concerned about my getting him up the ramp. I just didn't know which world he was speaking about. I couldn't get him up that ramp. He had to do that himself. Maybe he had been practicing for this crossing the whole month before. Perhaps when I saw him slumped in the van that night, part of him was already there at the threshold. He had managed to get himself through that door. He was now in the "living room" with all the ancestors.

While my main attention that morning went to comforting my mother, there was a moment when I turned my attention to my dead father. Strangely, on some level, seeing him dead felt like the most natural thing in the world. I remember walking across their small room to where he lay in his bed. Someone had placed a small, rolled-up towel under his jaw in order to keep his mouth from gaping wide open. As I walked across the room, I remember feeling like I was crossing a great chasm. Time stopped. I wasn't thinking at all but rather felt as if I were being called to act in some ancient play. Once by his bed, I reached down, gently placed my hand on his forehead, and then caressed his cheek. That moment is frozen in time. It was our final meeting, but it was so much more. It was life, my life, reaching out to touch death— without forethought, without fear, without revulsion. All of my thoughts and understanding about death pale in comparison with what I learned in my body as I stood there, caressing my dead father's cheek, that morning. The great truth of our dying sank more deeply into me. What I learned with that touch will be with me forever.

🌿 *Reflection*

Have you been with a friend or loved one as they sat at the edge of the great, wild mystery that is our dying? What did you learn? Find a tiny gift box and decorate the outside of it as a tribute to your loved one. On little pieces of paper, note the gifts you received in witnessing their passage. Put them inside the box. Keep your box in a special place where you will see it often.

Chapter 20:

A Powerful Turning

Our death is not an end if we can live on in our children and the younger generation.
For they are us; our bodies are only wilted leaves on the tree of life.
—ALBERT EINSTEIN

We had a family memorial in the days immediately following my father's death. He wanted to have his ashes scattered in the Ruby Mountains in northeastern Nevada, a place dear to his heart. Since he died in February, we had to wait for better weather before we could take his ashes up into that rugged mountain terrain. Soon, spring had come and gone and summer was turning to fall. Winter was not far behind when our family finally organized our trip.

My mother visited with her sister on that family's ranch while my siblings, their partners, my son Gabriel, and I went to scatter Dad's ashes. It was a cold and rainy morning when we left my cousin's house in Elko and headed out to the Rubies. As we came over a rise east of town, the snowcapped mountains appeared as if out of nowhere. While we crossed the valley, fall colors poured out of the canyons like rivers of gold. Entering the canyon on that gray morning, we were nearly blinded by the bright, almost psychedelic yellow of the aspen groves. I kept blinking. We sat in silence, taking it all in.

The Aspen Leaves

At that point, I was still uneasy with my siblings, but that much beauty began to open my heart. The small Marilyn who was still caught up in all the struggle began to disappear. I had the distinct feeling that what was about to happen would be guided by an energy much greater than my little personality, with all of its worries and concerns.

While we drove, the rain turned to snow, which soon stuck to the road. We were trying to reach the trailhead to Liberty Lake, where we hoped to spread Dad's ashes, but we had to turn around. We had just passed the largest side canyon, Thomas Canyon, and we decided that would be the best place for our ceremony. *Of course*, I thought. *Thomas Canyon—why didn't I see this before?* My father's name was Thomas Roy Hagar. I had always thought it was odd that there was a canyon with my father's name in this place that he loved so dearly. Now, it seemed to me that Thomas Canyon had just been waiting all these years to receive the ashes of another Thomas, the one who had held the Ruby Mountains with such affection for all of his ninety-three years. It felt like we were bringing our father home.

My sister had noticed a patch of bright orange aspens among all the yellow. She thought if we could get to them, that might be the perfect place. It was steep terrain, but we made it up there and found a small, open circle in the middle of the trees. She started our ceremony. "Dad, we brought you here because we know this was a place you loved."

I was gazing across the canyon while my sister spoke. Suddenly, a mountain goat stepped gingerly out of a clump of bushes and into my direct view. The trees in front of me had twigs jutting out from their trunks. The way they grew, they formed a perfect little rectangle in the foreground of my vision. The mountain goat had stepped right into this natural frame, and then the goat and the frame jumped out at me. "Mountain goat," I said, the words tumbling out of my mouth without thought. I pointed out the frame the little trees made, and the others gathered around to see.

The goat remained in the frame for the entirety of our ceremony. Over many years, I had gazed into those canyons, hoping to catch a glimpse of some of the wildlife that I knew lived there, but I hadn't succeeded until this moment. This wild creature's appearance, just as we started our ceremony, felt like a powerful blessing of our purpose there.

When we began scattering my father's ashes, instead of crying, I found my hand dipping joyfully into the box. I felt a profound honoring of my father's life. I was surprised to realize that I was scattering his ashes as if sowing seeds, looking more to the future than to the past, saying goodbye but also saying hello to new life and new possibility. I wondered what would grow from my father's remains returning to the earth. My joy increased with each handful. We saved some of the ashes and took them to where the stream cascaded down the mountain. Finally, all the ashes were gone, my father's remains now a part of this exquisite landscape.

We walked back down the trail. I felt the remains of my father's ashes on my skin, in my hair, and under my fingernails. At the trailhead, I wandered down to the creek to wash my hands. Cleaning up in this gurgling stream felt like part of the ritual. As I dipped my hands into the icy water, rubbing them together and scrubbing my fingernails, I was finishing my long journey with my father. When I was finished, rather than going back across the bridge the way we had come, I picked my way over the rocks until I reached the other side of the creek. Looking back, I saw the grove of orange aspen in the distance, yellow leaves shimmering in the breeze all around. I felt as if I had stepped back into this world, leaving some magical realm behind me there on the mountain.

Once we were back in our car, the road looked more passable than it had earlier. We decided to drive farther into the main canyon. Soon, the trees stood bare. White snow covered the ground. As we gained elevation, we moved from fall to winter in a matter of minutes. We made it to the end of the road and looked up at the 10,450-foot-high pass that led to Liberty Lake. After all that had happened, everything around me was dripping with metaphor. I was listening deeply to myself, and the landscape around me seemed to be speaking to me.

Looking up at the pass, I couldn't help but feel as if I were looking into my future. Metaphorically, I had completed half my task: I had seen my father to his end, but my mother was still living. The winter of losing both of my parents lay ahead. There was a steep trail yet to climb. I had hiked that trail up the mountain and over the top of Liberty Pass. I had fished in that beautiful lake on the other side. In this moment, it felt like freedom from my time of caregiving was up there over the pass. I hoped I had the stamina for the rest of the journey.

As we drove out of the canyon and descended, we moved out of the snowy winter landscape and found ourselves once again in the bright yellow of the aspens. But in the couple of hours we had been there, the storm had scattered the leaves; the trees were more barren, their branches more exposed, and the road now a carpet of gold. It was as if the world around us had participated in our letting go, honoring our arrival at the very peak of its fall beauty—a precious moment of fullness, not unlike the full circle of my father's life. As we drove away, the leaves were letting go as we were letting go, the great cycle of life supporting us with its powerful turning.

Later that evening, I was talking with my son Gabriel about the exquisite timing of the mountain goat's appearance during our ceremony. He recounted a memory: "Back when Grandpa died, I remember saying at his memorial that I believe we leave a part of ourselves in the places we love."

"Yes, I remember that," I said.

"Do you also remember that I said that when I was out in wild places where Grandpa had been, I expected to be with him there? I meant that metaphorically more than physically, but when that mountain goat showed up, it made me wonder!"

We both laughed and sat there looking at each other, wondering what might be possible.

❦ *Reflection*

Do you connect people who have died with the places they loved? When you visit their special places, take something from nature with you—a flower, a leaf, a stone—and leave it there in their honor. Write a letter in your journal, thanking them for all they have given you. Then let them write back to you.

Chapter 21:

Watching My Mother, Seeing Myself

Faith is the bird that feels the light
and sings when the dawn is still dark.
—RABINDRANATH TAGORE

I accompanied my mother through the immediate years after my father's death. We each grieved in our own way. I was comforted by going to the places around town that we had all been to together, as I felt my father's presence with us there. My mom preferred to avoid those places. We were able to talk some about our differences, but we never cried together, as crying around others was off-limits for my mom. I don't know how she was about it all when she was alone.

Things seemed to ease with my siblings. Perhaps our father's death left us more aware of the preciousness of life and the importance of family. We seemed better able to find more compassionate responses to one another. That helped tremendously. Both my brother and my sister visited more often, driving up for the day to have lunch with Mom and me. We fell into a nice rhythm.

My mother continued her slow decline. Watching an aged loved one deteriorate ever so gradually but inexorably—there in body but less and less capably, there mentally but less and less sharply—is a certain kind of torture. It is different than witnessing death from an accident or an illness. In those instances, it is possible to imagine that if we are really careful, those things won't happen to us; thus, we maintain our distance from the inevitable. But watching a loved one fade away gradually brings life's waning phase into the foreground of our awareness. It's like joining them on a very long hike. We accompany them as they head downhill. We see them struggling, passing through parts of the trail that are more challenging than others. We think their destination can't be that much farther, but the trail just gets steeper and their footing less steady. Then the trail disappears, and we watch as they slip and slide on loose rock and try to scramble over boulders. *How are they possibly maintaining?* we wonder, but they do. People used to die of "old age." We don't hear that diagnosis much anymore, but, to my mind, that was what was happening to my mother.

It had now been eleven-plus years since my parents had moved in with me. I was suffering from compassion fatigue and found myself needing for my time as a caregiver to be over. My daily visits with my mother had worn a deep groove inside me. For the most part, she was no longer able to have much of a give-and-take conversation. She had her stories, and she repeated them often. In almost every situation, I could predict exactly what she was going to say before she said it.

I couldn't keep up the pace I had set for myself. She lived so close that it seemed doable to stop by each day, but I couldn't do it any longer. Being me, I couldn't make up excuses or just not go—I had to try to talk with her about it.

After lunch at our favorite restaurant one day, we drove out to the headlands to enjoy the view of the coastline. I needed this expansive overlook to support me in delivering my message.

"Mom, I need to talk with you about something important," I said, already feeling my tears just below the surface.

"What is it?" she asked, looking surprised and a little concerned.

"I need you to know that I'm getting really tired. I'm overwhelmed with everything I'm trying to manage. I love you, and I really want to be available, but I don't think I can keep coming over to visit as often as I have been." I stumbled over my words as I spoke, trying to find just the right ones.

"Well, I'm so glad you said something," she said, looking somewhat embarrassed. Putting her head down, she added, "I should have realized that myself. Sometimes I'm just really slow to catch onto things like this, but then when somebody says it, it's completely obvious to me." She paused and then, with a deeply regretful tone, said, "That has been a problem for me all my life."

In my surprise, there was a moment of silence. She then added, "I'm so sorry I didn't realize what was happening."

"No apologies necessary, Mom," I told her, now unable to keep my tears at bay. "I just know I can't keep up this pace. Thanks for understanding."

I know now I should have considered asking her to move, but by then she was ninety-seven and I couldn't find it in myself to disrupt things that way. I just kept thinking her life would end soon—and then it didn't.

I watched friends and acquaintances move to the top of the generational ladder as they mourned the passing of their last remaining parent. Much to my chagrin, I found myself feeling envious. I felt like I did in my preteen years when all my friends were getting their period while I was still waiting for mine. That was a different stage, but what was so familiar was waiting for life to move on to its next, inevitable phase. I knew my mom couldn't live forever, but I began to wonder.

On her final Mother's Day on the coast, I took her out to lunch to celebrate, but I was quite aware that part of me was not celebrating. Everywhere we went, someone mentioned how lucky I was that my mother was still with me. On one level, I agreed, yet on another, I wasn't so sure. I was holding my love for my mother but, paradoxically, wishing that her life would soon come to a peaceful ending.

When I got in my car and drove away that day, I was in tears. On my way home, when my oldest son, Erik, called to wish me a happy Mother's Day, I couldn't hold back my tears. I told him about my difficult day with my mom and then said something that I really wanted him to know. "If I ever get really old like she is and you feel the way I do today, please don't feel bad about it." I surprised myself by adding, "I think it's the most natural thing in the world."

I soldiered on, but before we would celebrate another Mother's Day, my mother's assisted-living facility closed its doors. Out of nowhere, one day, all of the dear old ones living there received a sixty-day eviction notice. Panic ensued for everyone and their families, a state made worse by the fact that there were no other suitable options in our area. The residents were scattered in all directions. My family found a new facility closer to my brother and sister, two hours from my home. Thankfully, the decision about where my mother would live was taken out of my hands. Though I was furious about the way it happened, I was soon to understand it as a great blessing.

My mother moved just days before her ninety-eighth birthday. My sudden freedom was all a bit disorienting. One morning soon after that, I was walking on the headlands that surround my town. The tide was really low, exposing places underneath the sea that weren't usually visible. The sea birds were making a ruckus, delighted, I'm sure, to have found a whole new selection of food uncovered on the rocky shore. As I looked at that territory, I couldn't help seeing my own life. I was moving through a radical transition as my eleven and a half years of being a caregiver suddenly came to a close.

Like the birds exploring the newly exposed shoreline, I found a vast expanse of new possibility in my life. Time that I would have spent driving to medical appointments, running errands, making phone calls, visiting Mom at the Lodge, or taking her out was now mine to use however I wanted. Caregiving kept my life moving at a dizzying speed. Now, that scurrying had come to a screeching halt.

Friends witnessing my life were more than ready for me to leave caregiving behind and return to my "own life." I'm certain they were tired of hearing about my struggle. I was tired of my struggle myself, but I questioned if it were possible to make any kind of return to who I had been before. Those years with my parents had changed me. When they moved in, I took a different path than I might have otherwise, but I didn't ever feel as if I had stepped away from my "own life." All the while I was caregiving, it was my life I was choosing. Those years were ripe with lessons about aging and the far end of life. I walked away with gifts that will serve me. They already are.

My mother's adjustment to her new facility went surprisingly well. I made regular visits, but my brother stepped in as her primary caregiver with elegance and grace. It wasn't long before I saw his heart engaged in a way that it hadn't been when my parents had lived with me. I couldn't help but think of his comment about my having captured the high moral ground. Watching him step forward made it clear to me that he just wanted his chance to be the "good son." That he was, and he made it easy for me to step aside. My sister helped out as she could, bringing Mom roses from her garden and brightening her day with her bubbly personality. Wary of all I had learned from being on the other side, I tried to offer my support in whatever way I could and expressed my gratitude at every possible opportunity. My siblings and I had changed roles, but my mom was continuing to be cared for in the very best way possible.

One day, my brother commented, "It seems like I'm hearing way more expressions of gratitude from you than I remember giving when Mom was with you."

"Yes," I said, "and I mean every single one of them from the bottom of my heart!"

We both laughed. My sister joined in with her own thank-yous. No one did anything without gratitude all around. My brother was the lead caregiver, but that team I had longed for was finally manifesting itself.

In the years that followed, my mother's slow decline continued to leave its mark both physically and mentally. When she first moved, she would chat with me when I called, telling me everything she was seeing out of her window: the birds, the breeze in the trees, people coming and going. But eventually my calls seemed more disruptive to her than helpful. Sometimes she would quickly try to find a way to hang up. I guessed that internally, she was working so hard mentally to maintain some normalcy that it took most of her energy. If I called at 11:30 a.m., she would tell me she couldn't talk because she had to go down to lunch. I knew that lunch didn't happen until noon, but in her mind, it was already where her focus was and she didn't have the bandwidth for anything else. Eventually, she forgot how to use her answering machine; then, even answering the phone seemed like a burden. Sometimes I would wake her up from a nap and she couldn't orient.

I tried to visit once a week or so. As time went on, my visits recalled the painful disconnect I felt as a child with my mother. Once again, we were ships passing in the night. I had little to do with her physical care and no idea how she felt about her life. When I inquired about one thing or another that would have been bothering me if I had been living as she was, she responded, "I never think about it." Even when she was one hundred years old, any reference to the topic of death or dying elicited the same response—end of discussion.

I went on learning about the far end of life, about dissolution and decline. I had set an intention to embrace the Crone phase of my existence, but that was easier in theory than it was in practice. The universe seemed to be giving me a crash course in what that actually meant. First day by day, and then week by week, I watched my mother increasingly inhabit that archetype. I was learning that the power and wisdom we attribute to the Crone is hard won. It comes from letting our precious egos, with all their agendas, walk off center stage so the circle of life can come forward revealing its awesome beauty. I was reminded of that older woman in my collage, dancing in the mouth of the bear. *That is what it takes*, I thought, *holding the reality of both life and death and still finding the courage to dance with wild abandon.*

Mom became increasingly befuddled. Her confusion about time, names, and the generations seemed harmless enough, not really disruptive to her daily life, but after she turned one hundred, she began to slip into delusional states, seeing loved ones long dead living in her facility. Even that seemed explainable—maybe she wasn't fully awake, or maybe she was dreaming those things—but then she began having emotional outbursts of unexplained origins.

I visited her after one of those disturbances. She didn't recall anything about it. But, after a bit of silence as we sat looking at the flowers in the garden, she suddenly burst out, "I remember now: A guy came into my room and told me he wanted to fuck me!"

"Mom, what did you do?" I asked.

"I told him to get out and never come in there again," she said.

It was the only time I had ever heard my mother use the word "fuck" in my entire life. I looked into her face, searching for any hint that she knew what she had just said. I saw only a steely stare, not even the tiniest flicker of recognition of the huge chasm that she had just crossed. Though she was often her normal self, that was the day I accepted the fact that my mother now had dementia. As a child, I was afraid of death coming to take her; now, I found myself praying for it to come before she got even worse.

She became increasingly embedded in her physicality, unable to think of little else besides what her body needed in each moment—and her body's needs were enormous. Her care level at her facility was rising, as she needed help with showering, dressing, and grooming. She had managed to keep all of her teeth, but after a couple of them just broke off and fell out, she grew concerned about eating anything too tough or crunchy. She didn't want to trigger another dental emergency.

She was also careful about each step she took, judging the incline or decline of hills that were imperceptible to me, watching out for the smallest lump or bump or crack that might topple her, this after some falls. Before she sat down, she carefully evaluated whether she would be able to get up again, something that required many pillows so that she would have the strength to rise.

Eventually she became incontinent, which was a whole other world of concern. I often thought about a comment her doctor in Mendocino had once made to me: "What I've learned from all the really old people I care for is that they just want to be comfortable." I was learning that comfortable was not an easy place for a one-hundred-year-old to find.

My adventures in the wilderness earlier in my life were with me. I felt like I was witnessing the most distant frontier of human existence, the wildest part of our life on Earth. If things were going to get any wilder, it would be because Mom was ready to surrender herself to the big, wild mystery that awaits us all. It was as if her animal body was coming back to claim her. By the end, that was almost all that was left of her—that, her amazingly strong will, and her ever-ebullient appreciation of life.

❧ *Reflection*

It takes a lot of faith to watch ourselves or those we love slowly fade from their fullness. Collect materials from nature or whatever strikes your fancy, and fashion a little nest. (Clay works, too.) Hold the empty nest in your hand. Imagine all the life that was nurtured there. Write about the circle of life in your journal. Keep your nest for the next exercise.

Chapter 22:

Swimming with the Salmon

I would love to live like a river flows, carried by
the surprise of its own unfolding.
—JOHN O'DONOHUE

It took a couple of years after my mother moved for me to begin to feel restored. As my energy was slowly revived, I felt called to reflect on my own life as a way of gathering myself after that time of intense caregiving. At almost seventy, I was moving more deeply into my own Crone time. I wondered what still wanted to be lived. I began this book as a harvest of various life experiences I held dear. Was there a story that my life, my dreams, and my art were trying to tell? I was certain that was so.

Because my solo experience in Olympic National Park had been so pivotal in the vulnerable time after my divorce, I decided to return there to see what I could learn about my current life transition—as if that landscape might hold something vital for me.

On my first day, I found myself having breakfast at the Haven in Port Angeles, Washington, at the same table where I had sat so many years before. Back then, I was trying to find the courage to set out on my grand solo backpacking adventure. I didn't know what was in store for me, but I did know that I was stepping outside my comfort zone. On this day, I was the

251

only diner in the restaurant, and I sat quietly with my thoughts. *Is there a new comfort zone I need to step outside?* I wondered, as I sipped my tea and nibbled on my scone. *Is that what keeps us vibrantly alive as we age?* I suspected the answer was yes.

I could barely make a dent in this wild terrain. On this trip, I sat by the edges. I wrote. I reflected. I was there to visit the Elwha River. Construction blocked my access to the trailhead where I had hoped to take a short day hike. Instead, I'd have to be content to find a little spot before the construction barricades where I could at least sit by the river, listen to the water rushing by, and soak in its energy once again.

The landscape was familiar, and my heart warmed as I came through the forest to that clearing where the Elwha River tumbles along, framed from behind by the snowcapped peaks of the Olympic Mountains. I found a quiet spot and pulled off to sit by the river. The sky was blue and the water crystal clear. A brown duck with hints of orange underneath its belly made big splashes as it skidded along the water, taking flight. Suddenly, I caught a glimpse of a large salmon making its way upstream, and then another. I breathed in, relaxing into the moment. Returning my eyes to the riverbank, I noticed a dead salmon at the water's edge on the far shore. It was large, maybe two feet long. Easy food for forest creatures, it looked like some small animal had already feasted on it. It must have been out of the water for some time, as it was now somewhere between flesh and skeleton.

The river held this scene, including the salmon's demise, with absolute peace. The sound of the river rushing to the sea was as soothing as I remembered and held a deep promise of return. Its powerful flow was a picture of inevitability.

As my eyes shifted back and forth between the dead salmon and the live ones still moving upstream, a large one appeared in shallow water. It moved slowly and then in quick bursts of energy as it made its way against the current.

My mind wandered open and free with the sound of the water rushing by. My body remembered those sounds, the crispness in the air, and the smell of the cedar trees in the forest. As my senses awakened to this landscape once again, memories arose. I realized how much I missed that younger woman who had come here before, so full of heart, so needing to prove what she could do. She saw this landscape as a challenge, a way to find her strength. For some time, I had wondered what of her remains inside me. I realized that I had returned to the Elwha so that I might remember her.

As I sat there watching the salmon, I felt the transformation that had occurred. This wild place that I once pitted myself against and measured myself by had moved more deeply inside me. It was not so much out there as in here. Then, I had been the conqueror; now, I felt more like the conquered. Back then, I had been seeking strength—physical strength that I hoped might translate into the emotional strength I needed in my life at the time. On this day, I realized I'd found what my younger self was seeking, though, in the end, it didn't turn out to be what she thought she was looking for.

I have carried these landscapes and the experiences for all these years. They have become part of who I am. As I sat there that day, I felt just how much the domestication of my earlier life had receded. On this visit, I was more in touch with the wildness inside me. I was much more accepting of new life presenting itself, and, more important, I was more comfortable with life passing away. I knew for certain that all life is about change. *Perhaps it's not so much that this wildness has conquered me*, I thought, *as that I have found a way to recognize it inside me and learned to surrender to it*. At my age, accepting my place in wild nature left me feeling my belonging in a way I couldn't possibly have imagined when I was younger.

I know that our animal body, the sacred container for our life force, is a temporary home. We are nevertheless an integral piece of the ongoing story of creation. There is no way we can separate ourselves. We are embedded in creation, and it is embedded in us. I am comforted that when I die, I will in the end dissolve back into the larger story of which I am a part. I no longer look to a heaven in the great beyond but, like the salmon, welcome my dissolution into the arms of our Great Mother. Indeed, in that way, it is a home we have never left.

These twenty years have brought changes to my mind and my body, yet I am still swimming like those salmon, seeking to find home. The salmon find their way to the place where they were born. For me now, home is the place where I am most authentically me and from which my creativity springs. Once home, the salmon deposit their eggs in the nest they prepare in the gravel of the riverbed. I'm still hoping that the part of me that remains fertile can deposit my metaphorical eggs in the rich soil of my creative essence. At seventy, I still have a great hope that new life will spring from my efforts. And when life inside me is spent, I hope I'll be able to surrender myself to the shore.

Returning my attention to the river that day, I saw another large fish appear on the far bank. It was white on top, worn down by its life in the sea, its flesh already starting to decay.

It was moving very slowly in the shallow water, struggling every inch of the way. I thought of my one-hundred-year-old mother, inching through her days, doing just what must be done. She was as determined as this fish. Tears came as I watched its struggle.

A white flash caught my eye as another fish, thoroughly battered by its journey, appeared in the deeper water. Fighting against the current, it sidled off into the shallower water as it came to a riffle. There, it began to move upstream again, following the struggling salmon I had been watching earlier. I couldn't help but see my own life there in the river, my mother ahead of me while I came along behind, the generations moving upstream. I couldn't help but think, *I'm like these salmon. I'm here now in shallower water. Swimming where I can in this beautiful world. I'm here. I'm swimming. I know I'm headed home.*

🌱 Reflection

On little pieces of colored paper, write some things to which you would still like to give birth in your life. Fold them up and put them in your nest. Which of these things is the most relevant right now? Take a tiny step toward manifesting it.

Chapter 23:

Look, the Crone!

Every blade in the field—every leaf in the forest—
lays down its life in its season as beautifully as it was taken up.
—Henry David Thoreau

In late summer 2017, my mom took a turn for the worse. On one of my visits, I arrived just in time to see her inching down the hallway from the dining area to her room. Lurching her walker forward, she barely lifted her feet off the ground as she took her little half-steps. An occasional "ouch" slipped out of her mouth from a stabbing pain somewhere on the left side of her body, though she couldn't say where. She forged on with an iron will that would have put the bravest warriors to shame. "Am I almost there?" she asked, a little after the halfway point.

"Yes, you're almost there," I answered, but inside I was thinking about a much longer destination. I was thinking about death itself and wondering how she would ever cross that threshold. I was beginning to think that my mother was immortal. She was 101 years old.

Watching her walk was painful, but we had all been thoroughly trained not to suggest a wheelchair. Even so, later that day, when she wanted to have lunch in the garden, we did propose it, and she accepted without protest. My brother and I looked at each other, registering what had just happened. This was an admission that all was not "fine," her favorite word to describe herself no matter what her circumstance. My mother was endlessly positive.

She was put on hospice but soon taken off their rolls when her slide didn't take her to death's door. It turned out that she *was* "fine"; she had just reached a new stage in her decline: the end of her walking. Over the next months, she learned to cope with her wheelchair and her life continued on. There were crises here and there, and she was sent to hospice each time it looked like she was coming to her end, but she always bounced back and was removed from their rolls once again.

Then, in December that year, on the solstice, I got a call from my brother. "If you want to see Mom alive again, you should come now," he told me. She had lost consciousness and had fallen. She had been taken to the hospital but was now back in her facility.

I packed up and rushed down to be with her. When I arrived, she was in her bed, sleeping. We called hospice and signed her up once again. When the hospice nurse came, we learned that Mom was not at death's door but probably not too far from it.

In the days that followed, thinking that it might not be good to prolong her situation, my brother tried to talk to her about not eating or drinking, thinking maybe she was capable of taking a conscious action toward her dying. But, her brow wrinkled. She looked uncomprehending and responded, "Why? Why would I do that?" She was not going to "go gentle into that good night."

We began our long vigil, wanting to be with her as much as we could in the time she had left. But, as with my long stint of caregiving, we didn't know how long our vigil would last—would it be a day, a week, a month, or longer? We moved a rollaway bed into her room so that one of us could sleep there with her. One day, Mom asked about it. "What's that big thing over in the corner?"

"That's a rollaway bed so one of us can sleep here with you," we told her.

"Sleep here? In my room? Why would you do that?" she asked, crinkling her brow.

"In case you need someone with you in the night," we offered lovingly.

"Sleep right in here, in this tiny room? No. That doesn't make any sense at all," she said.

At first, we all gathered together with Mom, but we couldn't sustain that, so we started taking turns being with her in the daytime hours. It was a confusing time, because she would be in bed for several days and then wake up and decide she wanted to get up and resume her life as she knew it. I began to joke that my mother was like Lazarus. I was there one morning when she decided it was time to rise. I walked into her room and found her awake and trying to sit up in her bed.

"Well, I'd better get going on the day," she said. "I need to go down to breakfast."

"Mom, you've been in bed for six days," I cautioned. "I think it's going to take an awful lot of energy to get dressed and go down there."

"What? *Six days?* Well, then I'd *really* better get up!" she said, looking puzzled.

"Mom, really," I said, "I'm not sure you can."

"Well, of course I can," she said. "That's what we do here. . . . Six days? Really? How can that be? What was the matter with me?"

"I think it's because you're one hundred and one," I said. "I think you're just really tired, kind of worn out."

"Maybe so," she said. "But I'm good today. I know I have my bad days, but this isn't one of them. I want to go down and have my breakfast."

"Are you sure you want to?" I didn't know what to do. It all just seemed impossible to me.

"Yes, really I think I can do it today. I want to give it a try."

Surrendering, I reached over and pressed her button for the help to come. I wasn't about to try to get her dressed myself. I wouldn't even have known how to begin. She was so fragile.

Three caregivers arrived in her room. I watched as they lifted her legs off the bed and then lifted her to a sitting position. One held her from behind, as she didn't have the strength to maintain there, and they got her dressed. Every step of the way, she needed help. They lifted her into her wheelchair, washed her face, and combed her hair. They clearly had a practiced routine, but it took all three of them to accomplish their mission.

I knew my mother had a strong will—I knew that from my entire life with her—but her willing herself to breakfast that day was beyond my comprehension. As I watched, I felt as if I were caught in an old Western movie. Like someone being held at gunpoint, in my mind I was putting my hands in the air and backing up. There was nothing I could do to help my mom. She was going to meet her end in her own way. I just needed to stand back and be a witness.

I wheeled her to the dining room, which was by then empty. We sat silently while she ate, as she needed to use every ounce of her energy to concentrate on what she was doing. It took one and a half hours for her to eat a fried egg, a piece of raisin bread, and a tiny bowl of canned pears. At least half of the time, her fork went to her mouth without anything on it. I wanted to grab it and help, but the staff had instructed me that residents needed to be able to feed themselves in the dining room. All I could do was breathe deeply and find my way to being her calm, loving witness.

When she had finally finished, I wheeled her out of the dining room just as the residents were returning for lunchtime. "Oh! Is it time for lunch already? Maybe I should go back in," she said, confused but struggling to keep her life in the groove to which she was accustomed.

"Mom, you just finished your breakfast; we'll tell them you aren't coming to lunch. Let's go sit in the garden," I suggested.

I got some blankets to keep her warm, and we went out to sit in the sunshine. There were still a few flowers blooming, and we sat quietly, listening as the water tumbled from one layer of the fountain to the other. Soon she had fallen asleep, exhausted from her gargantuan effort to keep her life going as usual. I looked at her slumped body, which was listing to one side of her wheelchair. She looked beautiful sitting there, nestled in her soft blankets, like a baby but now at the opposite end of life. As I watched her, in my imagination I saw a crown of thorns resting gently and lovingly on her brow. She looked peaceful, not suffering or tortured but rather regal in her crown, a combination of Jesus Christ and the Buddha in female form. *Look, Marilyn, the Crone!* I thought. *She personifies it.* My heart filled with love and compassion for my mom and for us all.

Days turned into weeks, and then a month and more had gone by as my mom teetered between living and dying, a few days in bed, a few days up and about. The cycle repeated over and over again. My sister came forward over those weeks, spending many long days sitting by Mom's bedside. To pass the time, Laura found herself singing. She sang Mom's favorite songs: "The Red River Valley" and "Keep on the Sunny Side." Mom got stuck on those two songs, wanting to hear them over and over again.

I had just visited on a Sunday and planned to come again the next Saturday, but on Thursday morning I found myself packing things in the basket that I took when I went down to see her. As I watched myself do this, I told myself what was up. *I guess you're going to visit your mom today instead.* Soon I was grabbing my keys and heading out my door.

When I arrived, the caregivers told me that Mom had gotten up for breakfast but then asked them to take her back to bed. She told them that she didn't even have energy to undress.

I found her there sleeping, still clothed. I sat with her for a couple of hours before she roused. We chatted briefly about the day, and then she looked at me and said, "Marilyn, you live on the sunny side of life, don't you?"

My mother and my father were opposites in their outlook on life. My mother was an optimist, to the point of being a Pollyanna, and my father was a pessimist who often sounded like Eeyore. Mom so wanted everyone to join her in her sunny ways. I had explained again and again that I wanted off that coin entirely. Instead, I wanted to be with my feelings in the moment as they arose. I wanted to be able to hold the light and the dark. But right then, as I stood there contemplating whether to explain all that once again, I realized it didn't seem right even to try. We had covered that ground thoroughly already, so I answered simply, "Yes, Mom, I do."

She seemed comforted, and soon after that she fell back to sleep. When she awoke, she kept asking what kind of day it was.

"It's beautiful out," I told her.

"Oh, good," she said, again and again. "Sunny?" she asked.

"Yes, a beautiful, sunny day."

The afternoon disappeared, and soon it was time for me to go. When she next awakened, we visited, and then I told her I needed to leave. I got up and gave her a kiss on her forehead. "I love you, Mom," I said.

She looked at me intensely and then said, "I just love looking at you. You are so beautiful!" Those were the last words I heard my mother speak.

🌿 *Reflection*

As you walk through your world, experiment with looking for the beauty in the Crone phase of our existence: the soft petals of a wilting red rose; falling leaves; an old one's wrinkles. Photograph some of the things you see. Go out of your way to greet the elderly people you happen upon. What feelings are triggered in you when you look toward, rather than away from, life's endings? Reflect in your journal.

Chapter 24:

Letting My Mother Go

For life and death are one, even as the river and the sea are one.
—Khalil Gibran

We never know when we kiss a loved one goodbye if we will ever see them alive again, but after my father's death, every time I said goodbye to my mom, I tried to keep that in mind. So it was with this parting. But the problem was that, as much as I knew this might be our final farewell, I also knew that she might wake up the next morning and ask to be taken down to breakfast again.

I sat in my car with my tears for some time before I left my mom's that day. I was planning to go out to dinner and then attend a class. As I waited for my food in a nearby Chinese restaurant, I texted my sister and brother to keep them posted about the day. It had been incrementally worse than other visits. I wanted them to know about it.

"As far as I could tell, Mom was emptying her bowels from about three o'clock to four thirty. She kept saying, 'I wish I could just get it all out.' She was also gagging and spitting up thick mucus and blowing her nose on her bloody sheet. At one point, she looked at me and said, 'You live on the sunny side of life, don't you?' I lied! Difficult to do in that situation," I wrote.

"You have to wonder how much longer this can go on. Thanks for going down," my brother responded.

"LOL, so sunny," my sister chimed in.

"I wish I could have said to her, 'Mom, I love you and I'm concerned for you. If you have had enough of life now, the secret is to stop eating and drinking. If you want to do that, I will come down and stay with you to the end.' Can't help wondering if there is a point where that might register somewhere inside and allow surrender," I wrote again.

My brother reminded me that he had tried that. My sister responded with a very wise message: "Can't we just be patient with her own process? I feel like we're reacting out of our own discomfort, not hers."

It wasn't that I hadn't been thinking about reacting from my own discomfort, and I did want Mom to have her own process; it was just that on this day, hard as I tried, I couldn't tell the difference between my own response to the discomfort I had witnessed and my enormous empathy for my mother. *Is my empathy clouding my thinking?* I questioned. *What is the compassionate thing to do here?* My mind spun around and around, coming up with no answer. The compassionate response I was looking for was for death to come. Later, my brother put it this way: "I can't explain it, but at this point I wish nature would just take over and save her from herself."

My class that night was on the life of the imagination. In the middle of it, our teacher led us in a guided visualization in which he encouraged us to make a connection with a creature in the natural world. As soon as the visualization began, I was drawn to the energy in my jaw and was instantly aware that in my imagination, it was becoming a salmon's jaw. Soon, it was as if my body were becoming the salmon, my tail swaying in the water. I had fins and gills. I was no longer following the teacher's suggestions; I had simply become the fish. Afterward, we had time to draw the creature that had emerged.

The experience had been so physical. It was as if I could feel the dampness of the water on my skin and smell the mossy river bottom. In *Returning*, I picture the salmon having carefully prepared its redd and then laid those bright orange eggs in its watery nest. I spent a long time carefully drawing the river bottom. It was as if I were preparing a redd myself. I loved drawing those eggs, watching them find their way into the crevices in the gravelly bottom while all around me the environment supported the best outcome for new life to be born. I was the

Returning

salmon, and I knew that when I was finished, under that full moon, I would surrender my own life to this process.

I left class at 9:30 p.m. to begin my two-hour commute home, a little nervous at seventy-two about driving so late at night on our country roads. Barreling down the freeway, I passed my mother's exit, waved, and said, "Goodbye, Mom" out loud.

The freeway ahead was closing for construction, but I made it through just before the barricades went up. I breathed deeply as I turned onto the winding country road that would lead me to the coast. Relaxed now, I kept my eye out for deer and began to sway with the curves.

It was a beautiful moonlit night. As I drove through the Anderson Valley, I became aware that part of me was driving down the road but another part of me was over there, to my left, in the Navarro River. I kept thinking about the river as I drove along. It was a while before I realized that of course I was thinking of the river—I had been the salmon! What we seed in our unconscious minds stays around, even when we aren't consciously thinking about it.

As I wound up the hill at the Navarro grade, the place where in the daylight I love to see the river flow out into the ocean, my heart burst open. Though I couldn't see that in the darkness, I knew it was happening. I was so overwhelmed by the ecstatic return of the river to the sea that I pulled over to gather myself before driving on. I had witnessed so much that day: my mom, whose body was literally disintegrating, her skin breaking down, her muscles unable to hold her up, her heart so tired it was unable to keep up with its job. That is what dying of old age looks like. She needed to return to where she had come from, but she hadn't yet been able to find her way to dying. The river returning to the sea was so laden with the symbolism of homecoming, it had brought all my feelings abruptly to the surface.

I arrived home around midnight. I climbed into my pajamas and was about to go upstairs, when I just knew I needed to go outside and sit in my hot tub first. I tried to talk myself out of it—*Marilyn, you're exhausted. Go to bed!*—but another part of me insisted, *Just go out for a few minutes. It will be relaxing after your long drive.* Under the stars, I lounged in the warm water for about ten minutes before I realized that, of course, that salmon in me was still alive in my unconscious. I needed to actually get into the water before I could sleep.

I fell asleep at about 1:00 a.m. At 4:30 a.m., the emergency phone I had put by my bed many years earlier rang. It was my brother, telling me that our mother had not made it through the night. When I hung up, my sobs came quickly, but in the middle of my tears I found myself shouting out, "Mom, you did it!" I got up and got dressed, and within a very short time I stepped out into the darkness and headed back out onto the road, retracing my path of just a couple of hours before, now heading upriver—or uproad, depending on whether I was still that salmon or my human self, Marilyn.

I came over the grade into Cloverdale just as the sun rose over Sonoma County and my new life. Sixteen years of caring for my elderly parents had come to an end. I thought about the past six weeks. What an incredible will my mother had! I thought of my last moments with her, her question about the sunny side of life. I wondered if she had always worried about my penchant to live with more than just the sunshine. In the end, she must have been fighting with everything she had to maintain her own sunny side. Maybe she had just needed to hear me say yes before she had been able to let go. "Enough with all the rest of it!"

And her last words—I heard them now as a blessing, my mother looking at me, her adult child, in the way a mother looks at a newborn, seeing her little one as the manifestation of the miracle of life. *Each one of us is a manifestation of that miracle*, I thought. That insight is both powerful and, as we grow, easy to forget. I recalled my moment in the garden with my mom the day I saw her as awesomely beautiful in her final manifestation as the Crone. Whatever had happened in between, we had come full circle, from the beginning to the very end, mother and daughter, finding our true home in the gaze of unconditional love for each other and for life itself. What a gift for each one of us to give and receive at the very end of her life.

I thought about the seemingly endless night I had just passed through, my class, my drawing, how deeply I had been with the salmon. I heard my voice bidding my mother good-bye as I passed her freeway exit. The freeway closing behind me seemed like an odd detail reminiscent of the River Styx, I on one side now, Mom on the other. I thought about my ecstatic moment when I imagined the Navarro River pouring out into the sea in the darkness, my pulling over to collect myself, grieving my mother's physical disintegration. She was like those battered salmon I had watched in the Elwha. She had struggled against a strong current over these past six weeks, and then she had found it, the place from whence she had come. Her life had come full circle. She had made her nest and laid all of her precious eggs, and then had finally been able to surrender herself to the shore.

I had asked my brother not to have the mortuary come until I was there. I wanted some time with Mom in her room. When I arrived, my brother, his wife, and my sister had all gathered around her. My mother was lying on her back in her bed, her head turned slightly to one side. She looked very peaceful, as if sometime during the night she had just found a way to drift off, out, and away, her last breath a quiet pause, and then had been no more. I sat with her for a moment and later kissed her forehead, feeling the coolness of her skin on my warm lips.

We stayed with her for a couple of hours, visiting quietly, before the men from the mortuary came to take her body away. They were gentle and respectful as they moved her onto the gurney and wrapped her in blankets, covering her face last. They invited us to accompany them to the hearse if we would like to. When we walked out of her room, the director of her facility was waiting for us and handed us each a white rose. *Maybe we'll be taken out the back door*, I thought, but instead they wheeled my mom's body into the main lobby. All of the staff had gathered, and all of the residents who were there were holding roses as well. Our procession stopped while each person came forward and laid a rose on my mother's wrapped body.

In this unexpected moment of community, I felt like a child among others who were far more practiced in honoring the dead than I was. They knew how to hold this moment sacred. We followed suit, placing our roses on my mom. I looked into the faces of the staff, knowing my mother hadn't always been easy to help. I found such love there, in spite of it all. *How many of these ceremonies they must have witnessed*, I thought. *How do they remain so openhearted amid so many goodbyes?*

When the hearse drove away, we went back into Mom's room and stood awkwardly in the palpable emptiness. It was our first lesson in realizing that she was really gone.

However, it's amazing how quickly life moves on. We, the living, soon realized how hungry we were, so we packed up our things and went out to find some breakfast. While we ate, we realized we had things to do—the business of death was calling. Afterward, we went to the mortuary to make all the final arrangements.

A week later, I drove back down to be present for Mom's cremation. Making the decision to be cremated had not been easy for her. A few years before my parents had moved in with me, my father had written a letter to each of us asking for help with their end-of-life decisions.

"I can't get your mother to talk about whether she wants to be cremated or buried after she dies," he told us. "Can you help me with this?"

We talked it over and then assured him that if she couldn't deal with it, we would just handle it after she died. He made his own plans, and we left it at that.

Shortly after my father was cremated, out of the blue one day my mother asked, "Marilyn, do you think I should be cremated?"

I jumped at the chance to answer, "Yes, I do. If you want your remains taken to the Palisade cemetery, it's kind of the only realistic plan."

Without pausing, she said, "OK, that's what I'll do." Then she changed the subject, which let me know we were finished talking about it.

At the mortuary, I asked if it was possible to be present at my mom's cremation and learned that it was. In fact, we could roll her body into the cremation chamber and press the button that turned on the heat that would turn her to ashes. I felt called to be present in this way for my mother. I knew she was dead and that it didn't matter now to her, but because of her hesitation about it all, I just wanted loving arms sending her off and my loving hand pressing the button, committing to the process that would see her body to its end. I explained all of this to my brother and my sister, and in the end, they decided to be there as well.

I had planned to stay at the mortuary during the whole cremation process, but it became clear that it wasn't set up comfortably for families to wait. My brother and sister were hungry and wanted to go out to breakfast, something my mother loved to do. I decided to spend this time with the living, instead of the dead, and off we went. I could pick up her ashes later that afternoon. At the restaurant, we set the date for Mom's memorial: May 5, 2018, the day she would have turned 102.

❦ *Reflection*

Extraordinary things happen when we sit by the life-death door. People are born and people die. When loved ones die, they leave life to us. What do you want from yours? Open to something you have never done before. Take a risk! Commit to living a full life. What are your current hopes and dreams? Write about them in your journal.

Chapter 25:

And to Dust Thou Shalt Return

Life is a full circle, widening until it joins
the circle motions of the infinite.
—Anais Nin

My mother wanted her ashes buried in the Palisade cemetery in northeastern Nevada. Her family lived on a ranch just outside that town when she was born. Palisade is now essentially a ghost town; nothing is left of the place she knew except the foundations of a few old buildings. My mother's father, who died in the 1918 Spanish influenza epidemic, is buried in that cemetery, along with her grandparents and many of her aunts and uncles. We realized we would be bringing her ashes there one hundred years after her father died.

In the last years of my parents' lives, I had driven them from Mendocino to eastern Nevada several times to visit family who remained in the area. When the time for my mom's memorial neared, I decided I would drive her ashes across the state to her final resting place. The day I left, I placed a box on the front seat of my car and nestled the quilt I'd made for Mom all around it. I tucked the urn with her ashes in one side of the box and then placed a vase with two dozen long-stemmed roses of all colors next to her ashes. I was ready to make that final trip.

Our Final Ride

We had a graveside service at ten in the morning for the interment of Mom's ashes, followed by a memorial service at a community center on one of the cattle ranches nearby. Afterward, we shared a big lunch and visited for the afternoon. Nothing would have made my mother happier than knowing all of her family was together. So many came, from near and from far, from red states and from blue states, all with loving hearts, to honor her. There were only two remaining from her generation: a cousin, Wilfred, who was in his nineties; and my uncle Floyd, who had turned 102 just a couple of weeks earlier. The rest were from my generation, along with all the grandchildren and great-grandchildren, ours and theirs. Heartfelt stories were shared and poems read. There was as much laughter as there were tears. Noel, my brother's ten-year-old grandson, played "The Red River Valley" on his guitar and sang, touching the hearts of everyone there.

What I remember most from that day are two moments that happened at the cemetery in the morning. Palisade is an old railroad town. Freight trains still run through that narrow canyon. My grandfather was a conductor for the Southern Pacific Railroad all of his adult life, and my father spent a good deal of time working on the railroad in his early years as well. One of my mother's favorite memories from her childhood was of riding the narrow-gauge train that went from Palisade to Eureka, Nevada. When they wanted to visit their grandparents, that train would stop at their ranch in the morning, pick up my mom and her brothers and sisters, and drop them off for the day at their grandparents' ranch, which was farther down the valley. Later that afternoon, it would pick them up there and drop them back at home.

The cemetery is on the hill above the old town site. All around it is a low picket fence that separates it from a vast expanse of the sagebrush that makes up so much of Nevada's natural landscape. There are graves there from the 1800s, many with weather-worn wooden crosses. It's a picture-perfect pioneer cemetery in austere and rugged territory. The day of Mom's service, my brother, my sister, and I stood by the hole my ranch cousin Carl had prepared for her ashes. Behind us, across the Humboldt River, the palisades, the sheer rocky cliffs that gave the town their name, rose on the east side of the river. Just as I opened my mouth to begin our ceremony, I heard a rumble and felt the ground begin to vibrate underneath my feet. A train came around the corner and barreled along the tracks that ran next to the river. As it passed through the canyon, the engineer blew the whistle. We were just up the hill from this commotion and had to wait for the train to pass before we could begin. When that whistle blew, I smiled. I couldn't help but feel as if our ancestors were saluting our purpose there that day.

We thanked everyone for coming and did a couple of readings, and then my sister bent down on her knees in that dry, gravelly dirt and placed the urn with my mother's ashes in the ground. We each took a turn shoveling dirt over the urn until we had thoroughly covered it. When we finished, I read from my childhood Bible, censoring part of Genesis 3:19 and reading only, "For dust thou art, and to dust thou shalt return." In the full verse, these words are spoken as part of God's curse on Adam and Eve. I choose to hear them as a blessing.

We had given everyone a red rose to place on my mother's grave at the end of the ceremony. That time had come, and people stepped forward one by one and laid their flowers at the base of her headstone. I watched, tears streaming, as young and old approached the grave, leaving that token of their love for Mom.

I thought everyone had come forward, when I saw my son Gabriel emerge from the back of the crowd. Holding his hand, his little son, Chase, toddled beside him. Chase was fifteen months old and the youngest in our family. He was clutching his rose tightly in his other hand

My Mother's Grave

as he walked with his dad. When they got to the grave, Gabriel knelt down beside him and asked softly, "Do you want to put your rose on Grandma Rosie's grave with the other ones?"

Dutifully, Chase squatted down and carefully placed his flower with the others, but he didn't let go. He paused for a moment and then stood up, his rose still in his possession. Those of us watching chuckled. Then Gabriel gave him another chance: "Buddy Bear, are you sure you don't want to put your rose down here with all the others?" he whispered.

Hesitantly, Chase squatted down. Letting his rose touch the others, he paused again, and we all watched to see whether he was ready to let go. When he stood up, rose still in hand, there was laughter all around. Gabriel picked him up and carried him away, as Chase caressed the soft red petals of his rose with his tiny fingers. *Perfect*, I thought, *the youngest gets to keep the rose. It belongs to him. He will carry us all forward.* I ended the ceremony by looking out over the crowd. The words that came to me were, "We grieve because we love, and that is a great gift."

The kids were the first to disperse. I watched as they poured out of the cemetery gate and ran down the gravel road through the sagebrush, a flood of young life in all its exuberance.

Chase followed the other kids, holding his rose in the air like a trophy, sure-footed even as he headed down the hill. We were saying goodbye to my mother, but new life was streaming out in front of us like water flowing through this arid land, the next generation full of life, ready and willing to run toward the future.

🌿 *Reflection*

Make a wish for the generations to come, and write it on a tiny piece of paper. Construct a heart-shaped felt pouch that fits in your palm, by cutting two identical hearts. Decorate them however you like. Glue or stitch around the edge, leaving a little opening. Stuff the pouch with dried petals or lavender. Tuck your wish inside and close the edge completely. Hold that wish in your heart.

Epilogue:

Coming Full Circle

You must give birth to your images.
They are the future waiting to be born.
—Rainer Maria Rilke

One evening soon after I finished the rough draft of this book, I was listening to Beethoven while cooking my dinner when a disturbing thought popped into my head. The words, "It would really be all right if I died now," flashed through my mind. *What?* I thought. Those words threw me off balance. They seemed like the ultimate betrayal of my commitment to live to the fullest. I didn't think I was through with life. There was still so much I wanted to do and to experience. For certain, I wanted to watch my children and my grandchildren grow, and there was much more.

I sat with those feelings for several days, wondering about this dark moment and where it might lead me. It wasn't long before I came to realize that in circling my life with my writing, my wish to face death rather than turn away was coming to fruition. This thought about my own demise didn't have anything to do with not wanting to live; it was simply a sign that death—my own—had found a deeper home inside me.

I have no illusions that this insight signals the end of the process of accepting my own ending. Rather, I have crossed an important threshold, a step I think we must take as we get older if we want to live authentically.

Aging brings the circle of life into sharp focus. As we feel our circle near completion, the time we have left becomes increasingly precious. I feel it in a visceral way. The question of what yet wants to be lived looms large. I don't mean that in the sense of our accomplishments or our bucket lists; I'm thinking about our inner worlds, what we would still like to deepen in ourselves, and, in that deepening, what we still have to share.

In my writing, I've come to see that my life has indeed been telling me a story. An important part of it is just how much my wild self has urged me toward the deeply rebellious act of embracing the divine feminine energy inside me. Even as I grew up in a family and a culture that wanted me to look away, I was led in that direction. I find it a miracle that we are born with a deep inner wisdom that accompanies us through our unfolding future. Our wild voice is there, urging us this way and that way toward maturity, whether we are cognizant of it or not, but committing to opening to it in whatever way we can greatly amplifies its message and clarifies the direction our lives take. Our outer world can cloud our access to our deeper knowing, but fortunately we are born being drawn toward what touches us in the core of our being; our deep truth is waiting inside to find the fertile soil in which it can grow. The home of our deepest wisdom resides in the place I call our "wild inside."

I've dedicated my life to learning to listen ever more deeply to that wild place and let that wild voice guide me. It isn't a search as much as an openness to considering the deeper meaning of precious moments in our lives. It takes paying attention, curiosity, playfulness, a desire to explore, and learning how to think symbolically, all of which can be cultivated. Most of all, it requires a willingness to lay down our small egos and be receptive to awe and wonder.

We live because of the blessings we receive from the wild forces of Mother Nature here on Planet Earth and the universal forces where our earthly home finds its orbit around the sun. We are connected in every way to the ongoing story of evolution. That untrammeled place inside us is just a small piece of the larger wildness of which we are a part, the larger story that is being told, even as we think of ourselves as leading our own little lives.

Sometimes I wonder if we can feel the growing tip of evolution happening inside us. A pregnant mother feels the first flutter of new life as the baby grows long before anyone can place a hand on her growing belly and feel it externally and long before the baby is born. What if evolution is like that? What if this wild place inside us is the place where our psyches are dreaming up our next evolutionary step? If we could sense the growing tip of evolution in the psychic realm and pay attention to it, we would be consciously supporting that process, cocreators of the future. What if, in learning to listen to our wild inside and letting our lives be directed from that authentic place inside us, we can open the doors to the flood of new life that the world is just waiting to manifest?

These may all just be my outlandish imaginings, but I like thinking that when we engage with the invisible world inside us and make it visible, we are playing in the evolutionary field. I like to think that when we are making art, paying attention to our dreams and our intuition, being in touch with nature, and recognizing the synchronous moments that happen, we are playing with the growing tip of who we are becoming as humans.

The divine feminine energy is making a comeback. The counterculture of the late 1960s first brought this energy into my awareness. Earth energy seemed to be rising in those times, challenging sexual mores and resulting in the back-to-the-land movement that so many in my generation responded to. As the second wave of feminism swept the land in the 1970s, women woke up to new possibilities. From the emergence of research about the early goddess cultures to increased interest in black Madonna statues the world over, new images of the divine feminine have flooded our culture.

Cross-fertilization with other cultures, ones that are more at peace with the sacred feminine, also gives us a better sense of who we are and how we want to live that in the world. I believe that all of this is emerging from the backwater of history so that we can find balance with the overwhelming patriarchal energy that is currently running amok.

We live in dangerous times. Chaos abounds; the problems we face seem insurmountable. I realize that we have the power to destroy ourselves, but I look askance at dire predictions about our world coming to an end. I see those predictions as a symptom of a patriarchal mindset, something we have all absorbed to one degree or another. I refuse to join the ranks of those who despair, even to the point of thinking it unwise to bring children into this world. I see those sentiments as arising from a defeated perspective, one that has lost faith in the powerful forces that are trying to bring us into some kind of balance.

I refuse to fall into that pit of despair because I trust in the power of life's longing for itself. I have felt that power growing in my womb and been witness to its insistence on coming into being. As a mother, I hold special knowledge in my own body about the miracle of new life growing out of the darkness. As a grandmother, I remember when my body harbored life, and when I look into the eyes of my little grandsons, I see a spark eager to take on life. I want to be the one who holds a beacon of light for them, hands them the best and the worst of our world, and trusts their powers of manifestation.

I've always loved DuBose Heyward's children's book, *The Country Bunny and the Little Gold Shoes*. I read it to my sons when they were small. In it, the mother bunny gives her many bunny children tasks to accomplish at home so that she can be part of carrying out a somewhat magical mission that will be of great benefit to all. The reader senses that each little bunny is given an objective that fits their way of being in the world, complete with artists and musicians. In our lives, I suspect we all have our task in the big picture of things. When we live as our most authentic selves, we accept the responsibility for carrying our little piece of the much larger story that is revealing itself.

At the end of that little book, the mother bunny is tasked with delivering the most beautiful bejeweled egg the world has ever seen to a sick little boy who lives high up in the snowy mountains. In the illustrations by Marjorie Flack, the mother holds the fragile egg with loving care as she tries to ascend to the mountaintop, but she fails and tumbles all the way down. As she sits with the grief of her failure, the grandfather bunny appears out of the misty nowhere and offers her a little pair of golden shoes. The mother puts the shoes on and sets out on her climb once again. The shoes are magic—soon she is flying up the hill, and in no time at all she reaches the home of the sick little boy. She slips through a crack in the door, finds the sleeping child, and lays the beautiful egg on his pillow for him to find upon awakening.

This story touches my heart because I see it as a tale about divine masculine and divine feminine energy partnering to heal the sickness of our time. This union feels to me like what our world is trying to manifest. Finding my way back to my earthly mother in her divine aspect was life-giving for me, but I knew all along that that wasn't an end in itself. While I was exploring in the ways I have described in this book, I never imagined replacing the God of my childhood with the goddess energy. I have never lost track of the dream of the divine masculine principle and the divine feminine principle, working together inside each one of us to realize our greatest hopes for humanity and for our world.

Wholeness

I have had many dreams that point to this kind of mystical union. When I try to express the feelings behind these dreams, the words of Hermes Trismegistus, "as above, so below," come to mind. In my drawing *Wholeness,* the full circle of our lives rests both on the earth and in another realm. Here, I have earth above and sky below, each one reflecting the other.

In another, *Spiritual Marriage,* spotted spirit creatures that recall the characteristics of both cat and dog, bear and mountain lion, plant themselves into the earth, while the day sky, complete with sun, still shows the stars of the night world. Seeming opposites come together here. Everything is vibrantly alive in this colorful world in the forest.

Before the solar eclipse in August 2017, my first glimpse of what it might look like seemed to me to be a perfect pairing of masculine and feminine energy (the sun and the moon, respectively). I believe images can heal, and I felt as if this image could serve as a beacon by which we could chart our course toward a better future. I wanted to stand in a world where those two great forces partnered in the sky. I knew it would be profound and worth whatever I had to endure to get myself there to see it.

Spiritual Marriage

A friend and I piled into her car and drove to John Day, Oregon, which was in the path of totality. We found a spot in a cow pasture repurposed as a campground for eclipse viewing. That morning, eyes protected, we watched in amazement as the shadow of the moon bit into the sun and slowly made its way to the center. Through our glasses, the sun presented as a black disk. As the moon passed over, the disk of the sun began to look like a waning moon. It became a thin crescent, and then the moment of totality arrived. There was an audible gasp from the pasture. Safe now to view with the naked eye, we threw off our protective glasses and there it was, something I had never seen before in all my seventy-two years of gazing up into the sky: the black disk of the moon with the flaming white rays of the sun completely encircling it and shining from behind. A warm, sunny day had turned chilly in a matter of just a few minutes. Morning had turned to what looked like twilight, stars appeared in the sky, and an orange glow encircled the entire horizon.

Though the totality lasted just over two minutes there in Oregon, to me it seemed like an eternity. I had entered a kind of dream time where past, present, and future existed simultaneously. I felt linked to all the creatures, human and nonhuman, who had witnessed an event like this over eons. It awakened me to a universal perspective that leveled the playing field for all of us here on Earth. I had the thought that from this perspective, the political differences between my neighbors and me were irrelevant—they were so small in the big scheme of things as to be silly. The beauty of that image, the shining rays of the sun holding the moon's shadow, entered my consciousness as a healing image for our world.

I emerged from the totality feeling blessed by all that I had witnessed. I watched until the very last speck of the moon's shadow disappeared from the sun. Taking off my protective glasses again, I found the world as I had left it a short time earlier. There I was, on a sunny, warm day in a cow pasture in John Day, Oregon.

My friend and I decided to make some lunch before we got in our car to begin our long trek home. We spoke a little but were mostly silent, coming back now to our earthly reality after the unearthly event we had just witnessed. All seemed ordinary as I mixed a little aioli into a jar of home-canned albacore. I sliced open some vine-ripened tomatoes, turning them into little cups for a spoonful of the fish. I placed those bright red orbs on my plate and sat down with a sigh, hoping that some food might plant my feet back on Mother Earth after that cosmic adventure. When I brought the first bite to my mouth and experienced the explosion

The Eclipse

of flavor on my tongue, a surprising thought burst into my consciousness: *Ah! This is the true meaning of communion!*

I carry the shell of my early religious training with me, but I have filled it now with many other different colors and possibilities. The sacred in me is an alive, growing, and ever-changing energy. It is curious, open, receptive, and ready to be transformed in every moment. Sometime after, *The Eclipse,* appeared in my art journal. Here, I am holding a younger me under the eclipsed sun. Perhaps this young one is the one who walked home under the canopy of the starry night, so touched by the profundity of her baptism.

I am always surprised when I'm touched by the sacred. I think we are supposed to be. Experiencing awe is an important part of being human. We need to be shaken out of our rational minds now and then, out of the world where everything is known and explained. How else can we be open to what we have never seen, can't explain, and can't even imagine? How else can we be open to life anew? We need those moments of awe to crack us open and let the light shine in. The active, lightning-bolt energy of the masculine and the intuitive, earthy, womblike power of the feminine joining forces inside each one of us would make us powerful beyond all measure. Sun and moon, Mother Earth, and Father Sky, finding an equal and welcoming embrace in our world? I'm certain that would take us a long way down the road to peace, at last. Just imagine!

❦ Reflection

I wish you many moments of being touched by the sacred. If you were to write your own book focusing on your inner life, what are the names of the chapters you would include? Do you want to write it? For yourself? For others? Blessings on your journey.

Credits

The poem "You Darkness" is printed with permission from Many Rivers Press, www.davidwhyte.com. Rainer Maria Rilke, Trans. D.W., "You Darkness," *River Flow: New and Selected Poems Revised Edition*, 2012. © Many Rivers Press, Langley, WA USA.

Portions of an entry from my journal printed in *Spirituality and Art Therapy*. Reproduced with permission of the Licensor through PLSclear, Mimi Farrelly-Hansen (Editor), Suzanne Lovell (Contributor), *Spirituality and Art Therapy,* 2001. © Jessica Kingsley Publishers Limited, London, United Kingdom.

Pantheon Press, for allowing fair use of the opening lines of *Becoming Animal.* David Abrams, *Becoming Animal, 2010,* © David Abrams.

California Fly Fisher for permission to use portions "Finding My Way: The Making of a Fly Fisher," Marilyn Hagar, March/April 2000 Volume 8 Number 4.

Loreena McKennitt, Quinlan Road, for the use of her lyric, "Give These Clay Feet Wings to Fly," as the title of Chapter 8.

Brief excerpt from p. 29 from THE CRONE: WOMAN OF AGE, WISDOM AND POWER by Barbara G. Walker. Copyright ©1985 by Barbara G Walker. Reprinted by permission of HarperCollins Publishers.

Anne Baring, 2013. *The Dream of the Cosmos: a Quest for the Soul.* United Kingdom: Shaftesbury: Archive Publishing: p. 110 & 122.

Acknowledgments

I want to begin by thanking John Gunn, my childhood minister, because without his openness and inspiration in my young life, I might never have written this book. A big thankyou to my parents and to all my important teachers later in my life: Tyler Lincoln, Keith Whitaker, Monique Pasternak, Nina Menrath, Eloise Ristad, Dick Olney, and Jeremy Taylor. They all helped me open to realities I hadn't even dreamed possible.

Many thanks to my friend and colleague Joan Stanford for her inspiration and support as I wrote this book. She cheered me on whenever I came upon road blocks and reminded me again and again that the creative spark may dim, but it never disappears. I thank Joan and my other early readers—Kate Dougherty, Sharon Hansen, Lindsay Wansbury, Joanna Wigginton and Tansy Chapman—for their honesty and their encouragement. Much appreciation to Hal and Sidra Stone for their support and advice when I had completed my rough draft. A special thank you to my son Erik for photographing my artwork and to all three of my sons—Erik, Gabriel and Eli—for their encouragement in moments when I wavered about trying to publish my story.

I owe a huge debt of gratitude to my editor, Annie Tucker, for taking me under her wing and gently helping me to turn my book outward, toward my readers. Her steadfast support, her earthiness, and her great sense of humor made the editing process a complete delight. Finally, big thanks to Brooke Warner, Lauren Wise, and the team at She Writes Press for helping me navigate the world of publishing and get my message out into the world.

About the Author

Marilyn Hagar is a registered expressive arts therapist who owns and operates For the Joy of It!, a creative retreat in Mendocino, California. She has been in private practice and led groups and workshops at her forest retreat for more than forty years, dedicating her life to the belief that we are all creative and that expressing ourselves through the arts puts us in touch with our own wild essence. Marilyn has published articles about her creative life and her adventures in the great outdoors. She has also exhibited her artwork and her art quilts, inspired by inner-life imagery and her dream world. She has three wonderful sons and four precious grandsons. Her website is www.marilynhagar.com.

Selected Titles From She Writes Press

She Writes Press is an independent publishing company founded to serve women writers everywhere. Visit us at www.shewritespress.com.

The Art of Play: Igniting Your Imagination to Unlock Insight, Healing, and Joy by Joan Stanford. $19.95, 978-1-63152-030-3. Lifelong "non-artist" Joan Stanford shares the creative process that led her to insight and healing, and shares ways for others to do the same.

Think Better. Live Better. 5 Steps to Create the Life You Deserve by Francine Huss. $16.95, 978-1-938314-66-7. With the help of this guide, readers will learn to cultivate more creative thoughts, realign their mindset, and gain a new perspective on life.

This Way Up: Seven Tools for Unleashing Your Creative Self and Transforming Your Life by Patti Clark. $16.95, 978-1-63152-028-0. A story of healing for women who yearn to lead a fuller life, accompanied by a workbook designed to help readers work through personal challenges, discover new inspiration, and harness their creative power.

Note to Self: A Seven-Step Path to Gratitude and Growth by Laurie Buchanan. $16.95, 978-1-63152-113-3. Transforming intention into action, *Note to Self* equips you to shed your baggage, bridging the gap between where you are and where you want to be—body, mind, and spirit—and empowering you to step into joy-filled living *now!*

Tell Me Your Story: How Therapy Works to Awaken, Heal, and Set You Free by Tuya Pearl. $16.95, 978-1-63152-066-2. With the perspective of both client and healer, this book moves you through the stages of therapy, connecting body, mind, and spirit with inner wisdom to reclaim and enjoy your most authentic life.

Painting Life: My Creative Journey Through Trauma by Carol K. Walsh. $16.95, 978-1-63152-099-0. Carol Walsh was a psychotherapist working with traumatized clients when she encountered her own traumatic experience; this is the story of how she used creativity and artistic expression to heal, recreate her life, and ultimately thrive.